Probable Cause

To Meganne

With best wishes

John Hairland Williams

February 2020

An airliner crashes,
     Killing 47 passengers…

Probable Cause

Was it an accident?
     Or was it murder…

A Novel by

John Haviland Williams

ISBN: 0-75960-577-7

This book is printed on acid free paper.

1stBooks - rev. 12/27/00

This is a work of fiction. The events described are imaginary, and the characters and businesses are fictitious and not intended to represent specific living persons or companies. The National Transportation Safety Board (NTSB) and the Federal Aviation Administration (FAA), however, are actual agencies of the United States government. Even when settings are referred to by their true names, the incidents portrayed as taking place are entirely fictitious; the reader should not infer that the events set here ever happened.

Author's Note and Acknowledgments

Probable Cause is a work of fiction. While the circumstances of Coastal Airlines flight 193, a DC-9 commanded by Captain Anne Ryan, are patterned after an airline accident that actually occurred on February 17, 1991, at Cleveland-Hopkins International Airport, the story that grew from it is entirely the result of my imagination.

The National Transportation Safety Board (NTSB), the independent federal agency charged with investigating aircraft accidents, concluded that the *probable cause* of the Cleveland accident was icing on the wings, an insidious meteorological factor that continues to plague airlines today. However, things are not always as they seem, and hence the notion for the fictional plot you are about to read.

Of the many who gave assistance to me during the writing of the manuscript, I offer my thanks first to my wife, Suzie, who saw to it that I finished what I began, and who also possessed the ability to see the entire forest when I could only see the trees. Thanks also to those whose expert and objective eyes corrected my course where it was errant. They are: Captain Julie E. Clark, Northwest Airlines; First Officer David L. Leippe, United Airlines; Michael Batt, Merrill Lynch, Inc.; Pat Cariseo, Public Affairs Officer, National Transportation Safety Board; and to Frank Viernes, FAA Air Traffic Control Specialist, Sacramento TRACON.

John Haviland Williams
Placerville, California
September 2000

[The Board] "...shall investigate the facts, conditions, and circumstances related to...aircraft accidents and...determine a *probable cause* or causes for those accidents."

> --Congressional mandate creating the
> National Transportation Safety Board (NTSB)

"The board's vision is for the public to continue to have confidence in our nation's transportation systems, even when accidents occur, knowing that an independent body will determine the cause(s) of accidents and recommend corrective actions to be taken."

> --NTSB Vision Statement

--- **To Suzie** ---

ONE

He's up to something, I know he is, Anne Ryan thought as she sped down the ski slope after him, missing the deep mogul suddenly appearing in her path, her goggles frosting from a blinding sheet of white powder from Warner's skis ahead. Wind whipped her face as she wiped the snow from her goggles, tucked her poles beneath her armpits and leaned forward. Quickly her speed mounted, knees absorbing punishing blows from the choppy snowpack. In moments she was nearly abreast of him.

"Dead heat!" Warner Edelbrock shouted, laughing as he quickly swerved away and sprayed yet another blinding sheet of powder in her path.

In a heartbeat she was through it, again wiping the snow from her goggles, when suddenly the bottom fell out. Unprepared, she sailed high above the slope that fell steeply away beneath her, her balance lost and body tumbling as she dropped. She landed hard, flat on her back and skidding headfirst downhill. Jolting blows from the washboard of moguls pounded her as she slid wildly,

1

flailing her ski poles, when suddenly her body shot upward coming out of a deep dip, tumbled once and slammed into a drift.

For seconds that seemed minutes she lay gasping, disoriented, certain that the punishing ride down had busted something within. Gingerly she felt for her throbbing tailbone and winced.

Another sheet of icy powder swept over her and for a moment she thought it was Warner coming back to survey his kill. She could almost hear his derisive laugh. It didn't matter who his competition was—in the airline Boardroom, the racquetball court, or on the ski slopes with her—it was always the same: win at any cost. If he could sling a stinging barb as the coup de grace, so much the better.

A hand touched her shoulder. "You all right, ma'am?"

Anne turned quickly and a sharp pain shot up her neck, but she saw by his armband that he was a ski patrolman. "I...I guess so. My butt hurts though, and so does my neck."

"I'll bet. I saw you go off *The Leap* when the guy turned away—looked to me like he set you up."

She didn't doubt it. Warner Edelbrock seemed as adept at manipulating people as he was with corporate profits—the outcome always went his way. She rolled painfully onto her back and stared at the lumpy and threatening gray mattress of cloud reflecting her mood.

It had been a long time in coming, but at last she'd had enough of His Arrogance, Warner Edelbrock, president and chairman of the board of TransCon Airlines.

She no longer wondered how she could have been so foolish to become involved with a creature like Warner Edelbrock. She knew. It hadn't taken much to capture a forty year-old woman who had never married, who had been a loner by choice for most of her childhood as well as adult life, a woman who dated little and whose existence had become one-dimensional: Flying. She supposed it was the years of Spartan living on the meager B-scale salary of an airline first officer while seeking her goal of captain, alone, and with no interests outside of flying, that had primed her pump for the excitement and adventure of a walk on the wild side with Edelbrock. It had been heady stuff at first, yet over time his egocentric and sometimes cruel personality had at last overshadowed and tarnished any feelings she once felt for him.

So...had enough at last, old girl? she asked herself.

Yes, she supposed that she had. Until now, quitting Warner Edelbrock was much like before she had quit smoking—you knew it was harmful to your health and still you reached for another, hopelessly addicted. Maybe tomorrow, you said, until one morning you awoke with your chest in a vise and realized that it was your own hand ratcheting the jaws tighter.

The young ski patrolman patted her shoulder and reached into his parka for his radio. "Base, Patrol Four. Need a litter, ah, 'bout two hundred meters beyond—"

"Never mind," Anne said, sitting up slowly. "I'm okay. I got myself into this and I'll get myself out of it,"

"But ma'am, you might be injured, let me—"

She shook her head, "I'm okay, just bruised." *Bruised in body and stupid in the head,* she thought bitterly.

He closed his bag quickly and shook his head. "I can't leave you here, ma'am. You'll have to at least let me help you over to the chairlift landing. They'll have my butt if I don't. You know, lawsuits, that sort of thing, not that I think that you'd…"

During the ride down she sat stoically, arms folded, thinking. There at last came a time in life when you realized that a diet of peanut butter and jelly sandwiches packed cellulite on your aging thighs, that a demanding and stressful work schedule with too little rest inflated puffy bags beneath the eyes of forty year-old women, and that Warner Edelbrocks, like cigarettes, were bad for the spirit as well as the body. Yet even peanut butter and jelly and a demanding job had some redeeming values, but Warner...?

He stood waiting at the chairlift as she hobbled off, teetered, and quickly he grabbed her about the waist before she fell. "Take a tumble, did you?" he said, chuckling.

"You know damned well I did, Warner."

3

He threw his head back and laughed. "Too bad we don't have a video of it, Anne. Jesus, you were spectacular! Hey, have you ever seen the TV show, *America's Funniest Home Videos*? You'd have been—"

"Let's go. My butt hurts, my neck—damn, Warner, I hurt all over thanks to you."

"C'mon, Anne, be a good sport and don't be so testy." He grasped her elbow as he walked and she hobbled toward the parking lot. "First a drink and then into the spa, and then...well, you know."

Yes, she knew. There was a time when it had been fun, exciting, skimming the slopes with the most handsome of men, later getting fuzzy-headed with potent grog while soaking naked in his spa and still later feeling his strong, expert hands oiling her body for the delicious romp that would come. At sixty-one Warner Edelbrock looked mid-forties, tanned, muscular, a full head of hair just showing gray at the temples and framing ruggedly handsome features. His nose was hawkish, Roman, a feature she at first thought rescued him from prettiness, yet it matched the personality of the carnivore she now knew he was.

"You know I can't drink today," she said, easing into the passenger seat of his Chevy Suburban. He slammed her door shut, walked around to the driver's side, slipped on the ice and grabbed for the door handle. She wished that he'd fallen on his marvelous nose.

"Just thought I'd ask," he said, his voice taking on its predictable edge as he started the engine. "How about a little fun in the spa for your aching butt?"

She whirled in her seat. "Jesus Christ, Warner! Is that all you care about? Caressing my aching butt? Boffing my brillo? I could've been killed out there!"

Edelbrock stared ahead as he drove, his jaw set, the knobs at the corners bulging, fighting to control his anger. "You knew the drop-off was there, Anne, you should have followed me. Why didn't you?"

It would do no good to argue. It would serve no purpose to say that he had goaded her into competing on a dangerous and circuitous route, zigzagging at dizzying speed to disorient her, that his slashing turn at the last moment was expertly timed to raise a blinding sheet of powder and provide a curtain before that dangerous precipice, *The Leap*. That he had deliberately tried to harm her.

Anne glanced at her watch. It was four o'clock and she had only a little over an hour to catch the shuttle flight back to New York and be on duty at eight. *Go! Just go!* Never mind the useless argument that was certain to inflame him and upset her. Leave as usual—just don't come back. Lesson learned. "I've got to hurry, Warner, my flight leaves at five-thirty. There's just enough time for me to shower and change."

He nodded then slowed as they approached the driveway of the sprawling mountain retreat he called his "cabin". Compared to his estate on Long Island, it was. As he turned into the drive he gave only passing notice of the dark Ford Explorer parked on the shoulder a hundred yards up the road, steam rising from its exhaust.

The driveway wound uphill through a thick stand of conifers for nearly a quarter mile before revealing a rustic, rambling log structure of massive proportions. Also of log construction was the garage, and one of several doors raised when he punched a button above the visor, then eased the Suburban in between the Maseratti and the Lincoln.

Wincing with pain, Anne stepped quickly from the vehicle and stood waiting impatiently at the door before he had even switched off the ignition. Now it was her bladder that was screaming, but she wouldn't tell him that.

Anne turned the shower on as hot as she could stand it and stood beneath the drumming spray, turning slowly as the steaming warmth invaded her aching tissues, finally letting it beat on the bruised flesh just above the cleft of her buttocks. Gradually the

5

pain eased and at last she turned off the spray. Reaching for a towel, she stiffened when she heard a sharp explosion from outside the house. Backfire? The cannon used by Avalanche Control? No, too sharp, close.

She wrapped a towel about her and limped quickly through the house, calling his name. She stopped, suddenly wide-eyed, as he came in through the kitchen door stomping snow from his boots. He had a revolver gripped in his hand.

"Warner...what?"

"Garbage raiders. Got one."

Puzzled, Anne tiptoed barefoot to the window and peered out. There in the snow by an overturned trash can lay a dark form, the snow around it splattered with blood and brain matter.

Anne nearly vomited. "A dog? Jesus, Warner, you shot a *dog*?" she choked.

He slipped the revolver into a drawer and turned, grinning. "One shot, too. From the hip."

He reached for the corner of the towel tucked beneath her armpit and she spun away from him, the towel coming away in his grip. He chuckled as she sprinted down the hallway naked. "Cute little butt, Anne."

Mumbling obscenities, Anne quickly dressed, stuffed her ski clothes into her travel bag and slapped the latches shut, uncaring of the bra strap clenched in its jaws. She found him in the Great Room, brandy in hand, staring pensively into the fireplace. "Let's go, Warner. I have to hurry."

He turned and beamed, surveying her compact and diminutive figure, short-cropped blonde hair and sapphire eyes. Even though fortyish, she was indeed a beauty, he agreed. But the four gold stripes encircling the cuffs of her uniform tunic and the gold wings pinned to the breast seemed a stunning contradiction to the churning naked cheeks he had seen fleeing down the hallway only a short while ago. He had never become accustomed to seeing this woman in uniform even though more than two dozen now populated the cockpits of his airline.

6

He bowed. "Your duty calls, Captain Ryan. Alas, my loss. And where might your lucky passengers be off to tonight?"

"Detroit, if you can call that lucky. Warner, I have to hurry or I'll miss the shuttle."

He turned and plucked a glass of water from the mantle and pressed two tablets into her palm. "For your aching butt. Take two of these and call me in the morning."

"What are they? Dog poison?"

"An evil concoction of barbiturates with a dash of crack for a lift."

Anne threw the tablets into the fireplace. "You bastard, that's all I need."

Edelbrock smiled and handed her two more. "Ibuprofen, love. I was only kidding. Mediprin, Advil, hell, I don't know. Some generic store brand, it looked like. They're Sylvia's, but they're okay. Take 'em, you'll feel better. And, they're allowable in the cockpit, as you well know."

Anne nodded. They were, but she had to be careful what she took before a flight. She looked again at the plain white tablets, shrugged, and quickly downed them.

"Got everything?" he asked, backing out of the garage.

Got milk? might as well have been his question, for all he cared. "Yes, just...let's go," she said. "I don't dare miss the shuttle."

Warner turned sharply from the driveway and onto the highway, then stepped on it hard and the tires shrieked as the Suburban surged ahead. He didn't see the dark Ford Explorer still parked on the shoulder some distance up the road, now facing their direction. As he sped away, the Explorer eased onto the roadway and followed at a distance.

They spoke not a word as he drove her to the airport, and that suited her just fine—in ten minutes she would walk into the terminal building and he would be forever out of her life. The last of her unhealthy vices conquered. She peered out at the bleak, rolling countryside of upstate New York studded with trees now barren of their leaves and shrouded in an opaque mist. The weather was worsening and she guessed the temperature at near-freezing; the fog and mist would soon turn to ice and flying would be treacherous. She hoped conditions were better at La Guardia where the flight she would command tonight originated.

"Worried about the weather?" he asked, breaking the uncomfortable silence.

She considered his question while staring ahead into the gloom, a frown now creasing her brow. "Always," she said absently.

"You'll probably be de-icing the aircraft tonight—it's usually like that at La Guardia this time of year."

She turned and looked at him, cocking her head quizzically. "I know."

More minutes passed in silence as he drove, yet his moronic attempts at conversation had puzzled her. *"Worried about the weather? You'll probably be de-icing the aircraft tonight...It's usually like that at La Guardia..."* Well of course she was worried about the weather. What pilot wasn't? And of course they'd likely be de-icing the aircraft tonight—standard procedure in the industry of which he was very much a part. It was like one stockbroker saying to another that the market could have a brain fart if the President of the United States fell ill. Well, *doh!* Edelbrock was acting weird. Why?

"Anne?"

She sighed, "What?"

"It looks pretty bad out there, maybe you ought to trip-trade tonight. Let someone else fly the trip to Detroit."

Anne spun in the seat. "Just what in hell is *with* you, anyway? Why all the inane questions and now this sudden concern that you so carefully hid on the slopes this afternoon?"

Edelbrock raised his hands from the wheel. "All right, all right. Forget it. Just forget it. Christ, don't be so touchy."

Another mile passed in strained silence but Edelbrock seemed determined to make conversation. "So when are you going to come to work for us?" he said, reaching and squeezing her thigh. "We've got better equipment than Coastal Airlines, better pay, and I can get you assigned to a better base. Like Miami or San Francisco."

Her anger flared again, ignited by a worn issue. "Just like that!" she said, snapping her fingers and ignoring his kneading grip on her thigh. "You just say the word and people snap-to, don't they?"

He nodded, "I'm the boss."

And an insensitive tyrant in the industry. He'd made the offer before and it held considerable appeal, yet he seemed incapable of comprehending the harm of preferential treatment to flight officers, especially female. It disintegrated working relationships among flight crews, and a disgruntled flight crew was a dangerous crew.

"I'm happy where I am."

"You won't be for long."

She looked at him sharply, "What do you mean by that?"

"Coastal Airlines is going under just as surely as Pan Am and Eastern did. Next will be Coastal and soon most of the other old-line big names. You'll see. All fall down. The industry's about to undergo a series of consolidations, such that there'll end up being only about four major airlines. Maybe less."

Anne looked away and shook her head at his smug arrogance. Then, "I don't suppose you've had a hand in any of that. In Pan Am and Eastern."

He let it pass. "I was sorry to see them go, believe it or not."

She didn't. It was well known in the industry that Warner Edelbrock was a cannibal. He may or may not have had a hand in Pan Am and Eastern's demise, but he surely was helping Coastal to its grave. There had been TransCon's vicious fare wars aimed squarely at an already ailing Coastal; the much-publicized smear campaign against the line's president, revealing his homosexuality

9

and alluding to a penchant for boys, and who was later found shot to death—an apparent suicide. Then had come the union turmoil and violence, rumored to have been stirred by those having connections to TransCon, the timing of which had effectively shut down Coastal's maintenance facilities and crippled its flight operations. Many, including Anne, believed that Edelbrock and his public relations stooge, Philip Darcy, had been far more than just interested observers of the ills which had ravaged Coastal.

Such turbulence had been more than many of Coastal's passengers could tolerate, and the predictable exodus to TransCon had opened an artery that began as a trickle and later became a flood when the devastating accident of a month ago consumed the lives of all aboard one of Coastal's DC-9s. It was a flight Anne was to command, an accident that could have been hers had she not trip-traded with another captain at the last moment.

So Warner was right, Coastal was teetering over the abyss. But there was no way she would ever fly for TransCon; not while he was manipulating the helm. She would fly charter in the outback of Australia or the bush of Alaska in a rattling Cessna first.

"You're a good pilot, Anne, but I wonder about the others you fly with," he said, gripping the wheel and staring ahead. "Maintenance and pilot proficiency training are the first places an ailing carrier cuts costs. One more bad accident and the show's over for Coastal. Then you're out of a job."

He pulled to the curb in the passenger loading zone, set the brake and turned to her as she quickly grabbed her bag and stepped out. "Think it over, Anne."

She did—all the time. Airline flying was her life, a childhood dream instilled by her long-deceased father, also a pilot, but a dream realized only after years of great sacrifice and determination in what was then a hostile domain inhabited mostly by males. Years ago she had overcome the stigma of her gender and found her place among them, but here before her sat the son of a bitch who was bent upon destroying the airline that was now her home, however humble it had become. Without it her opportunities were few.

She stood on the curb and stared malevolently at him as he leaned over the seat and looked up at her. "Next weekend, same time, Anne?"

She fought back a stinging invective, calmed herself, and said simply, "It's over, Warner." With that she slammed the car door and strode briskly into the terminal building, a great weight suddenly lifted from her spirit.

The forward cabin door thunked shut and the shuttle's twin turbo-props spun up in a howling buzz as Anne sat among the passengers, staring absently out the window at the freezing rain. She felt their eyes upon her as she always did when she traveled to work in uniform. The flying public still regarded black or female airline pilots as something of an oddity; a black or female *captain* an even greater rarity. But in a decade that would change. Edelbrock had once said, *"Three-holers"* (his endearing term for women) *"and spooks were like a mountain of water behind a leaking dike—a drip becomes a flood."*

She shook her head. How very poetic. So like him to demean those whom he considered only marginally useful in the gene pool. She turned away from the window, unseeing of the man in the dark overcoat watching through the terminal windows.

As the shuttle taxied away from the terminal she leaned her head back against the seat, staring at the filthy nubby fabric covering the ceiling of the weary aircraft while digging absently at her cuticles. She nibbled at her lower lip, realizing only now that it was already raw and cracked, that she'd been chewing on it since Warner had destroyed that poor dog. God, what a vicious man he could be. And what must he be thinking of her now? She had bruised his famous ego not a little. Again. And Warner was a vindictive sort...

The shuttle braked to a halt and Anne peered out the nose-smudged window as the de-icing crew sprayed glycol on the wings. She thought of Warner's wife, wondered how she, or any woman, could have tolerated him for as many years as she had—and apparently still did. Anne felt great pity for the woman. And yes, she had felt guilt early on in their adulterous relationship, but Warner had convinced her that Sylvia, wheelchair-ridden with multiple sclerosis for most of her life, had sanctioned their extra-marital fling out of deep and abiding love and concern for her husband's well being. "Warner darling," Sylvia was to have said, "I want you to have what I cannot give you."

Lies. Gutter-ridden lies... Dead dogs and a smoking gun.

The howling of the engines at takeoff thrust broke through her troubled thoughts and she realized that her fists and jaw were tightly clenched.

"Nervous?" asked the smiling young businessman sitting next to her, his eyes dropping to the four gold stripes encircling her cuffs, then rising and fixing upon the breast of her tunic and probably wondering if there were any boobs in there.

She was accustomed to such inanities; still, she was tempted to tell him she was utterly terrified of airplanes. The shock effect would be marvelous except that the remark would likely find its way to her personnel office. "Only when I'm not up front driving," she said, turning away as the aircraft climbed into the gloom. She supposed even that sounded flippant, but there was much truth in her feelings. Like the sea, aircraft were terribly unforgiving of a pilot's carelessness, incapacity, or neglect. And like doctors, lawyers, accountants and other professionals, there were some pilots who just didn't belong. But you seldom knew who they were un-til--until it was too late. She had known some and they were very much dead.

The cottony void through which they climbed thickened and became darker, the wingtips now barely visible, and suddenly it spurred her memory of something Warner had said.

"It looks pretty bad out there, Anne, maybe you ought to trip-trade tonight..."

Yeah, right. Just like the last time, she thought, the guilt she couldn't shed once again seeping from that dark recess of her mind. The captain with whom she had trip-traded a month ago, as well as his crew and passengers, were dead; it should have been her. Ray Thompson had been reluctant to trade that night, especially at the last moment before the flight, but she had pressed him for the favor owed... Worse, she had needed the favor so she could spend a weekend in the sack with Warner.

Oh, god, Ray...

Her throat suddenly tightened and she squeezed her eyes shut again, wishing she could just pay her dues and make it go away...

John Haviland Williams

TWO

Coastal's flight operations office at La Guardia buzzed with activity as weary flight crews arrived and fresh ones departed. Captain Anne Ryan stood near the operations desk, punching codes into a computer terminal while the screen displayed dismal weather forecasts for her route of flight. She saw that La Guardia would be just above minimums for her nine o'clock departure, and Detroit, a destination she loathed, would be little better.

She glanced at the operations counter where her first officer stood preparing the flight plan, and saw that he was scowling, tugging nervously at his chin. Not a good sign. He was a recent hire, fresh from simulator school, and there was not a hint of sheen on the backside of his freshly creased uniform trousers. Although experienced pilots, many of Coastal's new hires were relatively uninitiated to the environment of large transport aircraft. She judged he would likely need careful watching while gaining experience at the controls of the DC-9, need to be coached through difficult landing approaches, and until she learned firsthand of his capabilities she would have to be poised at the ready to take over should he flub it. Well, not tonight. Tonight he could sit and watch; she would fly the trip.

Yes, the flight held much promise of a trying night in the cockpit, yet that's what she was paid for, wasn't it? And wasn't the challenge part of the allure of flying? Certainly, so get over it, girl.

She felt a touch on her shoulder and spun around.

"Whoops. Little on edge, Ryan?"

Captain Jimmy Truax, her nemesis of years, stood gazing down at her with a smirk tugging the corners of his mouth. His feral eyes still held promise that one day he would even the score that had smoldered since her first month on the line sixteen years ago. Early on she had endured his crude remarks of her gender until at last they had sparked a vicious clash and counter-clash, she the enduring winner, but with Truax you just never knew.

"I thought I smelled something foul, Jimboy. Now I know what."

The rangy Oklahoman blinked, deflecting the remark. "You flyin' in this shit tonight?"

"Any reason why I shouldn't?"

"No, not unless you're on the rag—which you seem to be most of the time." He nodded toward her first officer across the room, "Dumb-ass kid won't be much help if you are. I hear he hasn't even been in the military."

And neither have I, she thought. One more reason for his animosity toward her. To Truax's way of thinking, if you weren't a dick-swinging ex-jet jock, you just...weren't. Anne casually brushed his lapels then patted his cheek. "The next time you don't know what to do with yourself, Jimboy, I'd recommend hanging. But you can't use your family tree—there's no fork in it."

Truax snickered and swaggered on his way. Then he turned. "Don't bend the ship tonight, Ryan, we haven't that many left."

Seething, Anne punched the printout button then tore off the weather chart and strode quickly to the operations desk. Donald Overmeyer, her first officer, slid the dispatch release before her and optimistically offered a pen for her signature. She raised her hand for him to wait while she scanned it, frowned, then thrust it back.

"Not enough fuel, Overmeyer. Increase it to max gross."

The young man's left eyebrow shot up. "But captain, we're only going to Detroit. The company manual says we need fuel enough to reach an alternate airport plus forty-five minutes' additional flying time, and that's what I ordered put in."

Anne sighed impatiently, "Don't believe everything you read, Overmeyer. That's just a guideline, a minimum. Here, look at the weather chart, tell me what you see."

He examined the complex chart spread before him, lips moving silently as he deciphered the symbols. Then a slender finger with a crimson lacquered nail slid over the paper and tapped the symbol for Detroit.

"Not exactly sunshine and roses is it?" Anne said.

He shook his head. "It's just above minimums with a front expected to move through later. Maybe get worse."

"Which means?"

"Delays. Maybe get stuck circling in a holding pattern over Detroit."

Anne nodded. "Which means?"

His face flushed as realization dawned. "More fuel."

Anne smiled, relenting. "That would be nice. Now fill it up and check the tires, Don. See you in a few minutes."

Anne walked down the two flights of stairs to the crew lounge, wincing with each step as her lower back began aching again. It would be a long night, she had chosen to do all of the flying in rotten weather, they'd probably be delayed getting into Detroit, and the hotel shuttle would likely be late. It would be two a.m. at the earliest before she would get to bed—assuming she could sleep with the pain in her back. And people thought airline pilots lived exciting, glamorous lives. Anne sighed as she pushed the crew lounge door open. In truth it was flight after flight of boredom occasionally punctuated with moments of sheer terror.

She found her mailbox crammed with the usual stilted and officious memos from the high cockalorum of Coastal Airlines management and she quickly riffled through them, chuckled at a *Far Side* cartoon from her pal and fellow captain, Gordon "Gordy" Rosenberg; trashed a scratchy copy of a chain letter promising millions; and frowned at a scrap of paper on which was neatly typed, *Matthew 15:19 / Corinthians 6:9.* From some religious zealot, she supposed.

Glancing at her watch, she saw that it was near time to board and quickly grabbed her flightbag from beneath the row of boxes and stuffed her mail inside. She gasped with pain as she straightened, wishing she had another dose of Ibuprofen, but it was too late to walk to the concession stand to buy some. She would have to settle for the aspirin she kept in her locker.

She turned quickly and walked squarely into another pilot.

"Hey, Anne, long time no see. How you doin'?"

"Oh! Gordy! Jeez, I'm sorry. Fine. Fine. Look, I've got to go, I'm late."

"Aren't you always," he chuckled. "Did you get the dose of *Far Side* I sent you?"

"Yeah, thanks. Right now I need a dose of something else. Call you when I get back from Detroit, okay?" Anne scurried around the corner to the locker room, then stopped short. "Hey Gordo?"

The pudgy and light-hearted captain, her best friend, grinned and raised his eyebrows.

"Do you know anything about Matthews and Corinthians?"

Gordy frowned and shook his head. "Are they new hires?"

Anne wrinkled her nose and jabbed her middle finger at him, then stepped into the locker room. Hurrying, she fumbled with her combination lock and cursed when she saw that it was on backward. She never put it on backward, not even when rushed as she was now. But someone... Wincing, she crouched, twisted her head and squinted up at the tiny dial as she spun it, then yanked it open.

"Captain Ryan?" came a voice from the doorway.

It was Overmeyer. "What?" she said, impatience again edging into her voice.

"I'm going out to preflight the aircraft, anything else you want done?"

Anne sighed. *Back off from the guy*, she chided herself, searching for her aspirin bottle. She was letting the bad day with Warner spill over into her work. She turned. "Did the plane just come in or did they pull it out of a hangar?"

"It just came in from Cleveland—they said they had icing during the approach here."

"Who's they?"

"Captain Truax and—"

Oh, swell. Now she would have to disinfect the pilot's seat. She found the aspirin bottle, popped three tablets into her mouth, filled a cup from the nearby cooler, and downed them. "Okay. Get a ground crewman to check the upper surfaces of the wings— see if they're still warm or if there's ice and snow accumulating."

Five minutes later she again stood at the operations counter, this time reviewing Overmeyer's corrected dispatch release. She saw that he had modified the fuel loading to bring the combined weight of passengers, airplane, baggage, and fuel up to the DC-9's maximum gross takeoff weight of 90,700 pounds. She signed the release, slid it across the counter, then hoisted her flightbag and gave a nod to the operations agent.

On the floor above she knew that a substantial load of passengers stood milling about, waiting impatiently for the nine o'clock departure. They were her charges—all fifty-four of them. A slice of humanity who still held a kernel of loyalty and confidence, or perhaps other more obscure reasons, to fly Coastal in spite of Warner Edelbrock's vicious fare wars and slandering advertisements, and the fiery crash only a month ago, right here at La Guardia, that had claimed thirty-eight lives.

These passengers would be spooked a little tonight and she couldn't fault them if they were. The weather was particularly bad and it would likely not be a smooth ride, but she would see to it that it would be a safe one.

Maybe she was just a little spooked too. She stood looking out the door beneath the jetway and remembering again that it had been a night much like this only a month ago, cold, blustery, freezing rain that had become falling snow, that she had trip-traded with Captain Ray Thompson. Her flight had become his. Now Ray was dead. And so were his thirty-seven passengers and crew. His widow would forever bear the damning cross of "pilot error", the *probable cause*, so hinted by the hip-shooting media, yet still under investigation by the National Transportation Safety Board.

But pilot error was not like Ray, she knew. He had been a careful veteran, a pilot's pilot, her mentor, yet the conclusion seemed inescapable: Shortly after takeoff, less than a hundred feet above the runway, the aircraft inexplicably wing-stalled and he had lost it. Wing ice was thought to be a contributing factor, yet the NTSB found that they had thoroughly de-iced the aircraft shortly before takeoff and the notion was later shelved. The NTSB was now exploring the theory that Ray had been fatigued, perhaps distracted, and failed to act quickly or appropriately at a critical moment.

Anne didn't believe a word of it, yet there seemed no other explanation.

She peered upward at the shadow of the DC-9's nose and saw Overmeyer's silhouette in the glow of the cockpit lights, then glanced at her watch. Eight thirty-five. She had best get aboard.

Near the boarding gate for Coastal flight 193, Dominic Gugliotti and his wife, Antoinette, sat waiting nervously for their flight to Detroit. Their four children, all girls aged two to nine, stood side by side at the large windows, chattering and squealing eagerly and cupping their hands against the cold glass to see the airplane in which they would soon ride.

Dominic grinned and shook his head, squeezing his wife's hand and pointing, "See how they do that? Dem girls, they always line up from little to big. Justa like stair steps," he said with a thick Italian accent.

Antoinette mimicked him playfully, "And maybe thatsa because of the way you make a'love to me, Dom. You act a'like you climbin' the stairs."

Dominic grinned, nodding. "And then a'you yanka the rug, anna I go boom. Boom—more kids, huh? Boom—Toni, boom—Marie, boom—Teresa, boom—"

"A'right, a'ready, Mr. Boom-boom, quit beatin' your drum."

Only twice had the family flown before, and their forced humor did little to quell their fears of the flight to Detroit, yet neither would admit it to the children. For the youngsters it was an adventure and should remain as such; for Dominic and Antoinette their fear of flying seemed a sentence to purgatory. Once committed to visiting Antoinette's ailing mother in Detroit, the days since had become a cancerous foreboding, metastasizing as the day of departure neared.

It was too late to back out and offer a lame excuse to Antoinette's mother. Their tickets were deep-discount and nonrefundable. Money was tight.

Antoinette's moist hand gripped her husband's as she silently prayed, trying to shut out her paralyzing fear and the howling storm outside rattling the terminal windows.

Jack Wallach sat alone reading *Automotive News* while waiting for the agent to begin the boarding of flight 193. A purchasing agent for a large New York-based automotive parts supplier, Detroit had been his regular beat for years. Tomorrow morning he would meet with reps from Ford and GM to close some big deals. In the afternoon, his contact at Chrysler had assured him of a brief audience with the retired yet still influential automotive Pope, Lee Iacocca. Of course, there would be fifty or a hundred others there as well, but what the hell.

He smiled at the idea of at last meeting the great Iacocca, of how he could later inflate the fleeting acquaintance to those he sought to impress. *"Lee? Sure, I know Lee. We go back a long ways. Great guy, Lee. Hey, you know what he told me once confidentially--?"*

Yep, tomorrow would be a big day for Jack Wallach. Maybe a chance to move to Detroit would come of it. Join the major league. Maybe Iacocca would take a liking to him if he could just get him aside long enough...

A screeching toddler streaked past his crossed leg, knocking it from his knee.

"Toni no! Stop that! Toni, come here this minute!"

Jack Wallach smiled benignly at the middle-age woman and her family sitting across from him. The guy looked like the typical autoworker, he thought. He had the pallor of someone who never saw daylight. Hell of a life. Punch in, rat-tat-tat all day long on a noisy assembly line, then punch out and go home to an aging and dumpy Dago wife and a bunch of screaming kids.

Some people just didn't know how to live.

Sitting in a far corner of the boarding area by herself, an eighty-nine year-old woman rummaged in her purse, looking for her wallet. When she found it she opened it to the family pictures at which she often gazed for comfort in her loneliness. There were her three sons, Michael, Walter, and Donald, handsome men all of them. And of course, William, her long deceased husband, the handsomest of all. Lillian Attebury's "children", as she still called them, ranged in ages from 45 for young Donald, to 65 for Michael. Of the three, Donald, her baby, was the one she could count on most to stay in touch. The others? Well, they had their lives to live, but they called occasionally and never failed to send her a birthday card. But it was Donald who always sent her an airplane

22

ticket each year to come and visit him and his family in Detroit for two weeks.

She cherished those two weeks each year, being doted upon by Donald and his lovely wife, and spoiling rotten their three darling children...

A sudden gust of wind captured her attention, and Lillian looked up and gazed out the window at the blackness beyond. For moments she watched the huge plate glass windows flex inward, outward, fearing they would burst. She looked about the boarding area and saw that no one, including the gate agents, seemed concerned, and her fear subsided. But the weather was worsening and she hoped her flight would not be delayed—or worse, canceled. For too long she had been looking forward to this moment, enduring the creeping loneliness of her tiny flat in Valley Stream until at last the holidays returned and she could once again be with Donald.

For each of the past five or so years Lillian had become acutely aware of her age as friends and acquaintances of decades withered and died. Gone, most of them, and she had long outlived them all. And there indeed lay the root of her loneliness. She, the lone survivor. At 89 she was still healthy and relatively strong, alert, had all of her teeth—every single one of them. But most of those friends who remained among the living were not so fortunate. Most were now bedridden, incontinent, and cached away somewhere in a home to rot. Kenneled, they were. Incarcerated and largely ignored until their cycle was completed. Ashes to ashes...

No, there was nobody left anymore. Only young Donald cared.

"But mother," he had said a year ago, "surely you must have friends at the church luncheons, your club meetings, and the like. Why do you close yourself in so?"

Why indeed, as though it were a choice. Donald would someday come to realize when he reached her age that those ten and twenty years younger, and more, cared not a whit to be bothered with the elderly. And most of those near her age were either in-communicable, senile, or near death. But she would never tell that to Donald; the last thing she wanted was pity for her wretched loneliness.

A giggling child scooted past her feet, tripped and got up quickly and sped on, pursued by three others each a little taller than the one preceding, running in circles around the waiting passengers. Lillian smiled and shook her head. Oh, the exuberance of youth. They were so like Donald's children.

Suddenly a woman's agitated voice called, "Toni, Marie, Teresa, and Sophie—come here this minute! Now!"

Lillian watched the children gather quickly around their mother and father. The family seemed Italian, she thought. All dark-haired, dark eyes, lovely skin. The mother was scowling, her animated frown severe as she scolded the children, shaking a finger before each of their little upturned noses. Their heads nodded in unison.

"At'sa good girls," said their father. "Come on, Toni, come up onna daddy's a'lap, now. At'sa my sweetie pie. You wanna go see you gamma? You gamma love you, you know."

So Italian, Lillian thought, now wishing that she was as well. They were so close-knit and fiercely family-oriented. No one was left out. No one...

Lillian sighed, ashamed of her self-pity. But in another year, maybe two, it would all be over. God, let it be over, she thought. Ninety, ninety-one years was long enough. Too long. Lord knows, eighty-nine was long enough. Of what possible use was her kind to anyone, anyway?

Across the waiting area a frail teenage girl with frizzy hair and a tiny gold earring through her left nostril also sat alone, curled in a seat and clutching her arms about her small breasts while staring morosely at the worn carpet. For seventeen year-old Dodie War-nock, life had sunk to its lowest—or maybe it could go even lower yet. But Dodie Warnock had no intention of enduring any more of it. Tonight she would step aboard this airplane very much alive, but wherever it landed in a few hours they would carry her off. Dead. Her wrists slashed. And they would be sorry.

She had long ago given up wondering why her mother and father misunderstood her so. Almost a month ago she had given up. To Dodie Warnock that was a long time. An eternity.

But she would not do it in some filthy alleyway, an abandoned building, or even out at Jones Beach. Not even in her own bathroom. No, it had to be someplace bizarre, a place that would gain much attention and shock many. It would probably make the national news.

The bathroom of an airplane was perfect. She was sorry there would be so much blood to clean up...

A loudspeaker clicked and the voice of the gate agent filled the waiting area. "Thank you for waiting, ladies and gentlemen, we are now ready to begin boarding Coastal Airlines flight 193, DC-9 jet service nonstop to Detroit's Metropolitan airport. All passengers holding boarding passes may now..."

A whoosh of frigid air and swirling snowflakes greeted Anne as she pushed the door beneath the jetway open, and her mind flashed on the blinding sheet of powder moments before she became airborne at *The Leap* only hours ago. *Damn you, Warner Edelbrock!* Yet now, strangely, the grating pain in her back was nearly gone. A blessing, considering the long night ahead.

Skeptical of the thoroughness of Overmeyer's preflight inspection of the aircraft, Anne sighed and ducked her head against the icy wind and made a quick walkaround beneath the DC-9's wings, peering into the landing gear wells with her flashlight, checking for open inspection doors, obstructions or debris in the turbine inlets, then kicked a tire for the hell of it and knocked slush from her polished oxfords.

A familiar voice called out, "You don't trust *nobody*, does you, Miz Annie?"

Anne relaxed as she turned and saw the huge black man sling another suitcase on the conveyor. "Other than you, Titus, there's nobody left to trust in this rinky-dink outfit."

"That about right, Miz Annie, 'ceptin' Mr. Gordy. He an all right boy. Hey, you be careful tonight, you hear?"

Be careful tonight, you hear? had been Titus Wofford's parting comment to her for sixteen years, an admonishing blessing of sorts, without which her departures would be incomplete. If she could have a father again he would be Titus.

Anne set her bag down and hugged the huge man, her arms only half encircling his enormous waist. "Titus, you're an old worry-wart, but I love it. I'll be careful."

He cupped her shoulders in his great hands and peered down at her, his expression wary. "The bird look okay, missy?"

She glanced up at the shadowy DC-9 and patted its belly. "It looks okay, Titus. Now I've got to go."

He watched her climb the jetway stairs and disappear through the door. Turning, he surveyed the aircraft looming next to him. It looked okay to him too. But then so had Mr. Ray's. And now Mr. Ray was dead.

Anne stowed her flightbag and hung her tunic on the backside of the cockpit door, then slid quickly into the left seat and buckled in.

"Coffee, captain?" asked the senior flight attendant standing in the cockpit doorway.

Anne turned in her seat, "Ah, no. No thanks, Marlene. I'll only have to get up and pee later, and I don't think this is the night for it."

"Mr. Overmeyer?" asked the flight attendant.

"Hot chocolate, please. Uh—do you have any whipped cream?"

Anne rolled her eyes and handed him the before-start checklist. "Let's get with it."

She slid her seat forward and jacked it up three notches. She looked about the worn interior of the DC-9's cockpit. The ship was old by airline standards, an early 10-series built in late 1965 that had survived squintillions of landings—controlled crashes to some. Between her thighs foam padding bulged through frayed seat fabric; the enamel on the control wheel before her chipped and scarred, evidence of thousands of hours of nervous, bored, impatient if not sometimes tense thumbnails. Worse, it seemed she could smell the accumulated musk of every creature that had inhabited this "office" in the sky. Especially that of the animal known as Captain Truax.

Maintenance and pilot proficiency training are the first places an ailing carrier cuts costs... Warner Edelbrock's words echoed in her mind, nudging loose a bubble of doubt.

"Give me the log," she said to Overmeyer.

"What?"

"The *log*, goddammit." Instantly she regretted her testiness when she saw Overmeyer's rebuked expression. "Sorry," she murmured.

She scanned the aircraft's logbook entries, beginning with the most recent, Truax's. *Right main gear indicator lights burned out*, it read. She glanced at the instrument panel and saw that indeed both tiny bulbs were dark. And still the maintenance crew had not replaced them. No big deal, but illegal just the same. But it was yet another of the many hairline cracks that were becoming widening fissures in the soul of what was once a fine airline.

Anne examined the other logbook entries, saw five earlier write-ups for the errant ten-cent bulbs, a couple of squawks about the auxiliary power unit—later noted as repaired, but she was surprised to see that regularly scheduled maintenance appeared to have been performed as required. Okay, so the aging pelican seemed to be airworthy—score one for Coastal.

Be careful tonight, you hear...?

Yes, Titus, that's exactly what I'm doing, she thought, snapping the logbook shut. It was 8:59. Time. "Call out the before-start checklist, Donald."

"Right." He ran his fingers down the laminated list, calling out the obligatory challenges, awaiting her responses. "Circuit breakers?"

Anne trailed her fingertips over the panels. "Checked."

"Oxygen mask, regulator, interphone?"

They both checked their masks and Anne checked the regulator and interphone. "Checked."

"Cockpit voice recorder?" he called.

The black box. One of two which were the domain of the FAA and NTSB and already recording their conversation through the cockpit-area microphone. Grinning, Anne cupped her hands about her mouth and spoke in a low, gravelly voice, "Halo estatue?"

"Huh?" said Overmeyer.

"Never mind, Donald. Checked."

Two minutes later the forward cabin door chunked shut and the guideman's voice came through her earpiece. "Cleared to start engines."

"Starting engines," Anne replied, and nodded to Overmeyer.

From far to the rear she heard the low moan of number one spooling up, the ticking in her headset of the fuel igniters lighting off, then came the familiar hollow *thud* when it ignited, and the throbbing, muted banshee whine when it came to life. *Well, what do you know—it runs.* Then number two lighted and she felt the tingling throb of harnessed power through the seat of her pants, a delicious sensation of which she never tired.

"Uh-oh," Overmeyer said, pointing to a warning light on the annunciator panel. "Ventral door's ajar, or not sealed."

Anne glanced at the panel and saw that the amber warning light for the rear stair/door was indeed illuminated. She breathed a sigh; such annoyances were becoming too common at Coastal. She looked out her window and down, saw that the guideman was looking up at her expectantly and nodding toward the pushback tractor. She shook her head at him and spoke into her microphone. "Wait one, got a door light."

"I'll go back and check it, captain," Overmeyer offered, unsnapping his shoulder harness.

"Never mind," Anne said, "I'll get it." It was Overmeyer's job but it was also an unexpected opportunity for her to pee once more. If they had to circle in a holding pattern over Detroit two hours from now, which was likely, and then she *really* had to pee, she couldn't in good conscience leave Overmeyer in command. At least not until she knew more about him, how well he'd been trained. It would be just her luck to be sitting on the crapper in the back of the aircraft, her drawers down around her knees, when sure as hell something would go bump. "Tell Marlene I'm coming back," Anne said, unbuckling.

Overmeyer keyed his mike, called Marlene, then turned in his seat and watched the cockpit door close behind her. At last he could relieve the bloat in his belly, and he loosed a prodigious and satisfying fart. He reached overhead, opened the fresh air eyeball wide, directing its blast toward his crotch, then leaned back and sighed. She was a hard-ass, okay, just as they said, but he liked her nonetheless. He could learn much from her if he could overcome his fear and pay attention. He thought that when at last he was accepted into the airline ranks and donned the uniform of authority with the three gold stripes on his cuffs, that his fear would disappear. But it hadn't; if anything it was worse. In the simulator it was different, he had no problems there. But here, here it was real. He reached forward and gripped the control wheel, his palms sweating, and took deep breaths to calm his nerves. At least he wasn't the only one, he thought. He'd even heard of captains who had a deep-rooted fear of flying, yet were able to conceal it nevertheless. Well so would he, and someday he too would be a captain...

Anne strode quickly, but not too quickly, down the aisle through the passenger cabin, smiling benignly at dozens of questioning as well as appraising glances. *Hi, folks, I'm your captain--oh, yes I am--and I'm just going to take a leak, that's all.* Yes, it would be

a kick to someday say that. Maybe on her last day before retirement. Then she smiled brightly at the prettiest little dark-haired
child she had ever seen, sitting upon her father's lap. She reached
and gently touched her fingertip to the little upturned button nose,
winking as she continued past.

In the rear of the passenger cabin Marlene, the senior flight
attendant, stood arms crossed and waiting beside the errant exit
door. "Should I kick it?" she asked. "Again?"

"Probably what it needs," Anne said, easing past her. Quickly
she muscled the large door lever aside, pulled the heavy door inward a few inches, then slammed it shut and levered the handle
back into position. She snatched the interphone from the nearby
hook and called Overmeyer. "Light out?" Out it was, he replied,
and she quickly hung up and stepped into the lavatory.

Two minutes later she was on her way back to the cockpit,
hurrying now, and there again were the beguiling eyes of the little
girl-child watching her. But the child sat upon the lap of the most
frightened passenger she had ever seen; the man's eyes were filled
with sheer terror. Though the engines were running and the
guideman was waiting in the frigid air outside, Anne stopped in
the aisle and knelt by the child. "Hi, my name's Anne, what's
yours?"

"Toni." she said, hugging her father closely.

"Well, Toni, when we get to Detroit, would you like me to
show you the cockpit?" she asked, taking both of the little girl's
tiny hands in hers. "I'll even let you sit in the driver's seat, how's
that?"

The child was not in the least shy. "Yes!" she replied in a toy
voice, the dark pools of her lovely eyes enchanting Anne. "Can
my sisters come too?"

Anne had the feeling of being watched and looked around
quickly, saw three more pairs of child's eyes riveted upon her expectantly. "Why not. You, you, and you too," she said, pointing
to each as she stood up. "And now I've got to go." Again she saw
the frightened look in the father's eyes, and quickly she leaned

down and whispered, "You've got beautiful daughters, sir, and I'll see that the pilot takes extra good care of them tonight. Now sit back and try to relax, everything's going to be fine. Okay?"

"Okay," Dominic Gugliotti rasped uncertainly, trying to force a smile. "You tella the pilot to go low anna slow, huh?"

For once Anne was glad that a passenger thought her to be a flight attendant rather than a pilot, especially the captain, and she had purposely helped it along a little. Some people just couldn't become accustomed to a woman at the wheel, and this man was surely one of them. His fears didn't need enhancing. She winked at him and squeezed his shoulder. "I'll tell him."

The predeparture gong suddenly rang insistently in the main cabin and she knew they were getting impatient outside, and well they should, she thought, she had dallied too long. "Bye," she said to little Toni.

Anne settled into her seat, reharnessed, and spoke into her microphone to the guideman below, ignoring Overmeyer's perplexed expression that clearly asked *where've you been?* "Disconnect, brakes off and pushback," she said. She glanced out her window, saw the guideman nod and give her a thumbs-up. She blew him a kiss in return.

A gout of steam belched over the nose from the pushback tractor's stack and she felt the familiar nudge. It was the ritual of departure in which authority transferred from management to captain. From now until docking in Detroit the ship and its human cargo were her responsibility. Two minutes later they jerked to a stop and the tractor disengaged from their nosewheel.

She blinked the nosewheel light twice at the guideman below, saw his lighted wands signal wave-off, then gripped the thrust levers in her right hand and nudged them forward.

The fuel-gorged DC-9 bounced and swayed over uneven pavement as she taxied, and she envisioned fifty-six heads in the passenger cabin silently swaying in unison as though orchestrated. It had been her habit since early on to envision the whole of the

31

ship from all angles in her mind's eye before takeoff. It wasn't part of any checklist; it was her way of checking for the un- checked, a means to prod her consciousness for something over- looked.

As though detached from her body, her mind's eye floated about the aircraft and observed the cabin interior, its emergency exit doors armed and ready to blow the slides, the two flight atten- dants in the aisle demonstrating emergency procedures, checking that seat belts were fastened and tray tables up. Outside she saw the conformation of the DC-9's aging flanks as though seen by a bystander, the great wheels rolling through the slush and leaving ruts in their trail, the ship's T-tail towering above the howling en- gine pods. She waggled the rudder pedals and twisted and push- pulled the control wheel. Outside, the control surfaces on the wings and tail moved in response and she saw them as surely as if she were standing behind the aircraft. Then she focused her mind on the wings far to the rear and nearly out of sight from the cock- pit.

Wings. Their residual warmth from Truax's inbound flight was likely dissipating quickly now. They were probably accumu- lating snow since Overmeyer had them checked, and the circuits for the ship's own de-icing system were designed not to operate until after takeoff. Now she envisioned the snow accumulating on the wings, becoming slush, then freezing just as it was in the cor- ners of the windshield before her... If that was happening it could spell disaster on takeoff. There was now no question she would have to de-ice the ship.

She toed the brakes and keyed her mike. "Ah, La Guardia ground, Coastal 193."

"Go ahead, 193."

"Coastal 193's on the inner taxiway at Kilo, ah, we'd appreci- ate clearance to our de-icing pad."

"Hold for cross-traffic, 193."

Anne and Overmeyer watched as the ghostly shadow of a Delta 767 trundled past. Far ahead and to their right she saw that

Coastal's de-icing pad was vacant; at least there was some compensation for late evening departures. The delay would be minimal.

"Coastal 193 continue on the inner taxiway to taxiway Mike, then right turn. Cleared to the de-icing pad. Crew is on the way."

"One ninety-three, inner to Mike to pad," Anne replied, releasing the brakes and nudging the throttles forward. She instructed Overmeyer to make the cabin announcement.

Jack Wallach fumed and squirmed in the cramped seat as he listened to the voice from the cockpit, his forearm raised in defense of an adjacent child's flailing and outthrust foot. Delayed again, story of his life. He had hoped for a quick departure and an empty seat next to him, leaving room for his stuffed briefcase and providing insulation from the low-life that had boarded the aircraft. He'd drawn 9-F by the right window, the seat next to him now filled with the restless bulk of the Dago autoworker. And perched upon the man's lap was a kicking, shrieking child.

Swell. Welcome to Greyhound, Jack.

All he needed was for the wriggling and screeching youngster to later knock his drink tray over on his new suit, or worse—barf on him. That would do it. He'd pitch the fucking kid in a hoop shot across the aisle, landing square in its mother's lap where it fucking well belonged. Jesus!

Lillian Attebury settled back in her seat in the rear of the cabin, her fingers mentally crossed that they would soon takeoff, assuring that they were indeed on the way. Donald would be waiting, becoming upset if they were late.

She smiled pleasantly at the young girl seated next to her who only looked away, obviously troubled. She wondered how the child's parents could possibly allow their daughter to look so wretched with frizzy unkempt hair, an earring in her nose, and frightful satanic tattoos on her wrists. Family values...so little these days. So many young people today looked so rag-tag, were taught so little by their parents who were likely more focused on their own lives and absent much of the time.

Lillian leaned into the narrow aisle and glanced forward, seeing the Italian family seated well toward the front of the cabin. They understood family values, paid proper attention to their children, taught them discipline as well as how to love and be loved... They obviously had little means, but, oh, they had so much more...

Titus Wofford stood in the shadows beneath the jetway, securing the baggage conveyor for the night when the de-icing tanker rolled past. He grinned and raised his hand to wave at Willie standing on the tanker's cherry-picker platform, but as the tanker passed in front of the terminal lights he saw that Willie wasn't aboard. Whoever it was waved back. Willie must be sick, he thought. Lord knows, everyone else was in God's own weather. He coughed and swallowed a thick wad of mucous. Now he was coming down with it.

Anne watched the de-icing tanker circle them and stop by the leading edge of the left wing. The cherry-picker platform ascended, swiveled, and she saw the operator train the nozzle on the wing and open the faucet. A blast of glycol solution drenched the wing and fuselage, a steaming cloud of pinkish mist enveloping the hooded operator silhouetted in the glow of the wing lights.

Careful, fella, she thought, *watch where you're spraying*. There had been a time when another Coastal captain sat idled in conversation with a flight attendant while the de-icing operator gave the plane's left engine a thorough enema. That pilot now flew in the Alaska bush.

Anne arched her back and pressed her fingertips to the base of her spine. No pain. How odd... She hadn't thought that mere aspirin would do the trick. In a perverse sense she missed the pain, as it had fired her resolve to distance herself well away from Warner Edelbrock. Again she thought of his offer to fly for TransCon, to fly new and well-maintained equipment as well as being assured of continued employment in a profession she loved, and a better base...

Coastal is going under...think it over, Anne...

"Are you okay, captain?" Overmeyer asked.

She blinked her eyes open, realizing her face was taught, her small fists clenched tightly in her lap. *Damn, get a grip,* she thought. She turned and stared at him malevolently, nodding, but touching a finger to her pursed lips, for the cockpit voice recorder took down every word. Overmeyer had much to learn about the realities of the airline environment.

The de-icing tanker circled the nose, gave it a passing blast as though tweaking her own, and stopped at the right wing. "Watch them closely," she told Overmeyer.

He cupped his hands about his eyes and squashed his nose against the side window. For several minutes he watched them hose the aircraft with the steaming glycol fluid, then they hosed it again as if for good measure and gave his window a blast when they saw him watching.

Anne grinned at Overmeyer's exaggerated flinch while she listened to a monotonous nasal voice droning in her headset and telling of La Guardia's current weather conditions. At least it had quit snowing and the winds had calmed, but conditions were only in a lull; there was a SIGMET warning of the worst that would come howling through within the hour. Hopefully well after they were on their way.

When the de-icing crew at last finished, Anne taxied the now dripping aircraft to a holding position near the runway threshold while she and Overmeyer finished the challenge and response of the pre-takeoff checklist.

"Anti-skid?" called Overmeyer.

"Armed," Anne answered.

"Flaps?"

Anne touched the wing flap lever, noted its position in the detent and saw that it was correct. "Set. Checked." She scanned the cockpit a final time, double-checking, as was her habit. All was ready. "Call `em, Donald."

Overmeyer called the tower for takeoff clearance and Anne frowned when they replied, "Coastal 193, hold for runway obstruction."

She breathed deeply and sighed. The turbines whining patiently far to the rear were greedily sucking fuel, precious Coastal dollars, but it wasn't her fault. They waited five minutes and at last Anne called impatiently, "La Guardia tower, Coastal 193, what's the delay?"

"Ah, 193, the ah, the de-icing truck stalled crossing the runway. They're towing it away now. You'll have your clearance in a few moments."

Anne looked nervously at her watch. They were still safely within the holdover period before needing another de-icing, but doubt crept into her mind and it was her responsibility to assure that the wings were still clear of any ice or snow. Quickly she unsnapped her seatbelt and harness and went back into the passenger cabin. She excused herself as she leaned past an elderly couple seated over the wings and peered out their window. There was enough reflected light for her to see that the wings appeared clean, wet. On the opposite side it was the same. Satisfied, she returned to the cockpit and strapped in.

A minute passed. Two minutes. Then, "Coastal 193, taxi into position on three-one and hold."

"One ninety-three into position on three-one and hold," Overmeyer replied.

Anne released the parking brake and nudged the thrust levers forward. "Turn on the digital radar, Donald, I want to have a look at our departure corridor."

Overmeyer looked stricken. "Think there might be some storm cells out there *now*? The SIGMET said later—"

"What I *think* doesn't matter. With the radar there's no guessing. Remember that." She watched the shapeless yellow splotches painting the radar screen as she toed the brakes and swung the DC-9's nose in a wide arc, past the runway centerline, and then back to center again. She had seen no red splotches on the screen. Good, she thought. Other than blowing snow and pre-cip to the northwest there was nothing evil lurking out there at the moment, no storm cell signatures in their departure corridor.

A minute passed as they waited with the DC-9's nose pointed down the 7,000-foot runway.

Then: "Coastal 193, cleared for takeoff on three-one," the tower instructed. Overmeyer promptly repeated the clearance.

A thought ran through Anne's mind. *You don't trust nobody, does you, Miz Annie?*

"No, Titus, I don't," she murmured, leaning forward in her seat and grasping the glareshield. She squinted and stared down the length of the runway, saw the flashing yellow lights of a tow truck off to the side on a taxiway. It was clear, she saw, but not long ago a USAir had collided with another aircraft upon landing in Los Angeles when it was "cleared to land." Tower controllers weren't infallible.

"One ninety-three rolling," Anne said at last, pushing the thrust levers to takeoff power. The engines thundered far to the rear and the DC-9 surged forward. Though the takeoff roll ab-sorbed all of her attention, she caught Overmeyer's movement out of the corner of her eye and quickly glanced at him. He was tug-ging nervously at his chin again, as he had in operations earlier, and now she saw the sheen of sweat on his face in the dim glow of the cockpit lights. *What's his problem?*

Dominic Gugliotti clutched little Toni tightly in his lap as the en-gines suddenly roared at takeoff thrust. He felt the aircraft begin to accelerate and his breathing became shallow, his heart racing like a trip-hammer. In less than two hours it would be over, he told himself again and again. They would land safely in Detroit and then he and Antoinette could laugh about how frightened they'd been for nothing. Until time for the trip back.

Dominic glanced across the aisle at his wife seated by Marie and Teresa, saw her right hand gripping the armrest tightly, her knuckles bone-white. He watched her close her eyes and cross herself. Dominic did the same.

Fools, Jack Wallach thought, watching them. *Ignorant fools.* He loosened his seatbelt and reclined his seat, uncaring that it was against the fucking airline's rules. He'd paid for his ticket. And when you flew all the time like he did, you could bend the rules a little. The stewardesses knew a veteran when they saw one. Act like one and he'd be treated like one, right?

Dodie Warnock turned away from the old woman sitting next to her and reached into her book bag, feeling for and finding the single edge razor blade she had carefully wrapped in tape. In a way she hoped it wouldn't be there, but it was, and she knew what she had to do. There was just no other way.

The hurtling aircraft shook and roared as runway lights raced past Dodie's window in the darkness, becoming a blur and quickly widening the distance between her and her parents. In a little while when the seatbelt sign went off she would excuse herself and wedge past the old woman and go into the bathroom right around the corner. But she wouldn't be back. She supposed it would be the old woman who would come looking and find her. She would probably scream, and all that, you know? Cool.

Shivering in the frigid night air, Titus leaned against the pushback tractor, arms crossed, hands tucked into his armpits, when he at last heard the faraway thunder of jet engines at full thrust. He looked toward the east and saw three bright pinpoints of light gathering speed far down the runway. He knew it was Miz Annie. He watched as the dark shape of the DC-9 sped down the runway, passed opposite the terminal, then rotated gracefully and lifted off into the night. The ear-shattering blast from her engines was like a great ripping of canvas, raising goose bumps on his massive arms. It was a marvelous, powerful sound he loved, and his eyes misted as he turned away. "God be with you, Miz Annie," he murmured.

"Christ!" someone shouted nearby. Titus turned quickly and saw the guideman gesturing frantically toward the runway. His heart stopped when he saw the wing lights of the departing DC-9 rocking wildly as it clawed for altitude barely a hundred feet above the runway, sinking.

"Miz Annie! Oh my god in heaven, Miz Annie!"

A stream of sparks sprayed high in the air and he heard a rending of metal above the thundering of its engines as a wingtip dipped and scraped the concrete runway. Then the tail hit with a terrible shrieking and he stood frozen in fear as the doomed aircraft suddenly catapulted then cartwheeled and slammed upside down on the runway, careening in a shower of sparks. Then a brilliant flash turned night into day as an ugly fireball erupted and shot skyward. In a heartbeat came the concussive *thud* as the shockwave of the explosion thundered over the airfield.

"Annnnieee! MIZ ANNNIEEEE!" Titus shrieked, running and slipping on the icy pavement.

Inside the terminal throngs of terrified onlookers pressed against the plate glass windows, screaming and shouting as emergency vehicles sped past. A woman fainted, children screamed, and two men began shouting obscenities at one another and throwing punches, struggling for a view of the fiery spectacle.

Across the airfield a figure stood in darkness, also watching. He spoke quietly into a cell phone. "There's been a crash."

John Haviland Williams

THREE

"You're entirely too portly, Mitchell dear," Ethel Hardison re-marked, whisking away the bowl of mashed potatoes.

Mitchell Hardison sat across from his elderly mother, serving spoon poised for another helping as she set the bowl down well out of his reach. She was right, he knew, his girth was...well, it was significant, but then she should never have set the potatoes before him in the first place. His mind reeled back forty-five years, to his boyhood, to long before his notion to become an aircraft accident investigator. To when he had been a chubby boy of twelve and she had done the same with the bowl of mashed potatoes, and only his father of equally corpulent proportions, now long dead, had held any sympathy for his only son. Mitchell Hardison remembered well his father's startled expression when by chance they had met at the refrigerator late one night. Then began the nightly ritual that became their secret, their bond. Somehow Mother Hardison had never caught on.

Ethel Hardison interrupted his thoughts as he set the serving spoon down. "Don't think for a moment, Mitchell, that I never knew what you and your father were up to when you were a boy."

"Spiking frogs down at the pond?" he teased, admiring her aging yet still very much Patrician features. At seventy-seven she was still a beautiful woman, trim in body as well as mind. She would likely outlive her only child. She could certainly outthink him.

"Spiking potatoes. I used to watch from down the hall while you two had a go at my refrigerator in your most clandestine manner, whispering, giggling...and gorging yourselves silly."

"You saw all that...and never said anything?"

She sat primly with her hands folded in her lap and smiling tenderly, "I saw it all—including the farting contests afterward. You two were very good with `my coun-*try* 'tis of thee, sweet land of—'."

Mitchell Hardison rose from the table quickly, a muffled belch escaping his lips, his jowls flushing a deep crimson as he swept up the dishes and carried them into her tiny kitchen. *My coun-try 'tis of thee...* He had forgotten about that. Like two farting tubas he and his father had choreographed it pretty damn well, and with Brussels sprouts under your belt you could linger on the notes.

While she sprayed the dishes he palmed a drumstick from the platter with practiced skill, quickly wrapping the morsel in a paper towel and stuffing it into his jacket pocket.

"Mitchell," she said as they later sat in her small living room while sipping coffee, "have you made up your mind about early retirement? You said they had offered it to you."

Offered? It had been more of an ultimatum, but he wouldn't tell Ethel Hardison that. Ever. Thirty-five years he had been with the Feds, twenty-one of them with the Federal Aviation Administration, and the last fourteen with the National Transportation Safety Board as an aviation accident investigator. He was a sleuth of sorts, he supposed. The Board looked to him and others of his

42

cloth—collectively known as *Go-Teams*—to find out what killed airplanes. Pilot error? Structural or mechanical failure? Sabotage? All were questions he faced when one went down. Trouble was, the NTSB, the industry, the pilots associations, and the FAA had long wearied of his brash theories, which, admittedly, he lacked the polish and diplomatic demeanor to deliver effectively. He had the answers, he believed, but they thought them too simplistic and impractical to implement.

Mitchell Hardison simply believed that the cerebrums of many of the errant pilots who caused accidents were cruising at an altitude well above that of their bodies. Were they drunk? Usually not. Drugged? Some, perhaps. There were a few documented cases. But were they distracted, daydreaming? Absolutely.

"So what are we going to do, Mitch," his supervisor, Lucas MacDonald, had railed, "regulate the fucking mind? Have the FAA draft a notice of proposed rule-making that says, `Thou shalt not daydream in the cockpit'? Then link it to the eight-hour bottle-to-throttle rule? Don't think, drink, and fly? Oh, fine. And then maybe we could have the FAA's little minions skulking around and pouncing upon those pilots with a faraway look in their eye? Jesus H. Christ, Hardison, get real. You're a Neanderthal in the jet age. I think you should take an early-out. Retire. It's your right. Besides, the White House is cutting our budget again."

"So? Congress always fixes that. You telling me they're doing things differently on the Hill these days?"

"I'm telling you you've made some enemies under the dome, Mitch. And here as well."

"And I suppose I'm on the shitlist."

Lucas MacDonald's exasperation was total as he looked at Hardison incredulously. "On it? Mitch, you *are* the shitlist! Look," MacDonald said, plucking fingers point-by-point, "You're crude and profane with those to whom you should show respect, like Board members, for example. Your methods are brash and unorthodox, and you seem to take great delight in rocking the political boat like a canoe in a typhoon."

Hardison grunted and nodded. "Sounds about right. Gets their attention though. And, Lucas, I get the goddamned job done."

MacDonald shook his head and leaned forward, whispering hoarsely, "Even the Oval Office thinks you're an asshole. Mitch, an early-out saves a lot of face. Think about it."

He had. For the past two months it was all he thought about. Thirty-five years, and now they were holding the door open for him. The back door.

"Mitchell?" said Ethel, still waiting. "Mitchell?"

His eyes suddenly focused and he avoided Ethel Hardison's patient gaze and looked instead out the window. It was dark and raining. And it was cold. The rivulets of water streaming down the glass would soon freeze, he knew. Lousy night for flying. It was a night much like this when Coastal lost one a month ago, killing thirty-eight including the captain, Ray Thompson.

"I've thought about it," he said at last, "but I haven't decided. I...frankly, mother, I don't know what I'd do with my time if I did."

"I have that all worked out, dear."

I'm sure you do, he thought, heaving a deep sigh.

"First, we'll take a hundred pounds off you so you don't look so much like—"

Like a bowling ball with feet, which was what Lucas MacDonald had called him. But Ethel's comparison was kinder, gentler, usually naming some morbidly corpulent celebrity.

He looked at his watch and saw that it was nearing nine; late enough that he could comfortably excuse himself from another of their weekly dinners and chats, which of late inexorably led to her perceptions of what his future should be. Just as she had more than forty years ago, god love her.

Never married, he now wished that he had. At least there'd be a wife to come home to when the door slammed shut behind him at the NTSB. Something or someone providing a solid, defensible reason for not moving in with Ethel Hardison and spending the remainder of whatever lonely years he had left playing gin, watching soaps and game shows, and...oh god, withering away to a mere shadow at one hundred-eighty pounds. He hadn't weighed that little since boyhood. Mother Hardison would starve him to death.

"Thanks for a swell dinner, mother, but I really have to go."

She linked her arm in his and walked with him to the door. Of habit, he pushed his hornrims higher on the bridge of his nose then turned to hug her once again and stopped short. Her gaze was serious, knowing, as she stood in the apartment doorway and placed her hand against his chest.

Mitchell Hardison frowned, suddenly worried. "You okay, mother?"

She focused on his necktie, absently straightening the soiled knot that was always crooked. "Don't lie to your mother, Mitchell."

"Lie? What about?" Her words flustered him and he felt his cheeks once again flaming as though he were still a boy of thirteen. Her sharp words of decades ago still lingered, *"You don't masturbate, do you, Mitchell?"*

Ethel Hardison shook her head quickly then looked at him again. "Don't let the bastards force you out, Mitchell!" she hissed. "Do you hear? You're the best they have!"

He exhaled in a rush, his arms hanging loosely at his sides, and his voice came in a gravelly whisper. "How did you know?"

"I know everything, Mitchell. Everything that's important. You should know that by now."

Don't let them force you out, Mitchell... occupied his mind as he drove his old Ford slowly along the darkened and rain-slick streets of suburban Long Island, past rows of aging brick apartments like his mother's that populated the little town of Valley Stream. The wipers slapped a steady cadence in the thick mist, but Mitchell

Hardison was too preoccupied to notice the glazed smear now forming on the windshield. He automatically stepped on the brake as he approached an intersection and then felt the rear bumper exchanging places with the front. Suddenly alert, he turned instinctively into the skid, narrowly missing an also spinning Toyota with its horn blaring. In seconds his wheels slammed into the curbing across the intersection, the impact cracking his head painfully against the side window.

He sat there stunned for several seconds, engine idling, wipers clicking like a metronome, kneading a puffy bruise on his skull. Lucky, he guessed, he could have hit the Toyota, injured someone. He reached over the wheel and drew his fingers down the inside of the windshield, tracing the glaze now left by the wipers. Ice. And the streets were now covered with it. Deadly black ice. He should have known better. He did know better, only...*he wasn't paying attention!*

The irony of it gripped him. He, the outspoken crusader against inattentive pilots, sucked into the deadly vortex of daydreaming, of preoccupation when his mind should have been on the business at hand.

How easily the mind could drift...

Slowly he cranked the wheel and crept away in the darkness. The freezing rain soon became wind-driven snow and he envisioned the runways at La Guardia and JFK; they would be much like the streets, slippery, braking action poor. If they were smart they'd close down, but then whether to take off or to land was a decision left to the pilots. So long as ceiling and visibility were at or above legal minimums it was the captain's choice...sometimes his obituary.

No, be honest, Mitchell. It wasn't necessarily the captain's choice. At least not one he would want to make. True, the go or no-go decision was ultimately the pilot's, yet if ceiling and visibility were legal and he chose not to go he'd be damned-all by his airline for screwing up their on-time arrival and departure statistics. An airline seat that does not fly is a seat forever lost to the competition. It was a system with cross-purposes, Hardison grumbled as he parked in front of his apartment building. A system that attempted to balance safety with making a buck in an outrageously competitive environment of calculated risk, but too often the scales tipped heavily in favor of the latter. And the mindlessness of deregulating the industry in 1978 had upset the balance even more. It had turned orderliness into chaos.

The skies were crowded and no longer friendly, Hardison thought as he carefully ascended the icy steps to his apartment building in Flushing. And somewhere tonight, somewhere up there in those blackened skies, was a pilot whose mind would surely wander, if only for a moment, in spite of the dangerous elements. He would succumb to humanness. He would think briefly of his wife and children, or of his mistress, or of the shapely flight attendants in the back serving coffee and booze, or he may worry of rapacious IRS agents now perusing his tax return, or of a failed investment, or whether he could still pass his next medical, or still get it up...

These were the things that drew pilot's carefully trained minds away, caused them to miss a blinking light on the panel or the nearly imperceptible swing of a needle on a gauge; these were Hardison's self-coined "A" factor. One answer to "the why" of pilot error and the crashes that often resulted.

So what are you going to do, Mitch, regulate the fucking mind...? He would if he could.

He grunted wearily as he climbed the last step in the musty hallway, puffing from the three flights he forced himself to climb daily, sidestepping the creaking plank that probably wouldn't if he were a hundred pounds lighter.

Well that just wasn't going to happen.

He inserted his key into the lock and stepped in. There as always lay Dog in the middle of the frayed rug, chin resting on paws outrageously out of proportion to the rest of his body, ears splayed on the rug like overlong curtains, and bearing his usual beseeching stare that only Dog the Basset could render. *You're late and I am voraciously hungry.*

"I know, I know, I'm late and you're hungry," Hardison rasped. "Well so am I."

Dog stood at his heels, jowls dripping great strings of saliva while he scooped out a full can of the evil-smelling goo specially concocted for senior canines. He grunted with effort and farted a squeaker as he bent and set Dog's bowl on the floor, quickly withdrawing his hand as Dog dove for it.

Dog's charfing and woofling set his own juices to running and he patted his side pocket for the drumstick. Then he sat at the small kitchen table and began chewing thoughtfully when Dog signaled he was finished. He chuckled at Dog's rasping burp and answered with one of his own.

My coun-try 'tis of thee... He wondered if he still could.

A foul and unmistakable odor from Dog suddenly enveloped his nostrils and he rose with great effort and heaved a sigh. "You gotta poop now, Dog, right?" He shut his ears to Dog's sudden yet customary barking frenzy that could only mean, *yeah, real bad,* and snatched the leash from the kitchen doorknob. He would have to hurry, for while Dog possessed an incredible capacity for faithfully saving his *Foulness Giganticus* during the long days and sometimes nights alone, at precisely two minutes post-dinner his capacity was suddenly lost. Other than dinner, Hardison knew well that this was Dog's *Big Moment.*

He snapped the leash on Dog's collar and ambled toward the door. Then the telephone rang.

"Shit," Hardison muttered as Dog strained against the leash, whining with great urgency, his four stubby legs now swimming a sort of dog paddle on the slippery wood floor.

There was an unmistakable urgency to the ringing and Hardison hesitated, torn with indecision. He should let it ring; let the machine pick it up. He glanced at the kitchen clock, saw that it was nine thirty-five, and he felt a sudden sense of unease. *It was dark, icy, snow falling...* Visions of now treacherous runways at nearby JFK and La Guardia flashed in his mind, his own uncontrollable skid through a dark intersection... Still, he could call back in a few minutes, after Dog--

He strained against Dog's protestations and reached for the telephone. "Hardison."

"Mitch? Doug Westphal at the office. Coastal lost another one at La Guardia."

Hardison sighed heavily. "When, what, and how bad?"

"About twenty minutes ago. A DC-9, and...it's real bad."

The leash went slack in his hands as he listened to his assistant at the NTSB describe what had happened. Then, "Okay, Doug, I'll meet you there in fifteen minutes. You get hold of the rest of the Go-Team? Good. You know the routine, cordon it off, nobody touches anything, pee and blood samples of all the flight crew quick-like, hear?"

"Won't they do that in the autopsies?"

Hardison's heart sank. "Oh, Jesus," he muttered. "Okay, Doug, give me some more good news—who's the Board member assigned to our team?"

"Parghetti's on his way."

"We could do worse—see you in a few." He put the phone down and glanced at Dog, the aging canine's back now arched as he waddled about in a circle, pooping on the kitchen floor.

"You're excused, old fella. Sorry."

The grisly and chaotic scene awaiting him at La Guardia was a familiar one. Too familiar. America's airports seemed to have become synonymous with Africa's elephant graveyards, a place where the great ships of the sky came to die. Los Angeles, Little Rock, Dallas, Sioux City, Detroit... Over the years La Guardia had certainly had its share, but in the past month Coastal had boosted them into the forefront. He flashed his ID at a guard and drove through a gate to the runways where in the distance he saw the revolving lights of emergency vehicles and many glaring floodlamps clustered about the nondescript carcass of what had once been an airliner.

Within the carcass he knew that unrecognizable chunks of human detritus still remained, burned, blackened, often fused to shards of metal by incredible heat. He would have to paw through the putrid carnage while searching for clues, fighting back the gag reflex, often unsuccessfully. It was the part of his work he dreaded.

But somewhere in that god-awful mess lay the answer...*the probable cause*. As the investigator-in-charge he would have to find it.

A fireman dressed in asbestos gear flagged him down on a taxiway near the now steaming wreckage.

"I'm sorry, sir, you can't—"

"Hell I can't, sonny, this is my property now." Mitchell Hardison showed his ID and stepped on the gas. His wheels spun in the slushy mixture of fire retardant foam and snow when suddenly they bit concrete and he lurched forward.

NTSB investigator Doug Westphal stood near the smoldering wreckage jotting notes as he talked with airport and FAA officials. Body bags lay everywhere, some containing entire bodies, some not, and still the rescue crews emerged from the wreckage with more. The terrified and agonized screams from within had long ceased, yet miraculously some had survived. Some, not many, had even walked away with little more than scratches. Like the old lady he'd found wandering about in shock, wailing, *"Why me, God? Why did you spare me?"* It was a quirk of fate that he had seen occur frequently in airline disasters—the unscathed found sitting amid the horribly mutilated. God only knew how that happened.

He snapped his notepad shut and bent to examine a separated piece of the wreckage when he saw the familiar old Ford fishtailing its way through the snow toward him. He heard the Ford's engine race and he chuckled when the vehicle suddenly spun end for end twice before it stopped fifty feet away. The driver's door popped open instantly and he saw the short, rotund figure of Mitchell Hardison emerge.

"Over here, Mitch!" Westphal called, waving. "Be careful, it's—" Too late he saw Hardison's feet scoot forward from under him. "—slick." Stepping carefully he hurried to help his floundering superior.

"I don't need help, dammit," Hardison growled as he scuttled to his feet, "I just need some fucking...traction." He stood at last, puffing and brushing the slush from his clothing, surveying the scene. "Okay, now tell me what happened."

They stood beneath the glaring floodlamps, Westphal reading from his notes while Mitchell Hardison listened, nodding occasionally and scanning the grisly detritus of the forty-one who now lay dead. Six were still unaccounted for. There were eleven known survivors. Both flight attendants dead, the first officer dead, of the crew only the captain had survived but was in poor condition.

The doomed DC-9 lay on its back like a great dead bird, shorn of its left wing, the landing gear on the attached right wing jutting grotesquely skyward and silhouetted in the glare. Rescue workers in bright yellow slickers crawled on, in, and about the twisted and crushed carcass like so many maggots, still searching for human remains.

"Yo!" one yelled from within the wreckage, his head emerging through a broad fissure in the fuselage just forward of where the left wing had been. "Here's the six we've been looking for—they're all together!"

Rescue workers scurried and stumbled their way through the debris toward the worker inside the shattered and charred fuselage, hopeful that some of the six missing were still alive. Hardison stepped forward, hopeful as well, but he soon saw otherwise when a worker emerged with the unrecognizably charred remains of a child in his arms, his head turned away as he vomited into the wreckage. In minutes other workers dragged the remains of five more bodies free and laid them carefully in the snow, the coroner's deputies quickly stuffing them into body bags.

"Four kids, two adults," Westphal said quietly. "Looks like an entire family."

Hardison nodded, looking away. "Better that way, Doug."

When his nausea passed, Mitchell Hardison examined the wreckage more closely and saw that the aircraft's seams had split from the enormous impact, its fuselage eviscerated and leaving gaping maws ahead of and behind the remaining wing. The vertical portion of the tail was gone and Westphal pointed to it a hundred yards away. "There."

"And the left engine?" Hardison asked, seeing that the right was still attached to the tail section.

Westphal pointed in the opposite direction. "There." The huge cylindrical chunk lay steaming in the snow about seven hundred feet away. The aircraft had hit with such force that it literally shot apart.

Hardison stared thoughtfully at the wreckage for a few moments and then focused on what was left of the cockpit. He wasn't surprised that the first officer didn't make it.

Westphal snapped his notebook shut. "Looks like it rolled over after takeoff, sheared off the left wing when it contacted the runway, then cartwheeled and came down nearly flat on its back, the right side of the cockpit striking first. I'd say they maybe had a compressor stall or a flameout in one of the engines, then the wings stalled and it rolled before they could catch it."

"Maybe," Hardison said, preoccupied. "They expect the captain to live?"

"No, sir."

"What's his name?"

"Hers."

Mitchell Hardison raised his bushy eyebrows then crushed out his cigar and spat in the snow. "Okay, hers."

Westphal flipped through his notes. "Ryan. Anne A. Ryan."

A flicker of recognition passed through Hardison's mind. A number of women now flew as flight officers for airlines, but only a few were anointed with the fourth stripe of captain. The name *Ryan* was somehow familiar... He shrugged; it would come to him. "They recover the voice and data recorders yet?"

"Both of them. They're in my car."

Hardison nodded then took Westphal by the elbow. "Let's go for a hike."

They stopped by Hardison's car long enough for him to pull on his rubber boots, and then they began reconnoitering the hulk and debris. The stench of kerosene was everywhere and Hardison fought back the impulse to light another cigar. Instead he chewed on a dead butt while poking around with a flashlight. He squatted uncomfortably beside the flattened cockpit while Westphal greeted the arriving contingent of other NTSB investigators, the FAA, and pilot's association, then he reached and touched the crushed and shattered frame of the copilot's window. His fingers came away wet and sticky and he shined the flashlight on them. Blood. He swallowed hard and wiped his fingers in the snow.

In less than an hour they were fully organized except for the aircraft manufacturer's technicians and assorted other parties to the investigation who would arrive later. The remainder of the bodies had been located and removed from the wreckage, the area cordoned off, scattered debris was tagged and inventoried, photographs were taken from dozens of angles and a running commentary of observations was videotaped. Hardison assigned members of his NTSB Go-Team to interview the tower controllers, survivors, Coastal officials, and any eyewitnesses they could locate. He sent Westphal to get a copy of the control tower recording of voice transmissions to and from Coastal 193.

A thought struck him. "Doug!" he called as the younger man hurried away. "Find out if they de-iced before takeoff."

Hardison stood in the snow with his hands jammed in his pockets, oblivious to the goings on around him and staring thoughtfully at the wreckage while chewing a dead cigar and rocking back and forth on his heels. He envisioned how it must have been, apparently a normal rotation and takeoff and then something went awry, something caused the DC-9 to roll, then a wing clipped the runway and tore away, then the cartwheeling, then...splat. Boom.

He replayed the scenario in his mind several times. If they had been de-iced shortly beforehand, and the crew had checked the wings before takeoff as they were supposed to, then ice on the wings couldn't have been a factor. If they'd lost an engine, flameout or compressor stall or whatever, a DC-9 with an alert and responsive crew was capable of limited but continued flight. Structural failure? Not likely. Bomb? He would rule that out unless the picture wouldn't come together. But the picture so far *was* coming together—there had been two others within the past seven months much like it. Trans-Globe, Coastal, and now Coastal again. All crashes on takeoff. Here. The first two hadn't been his to investigate, yet there had been a commonality between them: Apparent pilot error.

There had been no structural failures, no bombs, and the notion of wing icing had been raised but later squelched when they learned that both aircraft had been de-iced prior to takeoff. All the evidence had leaned toward human failure. Somebody screwed up. The chief investigator had once said, "If it ain't mechanical, meteorological, an act of a saboteur or an Act of God, then by God it was an act--or lack of an act--of the pilot. In some measure."

He stared at the wreckage again. "Somebody screwed up here tonight," he murmured. "Big time." He sensed that he knew who and suddenly he wanted a lot more information. A dossier on Captain Anne Ryan would be a good place to start.

Doug Westphal saw the bright floodlights of the de-icing tanker parking bays ahead and he turned into the drive and parked outside on the ramp. Beside the building he saw a tanker parked in the shadows and two men in yellow raingear easing a thick hose from the tanker into a storm drain.

"Hey!" he called, walking toward them and waving.

The two men looked up as he approached. "Yeah?" answered the taller one.

"You the guys who de-iced Coastal 193?" he said, waving toward the crash scene.

"What about it?" answered the taller one.

"I need to check your load."

"Go ahead. Here, use my flashlight."

Westphal took the offered flashlight and hoisted himself onto the tanker, hunched down and opened the hatch. He shined the light in, saw that the tanker was quarter full and the de-icing solution of the proper color. Satisfied, he shut and dogged the hatch and leaped down.

"Any problems?" asked the taller man.

"None that I can see." Westphal reached into his pocket for his notepad, wrote his observations, then looked up. "I'll need your names." He took their offered IDs and copied the information, and then handed them back to the taller man. "Thanks, Mr. Darcy, appreciate your cooperation."

"My flashlight?"

"Oh. Yeah, here. Thanks."

As he drove away he glanced back at the de-icing crew still watching him. Strange, he thought. They had seemed so tense, wary. But then who wouldn't be? A crash killing many and here he was, a federal investigator, grilling them as though they were in some way culpable.

John Haviland Williams

FOUR

When the call came in at nine twenty-two p.m. the emergency room staff at Queen's Memorial Hospital went on full alert, expecting dozens of critically injured from the destroyed aircraft at La Guardia. Chief resident physician Dr. David Levinson knew what to expect. He'd seen it before, and they were ready when ambulance attendants brought in the first of the injured. Soon there would be more, many more, and he knew that their orderly efficiency would soon become a chaotic frenzy.

He stood waiting outside on the emergency room ramp, shivering in the cold with only his white hospital coat to protect him, while attendants from the second ambulance unloaded three more. He quickly surveyed their injuries and dispatched them inside to the waiting trauma teams. Now he watched the driveway for more flashing lights, listening for the wailing ambulances yet to come. He waited ten minutes, and then puzzled and freezing he turned and went inside.

"How many so far?" he asked Regina Dotzer, the head nurse.

"Ten. Four critical, four serious, two ambulatory. Amazing, isn't it?"

"What?"

"That some people can walk away from something like that."

He nodded absently. "It happens. Who've we got that's ambulatory?"

"Both ends of the spectrum—an elderly lady and a teenage girl who were apparently sitting together in the rear of the plane. Minor scratches, some bruises and contusions, but they're both in shock. I think you ought to look in on them, doctor, neither seems to have any family, but I think the teenager's a runaway."

Levinson looked up. "Oh? Why do you think that? That she's a runaway."

Regina shook her head and smiled. "Because I'm a woman, that's why. And a mother."

Levinson raised his hands. "Whoa. Understood. I'll leave her to you and Halstead. Obviously out of my field. Elderly women and little children, fine. Anything female in between is a complete mystery to me. Like, I can't relate, you know? Isn't that how they say it?"

Regina nodded. "That's how they say it. And, my good doctor," she said, tweaking his stethoscope, "that is why you're still single."

"And that I shall remain. Okay, where's the elderly woman and what's her name? I'll look in on her after they bring in the others."

Regina looked at the patient listing. "Attebury, Lillian. She's in observation room D."

"Was she hysterical?"

"Devastated, but not for reasons you'd think. She keeps saying, `Why me? Why me?' I think she means why should an elderly woman be spared when others much younger have died."

"A conundrum of life, Regina. That's the way it works. Random. I don't believe in the existence of predestination. And speaking of the way things work, I wonder where the rest of the survivors are? There should be many more than this. Maybe you should call the airport and find out what's holding them up."

"And maybe it was a small plane," she added. Then the telephone at her elbow rang. She answered it and frowned. "I see," she said, quickly writing a cryptic note and handing it to him.

David Levinson scanned the note: *47 dead, 11 survivors, last one on the way.* He crumpled the note and tossed it. Ten plus one on the way. Eleven. That was it; there would be no more. Then he heard the distant wail of a siren.

Regina Dotzer hung up the telephone and rose quickly from her chair. "I think that's the last one coming now," she said. "It's supposed to be one of the pilots."

The ambulance quickly braked and the tires shrieked when the driver threw it into reverse and backed to the emergency room ramp. Dr. David Levinson and Regina Dotzer stood watching when the rear doors flew open and three attendants hustled a wheeled gurney out onto the ramp.

"The airport people said they had to cut this one out of the wreck," Regina said.

The gray blanket covering the victim was splattered with blood, two IV's dangled from a rack, and an oxygen mask covered the injured pilot's bloody face. David Levinson glanced quickly at the victim, who seemed quite small for a pilot, then he saw the irregular and misshapen outline of shattered legs beneath the blanket and knew he was in bad shape.

"This way," he ordered as they hurried through the hallway.

Levinson quickly organized his team, ordered more IVs and an evaluation of the extent of the pilot's injuries, and had them prepare him for surgery while he scrubbed. A surgical nurse stood at his elbow, latex gloves held at ready as he turned, arms dripping.

"Cardiac arrest!" came a shout from the adjacent operating room.

"Damn," he murmured, diving his hands into the gloves and hurrying past the nurse. He saw a flurry of activity around the patient. "Paddles!" he shouted, quickly elbowing his way to the patient's side.

What he saw stunned him as he gazed for the first time at the complete and naked body of the critically injured pilot lying before him. He held the defibrillator paddles poised above two small and bruised yet perfectly formed breasts.

Regina Dotzer saw the obvious astonishment in Dr. David Levinson's eyes. "Yes," Regina said, "she is indeed a woman."

Quickly he slapped the paddles against her chest. "Clear!" he yelled. "Now!" As the electrical charge hit home the woman's diminutive body bucked violently beneath him. All eyes watched the monitor on the wall. Flatline. "Clear!" he yelled again as he held the paddles in place. "Now!" Again the woman's body bucked.

Nothing.

He sensed the tension among his staff, reflecting his own, certain they too were holding their breath. *Come on, come on little lady, live! Live, dammit!*

"Clear! Now!"

Again the pilot's small body heaved upward. He glanced at the monitor, willing the flat electronic green line to suddenly blip, to trace a mountain range of blips.

Still nothing.

A nurse swabbed his drenched brow and he exhaled heavily as he stood leaning over the pitifully broken figure, paddles still in place, and slowly scanned the length of her body. Maybe it's just as well, he thought. Lower rib cage crushed, fractured forearms, fractured pelvis, deep gashes everywhere, and both legs shattered. He looked at the swollen knot and gaping wound on her forehead and guessed massive head and internal injuries as well. She couldn't have lived, he knew, and if she had she would have lived out the remainder of her days in misery. Still...

Once more. One more try.

David Levinson took a deep breath. "Clear! Now!"

Again her small body bucked and the back of her right hand fell to rest on his forearm. He looked at her slender fingers, saw them slowly curl. It was involuntary, he knew; part of the process of death.

"Pulse!" someone shouted, and all eyes quickly fixed upon the monitor. There it was, the slightest blip, then another, then flatline. Then another blip, and another.

"Heart rate forty," droned the anesthesiologist.

"Aww-*right*!" a male nurse shouted.

Beneath his mask Dr. David Levinson smiled. Now he would have to get to work on her. And quickly, for he could lose her again at any second.

Twenty minutes later Regina returned to her station and sat heavily in her chair, massaging her aching temples. It had been tense in the operating room but Levinson had done it again. Not that the saving of lives wasn't part of his job, but it was the way in which he did it, as though each horribly injured patient were someone special to him.

The telephone rang and she reached for it. "Emergency, Regina Dotzer."

For moments she listened to the distraught woman on the line, nodding and quickly scanning the list of patients from the plane crash. The unfamiliar name wasn't there and she closed her eyes, gathering her thoughts. "I'm sorry," Regina said at last, "We don't have a Jack Wallach." She shook her head as the woman railed on, becoming hysterical. "No, ma'am, we were told that all of the survivors were brought to this hospital. I'm terribly sorry."

Somehow she couldn't bring herself to tell the woman to try the morgue.

Warner Edelbrock quietly hung up the telephone in his study and stood at the French doors opening to the balcony. He swirled the brandy in his snifter and pursed his lips, nodding. Then he quickly downed the fiery liquid, refilled it and settled comfortably into his favorite leather chair and placed his feet on the ottoman. He stared into the crackling fire and thought about the telephone call...

"Coastal has lost another one," his public relations vice president had said with obvious relish.

"Do tell. How many aboard this time?"

"Enough to matter," Philip Darcy replied. "More than enough to matter. The timing was perfect."

"What about the pilots?"

"Both dead, from what I could learn."

Warner Edelbrock shifted his large frame then inclined his head as he thought about it. He could see the morning headlines, almost hear the cries of public outrage. With so many more deaths close in the wake of the last crash, the litigation and huge settlements would be a lawyer's answered prayer. And his. Tonight's crash would effectively torpedo what remained of the floundering hulk that had been Coastal Airlines. Their routes and equipment would be ripe for takeover at a fraction of their worth, and he and TransCon were ready for them. It had been a long struggle, but the crashes had tipped the balance and at last Coastal would be theirs.

He raised his glass in toast to the fire and kicked off his slippers. He would miss Anne Ryan, but she'd been warned. She had every opportunity to get out of harm's way.

Restless, he rose and shuffled barefoot on the thick carpeting and stood again at the French doors opening to the balcony. He watched the snow falling steadily on the extensive and manicured gardens below, burying Sylvia's efforts of the previous summer. Well, at least burying the results of her *directing* of the effort. Often he had watched her below, thoroughly crippled yet comfortably ensconced on her motorized throne and scurrying about giving orders to the gardeners.

He thought of Romo, the head gardener, and how he seemed to humbly genuflect before her and absorb as his deserved punishment her furious tirades if he had planted the bulbs wrong or pruned the roses incorrectly. He visualized the meek and timid Romo nodding eagerly as she would at last dismiss him, how he would slink away, shoulders hunched and walking as though treading upon eggshells, and then, out of her sight, reach into the shed and grab a shovel. Warner Edelbrock fantasized how carefully, quietly, Romo would measure his steps as he crept behind her, then slowly he would raise the shovel high above his head and with all of his strength bring it crashing down upon her skull.

It could happen, he thought, sipping his brandy. Yes indeed, it could surely happen.

A faint mechanical whirring in the hallway broke through his thoughts and he carefully set his glass down. "Come in, Sylvia dear."

The ornate oak door to his study opened slowly and Sylvia Edelbrock rolled in. She stopped her wheeled machine in the doorway and set the brake. "Did I hear you talking, Warner dear?"

Quite possibly, he thought bitterly. He had been known to do that. He stared heavy-lidded at her as she sat stoically on her six-thousand-dollar throne. He detested the sight of her. Sixty-five looking eighty, Sylvia Preston Edelbrock sat hunched forward in her wheelchair and unable to sit upright. She smiled knowingly at him while kneading her gnarled arthritic fingers, an affectation he had long recognized as the precursor to conflict. Sylvia was up to something.

"I was talking on the telephone," he said at last, and stood and walked to the French doors, his back to her.

"Was it family, dear?"

"I suppose you could say that. Philip Darcy."

"That bastard," Sylvia hissed, "How dare you refer to filth like that as family."

Warner Edelbrock spun around. "Filth like that, as you put it, happens to be TransCon's vice president of marketing and public relations, Sylvia. I picked him myself."

She dismissed his sudden rage with an offhand gesture and whirred toward him. "Yes, I'm certain you did, Warner. He is the devil incarnate and you seem perfectly comfortable with having resurrected him. Tell me, who does whose bidding?"

Warner Edelbrock flew into a rage. "Goddamn it, Sylvia, I run TransCon, not you. Now leave it alone, for Christ's sake!"

"And it is *my* family's wealth that is the very foundation of TransCon, Warner! Preston wealth!"

He clenched his fists, eyes narrowing, "And you never let me forget that, do you? Do you, Sylvia?"

Sylvia stared at the carpet before his feet, suddenly morose. "I...I apologize, Warner," she whispered, covering her face with palsied hands. "I don't know what makes me say these terrible things to someone whom I adore so much. You've been so good to me...and I've been so..."

So predictable, he thought. Venom and honey. He forced himself to reach and touch her shoulder. "It's all right, Sylvia, forget it. Just forget it." He bent and kissed the top of her head. "Shall I call Pennington to help you into bed?"

She raised her head and shook it quickly. "No," she whispered, "I'll be all right. I can manage very well, you know."

"Yes," he said, "I know."

Sylvia took his large hand and held it to her cheek. "Did something happen at the airline? Is that why Philip called?"

"Everything's fine, dear. Just fine. Things couldn't be better."

Mitchell Hardison closed the file on his desk and leaned back in his creaking government-issue chair and sighed. It had been a long night since the crash and he'd had no sleep. His eyes were grainy and he rubbed his hand over his stubbled jowls, thinking how good a shower and shave would feel. He thought of Dog,

64

ever alone, probably lying at this moment in the center of his living room floor on *his* rug, waiting. He could see the sad hound-dog eyes staring patiently at the door, an ear cocking occasionally at any sound in the hallway that might be *Him*.

Dog's unfailing loyalty depressed and saddened him. Dog deserved better...

The intercom buzzed and he rocked forward and snatched the receiver, hoping it was Westphal with more information. "Hardison."

"Mitch, Lucas."

Lucas MacDonald, His Royal Highness, the boss, and offeror of the early-out. Hardison reached and plucked his cigar butt from the ashtray. "Mornin', Lucas."

"My office in five minutes?"

"Right."

Mitchell Hardison lateraled the butt about his mouth then gathered the Coastal 193 file and rose from his chair. The file was thin and the info scanty at best, but soon it would thicken as the bits and pieces from the investigative groups flowed in, and in a few months it would likely fill a cabinet, maybe more. From that would come the *probable cause*. If they let him have his way.

He opened the door to Lucas MacDonald's outer office, saw his bitchy secretary eyeing his left hand warily. He showed her that his gnawed cigar butt was safely out and harmless, but still her expression puckered.

"He's waiting for you, Mitchell," she said, nodding toward the closed door.

He straightened his tie and ran a hand over the sparse and brush-like bristle atop his head, then hitched his sagging trousers and entered.

"Morning, Mitch. You look dapper as usual. Have a seat and get comfortable. Be with you in a second," MacDonald said, pointing to the solitary straight-backed chair before his desk.

Hardison sighed and reluctantly took the familiar torture throne, well known to all who came before the boss. He yawned and drummed his fingers on the Coastal file while Lucas Mac-Donald, a starched and retired Air Force brigadier, finished scribbling a memo then tossed it into his out-basket and leaned back in his chair. "So, Mitch, what have you and your team got?"

Hardison grunted and thumbed the file open. "Okay, here's the long and the short of it. Coastal 193, a DC-9 of the ten-series crashed at La Guardia at 2116 hours, eleven December, nineteen ninety-nine. Forty-seven dead, including both flight attendants and the first officer. Eleven survived including the captain who is listed as critical and in a coma."

He turned a page. "Incident occurred on takeoff shortly after rotation. Witnesses we've contacted so far indicate that it rolled quickly to the left at an altitude of approximately one hundred feet, then quickly to the right, then a severe roll to the left again and continuing past the ninety degree position, at which point the left wing tip contacted the runway. Then the nose struck and the aircraft cartwheeled and rolled inverted, finally impacting the runway in an inverted position and skidding 800 feet until it came to rest 6,500 feet from the beginning of its takeoff roll."

"Meteorological conditions?" MacDonald asked, casually swiveling from side to side in his chair.

"Instrument meteorological. Ceiling indefinite, 1,500 feet obscured; visibility one mile and variable; light snow to the northwest; temperature 23, dewpoint 19; wind 220 degrees at four knots. Runway visual range 6,000 feet plus. Ice on the runways and braking conditions poor." He looked up from the file. "Nice night for a trip to Detroit."

MacDonald frowned. "Crappy at best." He spun quickly in his chair and stared out the window at the bleak weather. "So what do you think, Mitch, same as Coastal's last one? The guy—I mean the woman, flubbed up?"

66

"Maybe. We'll know better when the lab's finished analyzing the voice and data recorders. I've listened to the tower tape and nothing seemed abnormal."

"The crew say anything when the trouble started?"

Hardison shook his head. "Not to the tower. Probably too busy trying to control that rock and rolling mother, but the cockpit voice recorder ought to tell us something."

"Ice, you think? Wing ice?"

Hardison stared at the carpet, saw that his brogans were still covered with dried mud from the night before. Absently he polished the tips on the backs of his calves as he spoke. "Doubt it. It had quit snowing and they had de-iced less than ten minutes before takeoff. Wing contamination seems out of the question."

"But it stalled, no doubt of that, right? The rocking wings and all?"

"That's the way it looks to me," Hardison replied.

MacDonald shook his head in disgust. "Then that's it. Somebody in the cockpit screwed up. Again."

Mitchell Hardison shrugged and closed the file, tapping it on his knee. "Like I said. Maybe. And if they did I'll find out who and why."

MacDonald leaned forward on his elbows. "I don't need to tell you that this one's especially sensitive, Mitch. The administration's going to want more than just the *probable* cause. An entire airline could go down the tubes because of this if it's the pilot's fault or a mechanical failure resulting from poor maintenance. And because the captain's a woman you can bet there'll be an uproar among the I-told-you-so bunch. You know who they are, Mitch."

Hardison snorted. "Do we care? I mean about the I-told-you-so assholes?"

"Not as far as I'm concerned. But the Oval Office has been on the phone to me twice today. They want to know how it happened, what caused it."

"Crap. Coastal was a contributor to the president's party in the last campaign. There's probably a political link there."

"They just want us to be certain what caused it."

"And they want to know right now," Hardison retorted. "They think that all we have to do is go out and take a look, listen to the recorders, then snap our notebooks shut."

MacDonald let out his breath in a rush. "That's not the way it is. Those guys, the Chief of Staff, they know the score. They're not stupid. They just want a thorough investigative job."

They want us to stick it to someone, Lucas, and you fucking well know it, Hardison thought. Well, that just wasn't going to happen. He had never known the NTSB to be anything but painstakingly objective. And thorough. But still there were those who tried their influence upon them. "And a thorough investigative job they'll get. Business as usual," he said rising from his chair. "You going to give me carte blanche, Lucas, or the usual nickels and dimes to work miracles?"

"Whatever it takes."

Hardison raised his bushy brows. *Times change.*

Doug Westphal was grinning like a Cheshire and patting a tape recorder, waiting for him when he returned to his office, "Sit down, Mitch, and listen to this."

"The cockpit voice recording? That was quick."

"You've got a good staff, Mitch, you should be proud."

Hardison buried his face in his hands and slowly shook his head. *He who tooteth not his own horn, the same shall not be tooted.* Ah, the exuberance of youth. Then he looked up, "Roll it, Doug, and cut the crap."

For a few seconds there was nothing but the hissing of the tape. Then: "Coastal 193 cleared for takeoff." It was the voice of the La Guardia tower controller.

"One ninety-three rolling." Unmistakably the voice of a woman. Then came a roaring sound and Hardison knew that the engines had been pushed to takeoff thrust.

"...okay, airspeed's alive," a male voice said. The first officer, Hardison thought. It seemed an eerie voice from the grave. "...Engines stabilized, power's set..." Again the male voice. Then: "...fuel's even kinda balanced.....one hundred knots..."

Well that settles that, Hardison thought. The voice of the pilot calling out takeoff observations was usually that of the pilot not flying the plane. Thus the captain, Ryan, had been flying it.

"Vee one..." came the male voice again. "...rotate."

Hardison visualized the captain pulling the yoke back toward her lap, the nose rising as the aircraft hurtled down the runway...

"...vee two......plus ten....positive rate..."

Okay so far, Hardison thought. Normal takeoff, positive rate of climb. No sinking yet.

Then: "...Watch out! Watch out! Watch out!..." came a frantic voice.

It was the voice of the first officer and Hardison stiffened, the flesh on the back of his neck suddenly prickling. He looked at Westphal, saw his stricken expression. Then he heard the roaring of the engines surging, as though someone was jockeying the throttles, then came an insistent rattling sound.

"Stick-shaker," Westphal interjected. "Stall warning."

Hardison raised his hand, annoyed, listening intently. Then came the sound of the first impact, like a door being slammed, then a moment of frightening silence followed and he held his breath. The next sound was cataclysmic. An enormous and concussive impact burst from the recorder's speakers, followed by a great shrieking and tearing of metal as the doomed ship went through its death throes. He imagined the instant of final impact, remembering the crushed cockpit and the first officer's blood spilled on the shattered metal.

There was a prolonged hissing of blank tape and Westphal shut off the machine. "Scary, isn't it?"

Hardison nodded. Indeed it was. It was always spooky listening to the final words of those now dead. "I wonder what he saw when he yelled, `Watch out! Watch out! Watch out!'?"

Westphal shrugged. "Maybe the captain did something wrong, screwed up, maybe he was trying to warn her. Maybe she passed out or something."

Hardison looked at him curiously. "Play it again, Doug."

They listened to the tape three more times and each time Hardison jotted down another observation. At last he settled back in his chair, removed his glasses and massaged his stubbled jowls. God, he was tired, but already he had some answers. And many more questions. He glanced up and saw Westphal standing before his desk expectantly, a controlled smirk tugging at the corners of his mouth as though waiting for him to open a present.

"All right, Dougie," Hardison said wearily, "quit the silly theatrics and give me the punchline."

Quickly Westphal rewound the tape then checked the counter against his notes and nodded. "Wanted you to hear a piece of the pre-takeoff dialogue last."

The speaker hissed for a few seconds, then came the words of the first officer: "...Are you okay, captain?"

Hardison rocked forward quickly. *Well, son of a bitch.*

Dr. David Levinson adjusted the window blinds to deflect the glare of the midmorning sunlight. He moved to the bedside and stood looking down at his comatose patient. So sad, he thought, so terribly sad. It was times like this that made him regret his Hippocratic oath. He had saved a life, yes, but for how long he didn't know. Hours, days maybe. Maybe even months.

It had been a week now and she was at least stabilized, but her wounds were grievous and he had no notion of whether she realized the presence of others. He doubted it. He leaned close and examined her eyes through great puffy slits and saw that they were still dilated. A very bad sign. Neurosurgeons had drilled into her skull and relieved the subdural hematoma resulting from what must have been an enormous crack on the head, but he doubted she would regain her motor responses. In saving her life he had probably created a vegetable.

She had probably been an attractive woman before the accident, he guessed, judging from the structure and delicate shaping of the few uninjured facial bones. He reached for her chart: Ryan, Anne A., female Caucasian, blonde, blue, 63 inches, 118 pounds. Occupation airline captain. He saw by her date of birth that she was a little over forty, unmarried, no dependents. A blessing of sorts, he thought; there was no husband, no children to grieve.

He suddenly felt strangely self-conscious as he studied her chart, as though an intruder pawing about in someone's underwear drawer. He felt like he was being watched. He glanced quickly at her eyes but saw nothing, only the puffy slits.

"Dr. Levinson?"

He turned quickly, startled.

"Sorry, doctor," Regina Dotzer said from the doorway. "There's a Captain Rosenberg here to see the patient. Do you want to speak to him first?"

"Captain Rosenberg?"

"Yes. He says he grew up with Miss Ryan. That they're old friends."

Levinson sighed, "I was hoping someone from her family would show up."

"He says she has no family."

"I'll speak to him in the hallway. Maybe he can tell us something about her."

He saw that Captain Rosenberg was a stocky man of about forty. Roly-poly better described his moon-faced and boyish appearance that seemed at odds to the uniform he wore. His gaze and countenance seemed authoritative enough nonetheless, yet there was a definite aura of sensitivity about the dark eyes. He took Rosenberg's firm grip and introduced himself.

"Call me Gordy, everybody does. Can I see her now, doctor?"

"In a few minutes." He took Rosenberg by the elbow and led him into a small sitting room where he explained Anne Ryan's condition, cautioning him against optimism. He could see that the man was thoroughly shaken and bordering on tears, and he diverted the conversation.

"Tell me about her family—the family she once had, anything that will help us to know more about her, captain. Sorry, I mean Gordy."

Rosenberg paced the small room, his mind crowded with the memories of her as he tried to organize his thoughts and relate what she had told him long ago. At last he let out a heavy sigh and turned to Levinson. "Her mother disappeared--walked out, I guess--when she was two, and her father was killed when she was seven. She grew up with godparents." He shrugged and spread his hands wide. "That's it in a nutshell."

"How did her father—"

Rosenberg turned away and walked to the window. "Plane crash," he said woodenly, staring at the busy parking lot below. Then he turned, his expression stricken. "Ironic, isn't it? First him, now her? Ernie Gann was right. Fate *is* the hunter!"

"I don't understand."

Rosenberg waved it away. "Just a book title, that's all. Gann wrote it."

"Tell me about her father."

Her god, you mean, Rosenberg thought as he paced slowly at the window, his large hands jammed into the pockets of his uniform jacket. He doubted he could describe their relationship as she had, how she had worshipped him even in death as though he watched over her every move. "He flew for National Airlines back in the forties, fifties and sixties, and he and Anne were very close. Anne was an only child and she adored him, idolized him,

72

and swore that she would someday be a pilot like him. Then one day her father's DC-6B exploded in midair over the Gulf of Mexico with 62 passengers on board." He shook his head and continued, "I don't think she's ever really gotten over it. Her life of flying is like a tribute to him, a way of sort of memorializing her pledge to him when she was little. She said it was an 'I'm gonna be like you, dad,' sort of thing, you know?"

Levinson nodded. "Was it a bomb in her father's plane?"

Rosenberg shrugged and looked away again. "Probably. That was the official word, anyway. National had another one a couple of months later that was confirmed as a bomb. On the other hand I've read that DC-6s had a habit of catching fire and exploding during the forties, but the design defect was later found and fixed long before her father's crash. So who knows, a bomb—maybe, maybe not."

Levinson pondered this, then shook his head. "Must have been a hell of a blow for a little girl of seven, especially for the hero worship you describe." And because of that, he knew what he must say next. "Gordy, what kind of person was—excuse me, is she? I mean…" He hesitated, but it had to be asked. "I mean, was she socially adjusted, a drinker or non-drinker, ever use drugs, was there a man in her life? Or a woman? That sort of thing." He saw Rosenberg's eyes narrow for seconds. Clearly he had offended him. "I'm sorry, Gordy. I just have to know what we're working with here, should she become conscious."

Rosenberg relaxed a little. He'd anticipated the questions, knew they were necessary, but the implications stung and his response was caustic, a trace incredulous. "Socially adjusted? Just what in hell is that, doctor? Show me the model and I'll tell you how she fits, okay?"

Levinson raised his hands in defeat. "Sorry."

Rosenberg leaned close, "No drinking, no drugs, no shit, doc. Anne lives a clean life, a glass of wine now and then, but that's it."

"And her social life…?"

He had no quick come-back there. No smart-aleck remark. And Levinson had seen his hesitation. Anne's life was flying. Period. Anything and everything she could get her hands on. Everything from gliders to jets. It absorbed nearly all of her time, and when not flying she studied it, read extensively. There were few pilots that had amassed her knowledge, or had gained the finely honed skills that she possessed. As such, there had been little time throughout her adult life for much else. And that suited her. But some thought her too single-minded, too reclusive from the social mainstream. He told it all to Levinson, then sighed and shrugged as he fed him the tidbit that he knew of her social life, "She dates some. There've been a few men over the years," he said quietly. *Damn few.* "But I'm not one of them." He stood at the window and looked down again at the parking lot. "And she's not queer, either."

David Levinson rose from his chair and squeezed Rosenberg's shoulder. "Let's go see your friend."

The airline captain's eyes suddenly bored into his, any hint of grief now dissolved. "She's a strong woman, doctor. You have no idea how strong. Anne Ryan is one hell of a survivor."

Levinson nodded. *She'll need to be.*

Gordy Rosenberg sat quietly at her bedside, holding the warm yet lifeless hand of his best friend who for all purposes was the sister he never had. It had been that kind of relationship for more than twenty-three years…

He had met the slender and tomboyish Ryan in high school during their junior year, a year when everyone in the class taunted him as "that fat, shuffling Jew-dodo from the Bronx," or "Wiener Rosenberg." Everyone except Anne Ryan. It was she in the school hallways one day who had seen the leader of a group of taunting gentile youths jab his middle finger at the pudgy young Rosenberg, and it was she who had rushed in and with a mighty swing had fractured the upraised digit with a two-pound history book. Until then they had never met, but their friendship quickly bloomed...

"Why'd you do it?" he asked later as they strolled the school grounds.

Anne shrugged, "Character defect, I guess. But you are kind of pudgy. Mind if I call you Gordo?"

He chuckled, "Beats Wiener Rosenberg. But how about just Gordy, okay?"

Wiener Rosenberg... So long ago, he thought, watching the intermittent fluttering of her eyelids. He remembered well the ensuing years when they had washed planes together at the small airfield on Long Island to earn a few bucks for flying lessons, and later their late night studying for pilot examinations, she coaching and cajoling him into the wee hours until he got it right.

Theirs had never been a relationship of the boy-girl sort; he supposed that at first it was because he was too embarrassed to ask, and worse, feared that she might turn him down. Later they had talked openly about it, confessing that neither had ever had a close and enduring friendship, that both had been only-children orphaned at an early age. Absent marriage, which neither wanted, they agreed that screwing around in the sack was not likely to promote close friendships of the best kind. At least not those that endured. And so they had made a pact that theirs would be an inseparable buddyship, and together they would conquer the skies.

This they did as they earned their licenses and ratings and together sought still higher goals in the cockpits of airliners, until at last came the day that Anne ran headlong into the solid and unyielding wall of the male fiefdom that dominated the hallowed ground of airline cockpits.

The airlines opened the door to him but slammed it resoundingly in the face of Anne Ryan. Back of the bus, lady, they said in so many words, back in stewardess territory where you are better suited. Piloting commercial aircraft is a man's job.

He'd never forget her frustrating trials during the years when women were nearly an unknown commodity in airline cockpits, but she had been determined, tenacious, and she was a damn good pilot. Less than a year later when his own airline furloughed him for lack of sufficient passenger loads, he again joined Anne knocking on doors and together they found an open one at a new carrier named Coastal. Eight years later they were both promoted to captain...

He shook away the memory and raised her limp hand to his lips, a tear spilling down his cheek. He missed her humor that at times could be raunchy, her laughter, and enthusiasm. Her enduring friendship. So much they had gained together...now so much lost.

During the week following the crash of Coastal 193, Warner Edelbrock watched with great satisfaction as Coastal stock plummeted on the New York Stock Exchange. Fueled by the hue and cry of an angry as well as frightened flying public, journalists wrote scathing articles of Coastal's rocky existence, implying that the airline as well as the industry in general warranted a thorough house cleaning.

Adding momentum to the already tobogganing plunge of Coastal shares, one prominent newspaper quoted an unidentified official of the FAA as saying that "the case of Coastal 193 appears to be yet another in a series of incidents involving Coastal in which pilot error appears to be the cause."

Warner Edelbrock nodded. *Pilot error.* Their mole at the FAA was doing his job according to plan. He laid the newspaper down and reached across his desk for the markets section of the *Wall Street Journal.* Coastal was down another three points, he saw. His plan was going well, on schedule as well as target. He turned again to his full page TransCon ad trumpeting their fine safety record, opulent service, adherence to arrival and departure schedules, and their new low fares. *"You can depend on us!"* appeared at the top in bold print. The antithesis of Coastal, he thought, he had seen to that. And Darcy was right—the timing of their plans couldn't have been better. And the crashes had tipped the balance. The end of Coastal was at hand.

"You did good, Philip," he said at last, rocking forward in his chair and carefully folding the newspaper. Philip Darcy, vice president of public relations and marketing, sat across from him in the luxurious office, lounging casually in a leather chair. Edelbrock beamed at the younger man. A streetfighter he was, unafraid of the risks they were taking and he knew the business well. They made a good team.

"It's working," Darcy said. "You should see the ticket counters at La Guardia, JFK, and Boston. I've increased the staffing by forty percent to handle the load, cordoned off larger areas for the waiting lines, and I've got passenger service agents floating around in the crowds to speed up the check-in process. Plus we're giving away free round-trip vouchers for each passenger holding a Coastal ticket."

Edelbrock nodded. "What do the Coastal counters look like?"

"Like death warmed over. They're sitting there with their chins in their hands and cobwebs growing on their eyelids. It's deserted, Warner. Their morale's shot to hell. Already we've hired twenty percent of their ticket and reservations staff."

And soon we'll have their routes and equipment. "Have you talked to Donnelley this morning?"

"I have, and he said Coastal was down another two and a half at the opening bell. The institutional trading is running scared and now the smaller investors are knee-jerking and dumping as well. Coastal is down thirteen points since the crash, and Donnelley says the SEC is talking about suspending trading. Looks like the end is near; I think we'd better hurry."

Edelbrock raised his hand in abeyance although he knew Philip Darcy was right. Coastal's stock plummet that had been their personal treasure trove was about to come to an abrupt halt if the SEC acted swiftly. "Let's see where we stand first," he said, rising from his chair. He slid an elegantly framed Reubens aside on the opposite wall, exposing his safe, and spun the dial.

Edelbrock settled back into his desk chair, unfolded a computer printout and spread it on his desk. He studied the listing of Coastal stock sales, his and Darcy's, that they had sold short on the market since the beginning of the year. But most of the sales had occurred within days of each of the two crashes.

Their broker and silent partner, A. Milton Donnelley, had taught them that "short sales" were Wall Street lingo for a form of stock market wagering, a sort of playing the market in reverse. Betting on the downside. Legal, he'd said, so long as you didn't control the market in which you were playing. Donnelley had shown them how they could put the cart before the horse and sell stock they didn't own at, say, $25 a share and later buy it at $20 when the market dropped, thus completing the transaction and reaping a $5 a share profit. In and out. Quick and neat and no investment. The trick was to know that a stock would drop in value, Donnelley had said. Inside information, if you could get it—or create it.

Ah. *Watch*, so replied Edelbrock and Darcy.

Since the beginning of the year he and Darcy had collectively sold short nearly 100,000 Coastal shares, taking handsome profits on the spread between current market value and a future price at a lower value. Each time they completed a short-sale transaction at the lower market they waged yet another damaging war upon Coastal, further driving down the market. They slashed fares on competing routes, delivered warped hype and innuendo to eager journalists, and fomented labor disputes that further crippled and demoralized the ailing carrier. With calculated timing, they placed new orders for short sales.

And then came the crashes of Coastal 288 and 193. The Mother Lode.

"One point three million for me and $600K for you, Philip," he said at last. "We've done well, I'd say. Best not to become greedy. So let 'em suspend trading; who gives a fuck?"

"You don't want to roll the dice again?"

"Philip, if you have the dice in your corner for too long people get wary, suspicious. The wrong people."

Darcy leaned forward, "But we're trading under a fictitious name as a foreign investor group with phony tax ID, nobody can—"

"Donnelley can. He knows who we are."

"But he's a partner in this venture as well as our broker—he'd implicate himself too. Why would he—"

"That fat fuck would plea bargain with the SEC and IRS to save his own ass, Philip, and keep the change. The time to quit is now, understand? We're on the verge of a major coup when Coastal goes under, so don't for Christ's sake fuck it up."

Darcy nodded and rose to leave.

"Oh, Philip?" Warner Edelbrock reached into the center drawer of his desk and withdrew a thick envelope. "Give this little bonus to our friend at the FAA, will you?"

"He'll want to know if there's going to be more," Darcy said. "What should I tell him?"

"Tell him...tell him to watch the market. Like any wise investor."

Darcy grinned. "Any particular market?"

Edelbrock looked away and stared at the Reubens on his wall. "I'm not going to single one out just yet, but there are several major carriers that would make good candidates. All are hurting for cash, are debt-heavy, and passenger loads are lagging." He rose from his chair and walked to the windows. He stood hands braced wide on the sill, surveying his aluminum armada below. "And there are two in particular with financial problems so great that it would take only a scrotal tug to tip the balance. Some union unrest, a little picketline violence, well-targeted fare wars, some appropriate rumors, and then of course would come the resulting layoffs and cutbacks on maintenance... And who knows? Such things could lead to their losing a ship or two... And if that were to happen, we can count on our man at the FAA to raise the specter of pilot error."

"It could happen," Darcy said, laughing. "You just never know."

FIVE

"Easy now," Regina Dotzer said to her assistant as they slid their arms under her body. "Turn her onto her side gently. That's it. Careful, don't twist her back. There." She quickly unfastened the ties on Anne Ryan's hospital gown and exposed her back, then turned to Dr. David Levinson and the chief of neurosurgery. "She's ready now."

The neurosurgeon scuttled his stool over to the bedside and gently ran his fingers along the vertebra of her lower back, found the area he sought and held his finger there while he reached for the syringe. He carefully positioned the large needle next to his finger and between the vertebras, then gently slid it home. "So. Easy as can be."

Dr. David Levinson stood behind the neurosurgeon, watching while he withdrew spinal fluid. "You know, I'm not so certain she can't feel that," he said.

"She can't feel a thing, doctor," the neurosurgeon replied. "She doesn't even know we're here."

"Maybe."

Puzzled, Regina Dotzer watched David Levinson until he felt her gaze. When he looked up she inclined her head toward the hallway and he followed.

Out of earshot, she whispered, "Do you know something I don't, David?"

He glanced quickly into the room, saw the neurosurgeon preparing to leave and the nurses rerigging the traction slings. "Not really, just a gut feeling."

"Do you think she's awake?"

He sighed and shook his head. "I don't know. Maybe, but professionally speaking I don't think so. I've been watching her closely since they brought her in two weeks ago and I haven't seen any tangible signs, but..."

"But what?" Regina urged.

He looked cautiously toward the doorway then whispered, "Regina, when I'm in there alone with her I get the feeling I'm being *watched*."

His Go-Team and the investigative group chairmen were waiting when Mitchell Hardison walked into the small conference room adjacent to his office and tossed his files on the table. It was time for another of the lengthy progress meetings to compare notes, listen to theories, challenge speculation and play devil's advocate with each other. The results laid the groundwork for what to do next.

"Mind if I smoke?" he said, the smoldering butt jutting defiantly from the center of his mouth. He grinned at the sudden howls of protest from his coworkers. "Didn't think so." He hooked a chair with his foot and took a seat at the head of the table.

"God," Westphal complained, "It's a clear day outside, but we're gonna go below minimums in here. Somebody call the EPA and report this guy."

"A do-nothing agency," Hardison said. "You'll get no remedy there. We're the only government agency on the planet that does any work."

"Hear, hear," said another investigator wearily.

"Okay, okay," Hardison said, then took a long pull on his cigar and exhaled a suffocating cloud. "Let's see what we've got so far. Westphal, we'll start with you."

"Right." He consulted his notes for a moment and began. "We checked the manifest and load factors and found that the ship was full of fuel and at max gross weight at departure, and the center of gravity was well within the operating envelope. They de-iced about ten minutes before the takeoff roll which was delayed about five minutes by runway obstruction, and—"

"Wait a minute," Hardison interrupted, "what runway obstruction?"

"The tower people said the de-icing tanker stalled on the runway after leaving the pad."

"On the *runway*? What the hell was it doing on the runway?"

Westphal shrugged. "Shortest distance between two points, I guess."

Hardison thought about that, puzzled, but decided to let it go for the moment and wrote a quick note to himself. He blew another billowing cloud and looked at Westphal. "You check the tanker's contents after the crash?"

Kaminski, chairman of the systems group, interjected, "You think maybe they didn't give 193 a blow job after all?"

"No, Brad, like maybe somebody forgot to add enough juice to the solution. Like the Air Florida problem in '82 at Reagan, back when it was still Washington National." He looked back to Westphal. "What'd you find, Doug?"

"I talked with the tanker crew, then I climbed up on the tanker and shined a flashlight in the tank. It was, oh...I'd say only about a quarter full, so they must have given 193 a hell of a squirt. Then—"

"I'd agree with that," said another investigator. "La Guardia closed down right after the crash, so they couldn't have de-iced another ship after 193—"

Mitchell Hardison stared at the table top, thinking, tugging at his bulbous nose. "What color was it, Doug?"

"Green and white. Like all Coastal aircraft."

Hardison sighed, ceremoniously set his cigar down and pinched his brow. God, but he was getting a headache. He gave Westphal a pained expression. "No, no, what color was the *juice*? The stuff in the tanker?"

"Oh. Pink. Like it's supposed to be. Like Kool-Aid."

Nodding, Hardison wrote himself another note. Westphal's findings squelched his notion that maybe someone had forgotten to spike the punch, to add glycol to the water for an effective de-icing solution. He remembered well the tragedy he'd seen and investigated years ago at what was then Washington National Airport, at which shortly after takeoff an Air Florida 737, unable to gain altitude, had ricocheted off the 14th Street bridge and plunged into the frozen Potomac, claiming 73 lives. Among other errors, the aircraft had been accidentally "de-iced" with a very weak solution that had promptly frozen into a clear glaze and later disrupted the airflow over the wings, such that they couldn't gain sufficient lift.

Okay, Hardison thought, rule that notion out. He crossed off one question on his list. At least the playing field was narrowed somewhat. He turned to Tom Walker, "What have you got from analyzing the flight data recorder?"

The bearded and bespeckled Walker, a former commercial pilot and aeronautical engineer now in charge of the NTSB's aircraft performance group, rose and gave them copies of a lengthy computer printout, then taped an enlarged version to the chalkboard and withdrew a telescoping pointer from his shirt pocket. He was a bit too professorial and pedantic for Hardison's liking, but damn good at his work. You paid attention to Walker. Hell, you paid attention to all of them. These guys were good.

"This is a schematic diagram of the takeoff sequence," Walker began, "in which I have correlated data from the cockpit voice recorder and the flight data recorder. As you can see, the aircraft traveled 6,511 feet from here, at takeoff position, to here, where it finally came to rest thirty-six seconds later.

"According to our structures group, the first impact marks were here on the right edge of the runway where the left wing struck. That's exactly 5,078 feet from the beginning of the runway. Fractured pieces of the left wing were found strewn along an approximately 1,600-foot path of wreckage and continued to the point at which the fuselage came to rest.

"The cockpit and a section of the cabin forward of the front wing spar were separated from the remainder of the fuselage, as were electrical cables, hydraulic lines, and flight controls. It was this separation that spared the flight crew from incineration. But there was severe crushing to the top and upper right portions of the cockpit and forward fuselage.

"Now let's back up and turn our attention to a point 3,440 feet from the beginning of the runway. It was here that we found a faint scar in the concrete, about a hundred feet long. That got us to thinking, so we examined the bottom of the tail of the aircraft which revealed a worn or flattened area on the hard metal tiedown eye. The scar on the runway was about a quarter-inch wide, and so is the tiedown eye."

Westphal raised his hand. "So it appears that the captain overrotated—pulled back on the wheel too quickly and scraped the tail on takeoff, right?"

Walker nodded. "So it would appear. However, even so, such action is not necessarily problematic. It's not an entirely uncommon occurrence."

"Did any witnesses see this happen?" Hardison asked. The witness group chairman shook his head. Hardison grunted and wrote himself another note. "Go on, Tom."

For the next fifteen minutes they listened while Walker explained that, even with the probability of tail-scraping, the takeoff had been properly executed. According to the flight data recorder the takeoff occurred at the proper airspeed considering the aircraft's weight and the wind and temperature conditions, a positive rate and angle of climb had been established, and the engines were producing takeoff thrust.

Kaminski added, "We also examined the wings, fuselage, and the engine pods and found no evidence of explosion. I'd rule out a bomb, but we're still checking."

"What about the engine surging we heard on the cockpit voice recording?" Westphal asked.

"I was coming to that." Walker turned to the diagram and pointed. "Thirty-four seconds after the beginning of the takeoff run, and at a point approximately 4,000 feet down the runway, while airborne, the engine surging began. One second later, you will recall that we heard the rattling sound of the stick-shaker warning of a stall condition. You see, turbine compressor surges in rear-engined aircraft can occur when the airflow over the wings becomes disturbed, turbulent, such as in a stall condition, and the airflow is deflected away from the turbine inlets on the engines. The result is similar to someone being strangled, gagging and gasping for breath."

"So loss of power brought it down? Is that what you're saying?" asked Brad Kaminski.

"Not at all," answered Walker. "It was too late for that. The aircraft's wings had already stalled. The engine surging was a byproduct of the approaching stall which occurred quickly." Walker consulted his notes then reached and turned on a tape recorder. "Listen."

"...Watch out! Watch out! Watch out!..."

Walker snapped the recorder off. "Those were the first officer's warnings two seconds before the surging began. It was at that point, according to my analysis, that the aircraft rolled sharply to the left...the first time. The stall was already in progress and the engines had nothing to do with it."

Westphal tried to sum it up. "Okay, so we rule out engine failure and a bomb—at least for the moment. That leaves us with the stall, and I keep coming back to the tail-scrape evidence. Of overrotation at takeoff. She could have been climbing at too steep an angle; that could have caused the wing stall, which caused the rolling, and finally the crash. Looks to me like we've got the probable cause."

"We haven't got jack-shit, Doug," Hardison growled. "Tell him why, Tom."

Walker pointed to the printout again. "The digital flight data recorder copies all pertinent flight data, including the angle of climb. Granted, there may likely have been a tail scrape, as the data do indicate that the wing angle of attack at rotation was steeper than normal. Yet the captain rotated at 132 knots, the proper airspeed and with sufficient cushion to avoid an incipient stall, and the initial climb-out was also at a speed sufficiently above that at which there would be an aerodynamic stall under normal conditions."

"And still it stalled and went boom," Hardison added. "Any ideas why, Tom?"

"I'll say this: Considering that the flight crew properly calculated the takeoff speed during flight planning and took into account the aircraft's weight, the wind, and the outside air temperature, all of which are factors in aerodynamics, the stall shouldn't have occurred."

"Brilliant," Hardison barked, stubbing out his cigar.

"*Did* they properly calculate those factors beforehand?" Kaminski asked.

"Yes," said Walker. "We examined the flight plan, compared their calculations to the parameters contained in the airplane flight manual, and cross-checked it to meteorological conditions and the flight data recorder."

"So what could account for the fatal stall?" Kaminski pressed.

Walker stared at their puzzled faces for several moments. "Two things," he said at last. "Wing ice, for one. The presence of wing ice, not anticipated during the flight planning, would erase their stall margin. With wing ice, most of you know that an aircraft's wings will stall at a higher than anticipated airspeed. The hard-wing DC-9 ten-series is particularly susceptible to stalls when the wings are contaminated by ice—exacerbated by cold-soaking fuel within, and the conditions at La Guardia that night indicated an icing environment. Thus, with the unknown presence of wing ice a stall can occur quickly and when it's not expected. At low altitude, as was the case here, there is virtually no opportunity for recovery."

Mitchell Hardison rose from his chair with great effort, walked to the window and stared at the slushy streets below. On the corner stood a Santa as portly as himself, ringing a bell. Christmas tomorrow; he would have to hurry to buy a present for Dog. And Ethel.

He focused his thoughts. No, ice wasn't the culprit here; that possibility had been settled by those in the control tower who had observed the de-icing and confirmed that it was no longer snowing, and by Westphal's investigation of the tanker's contents. It was something else...

At last he turned and stood with hands braced on meaty hips as he slowly surveyed his staff. Then he looked to Walker. "You said *two* things could account for the fatal stall."

Walker looked uncomfortable, his professorial composure rattled. "This is out of my line, but..." He bent and rewound the tape recorder then punched it on.

"...Watch out! Watch out! Watch out!..."

The first officer's words from the grave were frantic, terrified, and again they galvanized the listeners. Quickly, Walker shut the machine off, his expression stricken.

Hardison now knew what was coming. "Say it, Tom."

Walker wiped his mouth with his handkerchief and tugged at his beard. "It seems to me that the first officer may have observed something...something untoward occurring in the cockpit. As though the captain, who was flying the aircraft, had suddenly...taken leave of his senses, and—"

"Hers," Hardison added. "And flew the son of a bitch into the ground."

"Yes."

A. Milton Donnelley sat at his desk in the brokerage offices of Pickard, Wilmott, and DeLeury quickly jotting notes while talking on the telephone to a client. Then he thanked the client, offered lunch that was declined for a rain check, and hung up. It was a large order to short-sell another block of DeccoTech stock, a U.S. Senator's former company, and over the past year it seemed that everyone had become risk-takers in the volatile and see-sawing markets. It seemed also that more and more people were able to predict with uncanny accuracy that the market for a particular stock would fall and they would profit from it. Short sales were now in vogue. Among others there had been Worthington with InterCo Tool; Copenhaver with International Computer Systems, known as ICS; and now Fortensky with DeccoTech. All had been insiders and reaped handsome profits funneled to Swiss accounts without the investment of so much as a dime, but none had profited as handsomely as Warner Edelbrock and Philip Darcy.

The wily and close-mouthed Edelbrock had somehow positioned himself to control Coastal's plummeting market; Worthington, with his ties to the unions, knew in advance that they would launch a crippling strike against InterCo Tool; and Fortensky had concocted something about the senator's ties to his former company that would lead to scandal and the canceling of many of DeccoTech's profitable government contracts. Then it had been Jack Copenhaver who knew that DigiSpeed and other Silicon Valley makers of the popular electronic home

89

number-crunchers were ready to launch the low cost technology to effectively neuter the market share of ICS, the staid and seemingly myopic giant of the east which believed its carmine logo and hence its market share preordained by God. Indeed, Old Red had taken a mighty tumble.

He sighed audibly as he sat in his glassed-in office and watched the electronic ticker symbols flash past on the screen in the adjacent "bullpen" where the grunts took stock orders. Abbott Labs 29½ flashed past, down one point, he calculated; Bank of America 32, down a half; then came CitiCorp, Coastal, Delta...

Coastal... Soon it would no longer be on the ticker screen. He sensed that probably at this very moment Warner Edelbrock and his legals were behind closed doors with a frightened and demoralized Coastal Airlines CEO and board of directors. Agreements would be signed, money would change hands, and in weeks, maybe even days, Coastal would drop from the ticker screen just as surely as its planes dropped from the sky.

A. Milton Donnelley, senior account executive, leaned back in his chair and spread his fingers wide across his vest girdling an ample belly, nodding as he thought about it. Being not only the order-taker but also a partner in Edelbrock's well-timed and substantial short-sales of Coastal stock, had carried considerable risk that he too could become implicated in tax fraud and insider trading, and the subject of IRS and SEC investigations. He stood to lose not only his position with Pickard, Wilmott, and DeLeury, but his stockbroker's license, the substantial profits and commissions he'd earned on their Coastal transactions, as well as his freedom. Indeed, it was conceivable that he could go to jail if caught. More specifically, if Warner Edelbrock were caught. The convoluted yet visible paper trail would lead directly to the chair in which he now sat.

But A. Milton Donnelley knew also that without risks money was not made. At least not Serious Money. Oh, the high-rolling fools of Wall Street and other lesser entrepreneurs with their junk bond scams and the like had been caught, but there had been a simple common denominator among them: greed coupled with high profile. But the InterCo Tool, the ICS, the DeccoTech and the Coastal deals he had done were mere ripples on an ocean in comparison. The trick was to do smaller and lower profile deals like those, and many of them. And of course, be a partner in them.

He knew that he could count on the successes of Edelbrock, Fortensky, Copenhaver, and Worthington to become his springboard into more of the corporate inner circles. And someday perhaps he would be allowed to gain a larger share of the action.

But unlike the gimme-now fools, A. Milton Donnelley took great satisfaction in knowing that he was a patient as well as intelligent professional and he could well afford to wait. He sat fondling the tiny Phi Beta Kappa key bridging his vest, kneading it like a rosary as he dreamed of what was to come.

"Good morning, Milton."

Startled, he quickly spun and rocked forward in his chair. There in his doorway and waiting patiently in her motorized wheelchair with her Neanderthal attendant in tow, was none other than old ironsides herself.

"Why, Mrs. Edelbrock, what a pleasant surprise. Do come in, please." He stood quickly and shuffled the chairs opposite his desk as she whirred forward.

"Pennington, you may wait for me in the reception area," she said to her attendant, giving him a deferential wave.

A. Milton Donnelley locked eyes briefly with the large and powerfully-built man who stared back at him with a blank expression. He abhorred this creature with large, wide-set eyes wedged deeply beneath a shelf of brow that quickly receded to a bald plateau of hideously scarred flesh. At first meeting years ago he had thought the man a moronic, a victim of a safe falling upon his skull, yet in time he had sensed that far more than a mere flicker of intelligence resided in that repulsive and fearsome countenance.

Lyle Pennington nodded once at her command, his eyes never leaving Donnelley's as he slowly backed out of the doorway. Then he turned and quietly stalked away.

Donnelley took his seat and folded his hands before him, offering his most ingratiating smile. "My dear Mrs. Edelbrock, how nice it is to see you this morning. You look especially well. Now, how may I help you today?"

He watched as she withdrew a slim, fine leather briefcase from beneath the shawl covering her withered legs. "I have met with my attorneys concerning my trusts, Milton, and I have decided as to the disposition of some of my portfolio." She handed him a single document. "Is this a fair analysis of my current holdings?"

A. Milton Donnelley took the document bearing the letterhead of a prestigious law firm and adjusted his eyeglasses as he scanned the listing of her securities holdings. "I believe so, but let me compare it to your current accounts."

He tapped her account number into the computer terminal and gazed at the screen as the summary scrolled up. There it was, an enviably formidable block of assets known as the Preston Trust, of which she was sole beneficiary until her death when fifty percent would pass to her husband, Warner, and the balance to a distant cousin. In it was controlling interest in the voting shares of TransCon Airlines, Inc. and its subsidiary, Preston Aeroservice Enterprises, left by her father, C. Gordon Preston, founder of TransCon, and valued at nearly $1.4 billion; a large block of U.S. Treasury notes valued at over $156 million; and a scattering of tax exempt municipals valued at $120 million.

A. Milton Donnelley's fingers trembled on the keyboard whenever he gazed at her enormous wealth. He glanced at the listing she had given him and compared it to the screen. They agreed. He nodded and tapped the "clear" key, then passed the listing back to her.

"To the penny, Mrs. Edelbrock. What changes did you wish to make?"

"I have already made one that doesn't concern you, Milton, but your firm shall be receiving a letter from my attorneys indicating that there has been a change in beneficiaries of the shares held in my account should I predecease my husband."

"I see." Now that was significant. Someone, either the cousin or Warner, had no doubt somehow stumbled into her disfavor. How very stupid. He looked across the desk at her, saw that she sat hunched forward as usual but staring at him intensely as though expecting a reaction. He gave none.

"What is it that I can do for you, Mrs. Edelbrock?"

Sylvia Edelbrock smiled pleasantly, draining any hint of animosity from her expression. Then with an arthritic finger she pressed a button on her control console and whirred to the edge of his desk, reached and placed her hand over his.

"Milton, I wish to make a gift to someone greatly in need."

"Oh really? How very kind and generous. A belated Christmas gift, perhaps?"

"Oh, I suppose you could say that. Yes, really, I guess that it is. But first..." Sylvia Edelbrock reached again into her briefcase and withdrew a check for five thousand dollars. "Happy new year, Milton."

He took the check and saw that it was made out to him. "Why, Mrs. Edelbrock, I—I don't know what to say. We try our best to service your account with the utmost care and efficiency, but really, I certainly have done nothing whatever to deserve such a generous gift as this."

Sylvia patted his hand. "For your loyalty, Milton, a rare commodity indeed, these days."

"No. I can't accept this. Absolutely not. My loyalty to you comes without price." He attempted to hand the check back but Sylvia Edelbrock was already in reverse gear.

"It is indeed priceless, Milton, but I insist that you accept it."

He relaxed. Of course there was no choice; he must not offend her. "Then I shall, but on the condition that I donate it to a worthy cause."

Sylvia laughed gaily. "Condition accepted. Now I have another gift I wish to make while I'm in the spirit, and I need your assistance. It will involve disposing of some of my shares."

"I'd be delighted. You said that you wanted to give a gift to someone greatly in need. I trust that perhaps you wish me to be the messenger?"

"Exactly, Milton. Oh dear, this is so exciting, and..." she leaned forward in the wheelchair and whispered, "clandestine." Again she whirred forward, this time pushing a note across his desk. "These are your instructions. You must be absolutely discreet in executing them and there is to be no link whatever as to the actual source of the funds."

He read the note quickly then frowned and read it carefully twice. Puzzled, he looked up and found that her expression had become intense again.

"This is a very generous gift, Mrs. Edelbrock, but backdating it is technically illegal. And your husband, if he should learn of it, might become, ah, agitated?"

Sylvia Edelbrock quickly retrieved the instructions and placed them back in her briefcase. She reached and squeezed his hand again. "I knew I could count on you, Milton. This will make me very happy. Very happy indeed."

And so the recipient. "I'll take care of it immediately."

"As I said before, Milton, your loyalty is priceless. Now I must go."

He rose from his chair as she whirred toward the doorway. Then she stopped abruptly and spun her wheelchair around. "Oh, I nearly forgot, Milton. I'd like copies of my husband's accounts."

A. Milton Donnelley's heart stopped. "I'm sorry, Mrs. Edelbrock, your husband has no accounts with us."

She held his gaze in silence for moments then smiled, "I must have been mistaken, Milton." She tapped her right temple. "Age, you know."

He watched her roll swiftly down the hallway toward the reception area where her aide, Pennington, stood waiting, then he edged behind his desk and sat heavily, his heart thudding. Had she caught that?

He considered the strange instructions she had shown him, understanding well why she would not leave them. They were certainly something he would not want found in his office. But where had he heard the beneficiary's name? He shook his head. Indeed, a most fortunate individual to receive a gift of this magnitude.

He looked at the $5,000 check that bore his name, then pocketed it with satisfaction. Adequate compensation for the technical indiscretion he would execute on her behalf, and well worth the risk...so long as Warner Edelbrock never learned of it.

With her attendant following close behind, Sylvia Edelbrock entered the empty elevator outside the offices of Pickard, Wilmott, and DeLeury and whirled her chair around as the doors closed. She sat hunched forward and nodding with satisfaction while kneading her gnarled hands as the elevator hissed downward.

"Pennington, I want copies of Warner's accounts. Milton didn't for a minute fool me. Get them."

Dr. David Levinson sat in a swivel chair beside Anne Ryan's bed, making notations on her chart. Behind him Regina Dotzer finished adjusting the traction slings about the patient's waist and legs.

"Will there be anything else, doctor?" she asked.

He looked up and scanned his patient's cumbersome casts and harnesses, saw that all was as it should be. "Uh, no. That'll be all, Regina, and thanks."

For moments he sat legs-crossed while tapping his pen on her chart, thinking. It had been nearly four weeks since they brought her in from the crash, and her wounds were healing nicely enough, the fractures set and mending, lung, kidney, liver and heart functions were near normal, yet still she lay unconscious. He now had no doubt that she would recover at least physically, although she would likely be confined to a wheelchair for many months, possibly longer. Whether she would ever walk again unassisted was another question. A still greater question was whether she would ever regain consciousness.

All of the specialists with whom he'd conferred believed that there now seemed no physical reason for her detachment. The tests had shown neither causal brain damage nor permanent injury to the spinal cord. They believed that she was no longer comatose but catatonic. They also believed that somewhere within the psyche a sort of protective circuit had snapped, mercifully shielding her from the agonizing pain and the terrible post-crash trauma, and that only time would heal the mental wounds and eventually restore her consciousness. Just how much time, they didn't know.

He felt deeply sorry for her should she awaken, for the news media had been brutal in the aftermath of the crash. He had read of her immediate defrocking by the airline, of the suspension of her license by the FAA, and of the innuendo of probable causes for which she was said to be responsible.

He shook his head sadly. Should Anne Ryan ever regain consciousness she would be thrust into a scalding cauldron of conditioned public opinion; they would devour her for the apparent careless taking of forty-seven lives. But had it been careless? He looked at her peaceful and innocent face, the puffiness now gone, and wondered.

She's a strong woman, doctor. You have no idea how strong. Anne Ryan is one hell of a survivor.

Dr. David Levinson nodded absently, remembering Gordy Rosenberg's words. He braced an elbow on his knee and sank his chin into his hand as he watched her chest rise and fall. *How to reach her*? Over the weeks he had become even more certain that she was aware of his presence and that of others. Occasionally he had seen her eyelids flutter, but when he would pass his hand before her face there was not a flicker of recognition.

Her eyes were open now, only slits, but open. Again he passed his hand in front of them and snapped his fingers.

Nothing.

It was like being encased in a sealed tomb, or a body within a body, or like one of her nightmares as a child when the frightening monster pursued her and her legs were leaden, unmoving, and the screams wouldn't come. Her churning thoughts echoed as though in a chamber and surely someone must hear them.

Help me, please!

She watched helplessly through veiled slits as the doctor moved in close and snapped his fingers before her eyes.

Anne Ryan had no idea how long she had been aware of their presence, of when the terrifying nightmare had become reality. It hadn't happened suddenly, the scenarios had blended subtly and there was no clear transition from one to another...

It began with the bone-shattering impact of the crash, the searing pain, then blackness. For what seemed a millennium she had drifted in a dreamlike world, awash in a sea of darkness yet floating gently toward a faint ray of light on a far horizon as though dawn were coming. She had no body, no essence of form; she was but a tiny mass of swirling invisible energy drawn toward a vortex in the universe of deep space. It was *The Source*, she knew, the source of life after death and of lives to come. It was a cycle of perfection that she now fully understood as though she had known it all along.

She was going home.

There were no shimmering castles in the sky nor strains of lovely music embracing undulating fields of waving grain, nor were there bodily forms of loved ones long passed and cheerfully greeting her arrival at some utopia in the heavens. But there was a deep and abiding sense of well being, a sense that she was not alone, that the swirling particles of energy comprising her soul had at last blended with all that was the universe and that she was an integral and meaningful part of the whole.

There were no voices, no echoing words from heavenly angels as she drifted nearer to the zenith of light and *The Source*. Yet the light gave a living sense of warmth, an awareness of being loved without condition, and there were gentle and comforting thoughts implanted as surely as though spoken.

Then had come the sudden and jarring turbulence as the placid universal sea in which she drifted became a swirling and disconsolate maelstrom, and she became frightened, the once beckoning light in the distance dimming as she receded in what seemed a swift outgoing tide. Then came the spinning, dizzying spiral as she felt herself sucked into a whirlpool, sinking in a darkened void that became a tunnel filled with frightening echoes. She saw hazy images far below as if seen through the opposite end of a telescope, images of frantic and scrambling humanity shouting and cursing, and she fought the spiraling current that pulled her inexorably downward.

No! I don't belong there! No, please, I don't want to go back!

The voices suddenly became louder, clearer, the images sharper as the aperture at the bottom of the tunnel in which she sank quickly grew larger.

"Clear! Now!"

Her momentum increased and suddenly she was in a flailing free fall, her body tumbling end over end...

"Clear! Now!"

Headlong she sped toward the widening aperture and she saw the human images clearly, images of doctors and nurses hovered over a body...

"Clear! Now!"

Suddenly she felt a crushing impact as though a tether had quickly checked her fall, and she hovered only feet above the activity below. She watched curiously as they worked, saw the bloodied sheet covering the small body over which they ministered. She saw a tall and lanky man who seemed to be in charge slump his shoulders in defeat, his hands hanging at his sides and clutching what looked like ping-pong paddles. *How very strange.* Then she saw that the body was hers, and in a detached fashion as though it were another's she felt great sorrow.

Slowly she began to ascend, once again feeling a sense of weightlessness and well-being, secure in the knowledge of her destination. Soon she would again see the light on the zenith and this time she would complete her journey.

"Clear! Now!"

Suddenly she felt a tremendous lurch and saw a blinding light overhead. Agonizing pain seared through her body and her senses shrieked in deafening echoes until she could tolerate no more and all became blackness.

For what seemed eons she floated in a darkened hell populated by all that she feared most. They were her worst nightmares, the personification of the worst evils imaginable, and she lived all of them. Over the weeks that were lifetimes she couldn't measure, one frightening nightmare merged with another until she found herself in a strange room and lying in state beneath crisp sheets, immovable, and watching gauzy and translucent figures hovering about her, their voices an insistent and unintelligible buzzing like creatures from some distant planet, and she strained to see through the haze in which they were encapsulated before the blackness came again.

As the nightmare wore on the gauzy webs through which she peered gradually cleared, the shapeless images assumed definition, and the buzzing voices took on inflection, meaning. They were talking about her, clucking, shaking their heads. She saw their faces clearly now, a man, a woman, leaning over her. She felt a soothing and gentle coolness on her brow as she watched a hand reach above her eyes. She thanked the loving hand that had interceded in the nightmare, but still they didn't hear.

The nightmare soon came in cycles, alternating between darkness filled with repulsive creatures feasting upon her flesh and that *place* again, that room where she lay in state, where she lay in death. They talked to her and she answered and still they ignored her and took great delight in prodding her pain-wracked body. Yes, she was dead. This was where hell was. She had been given a glimpse of the afterlife in another place, a cruel teasing to show her what might have been had she lived her life otherwise. She would never again sense the comforting, loving implanted thoughts that existed *out there*, never again feel the warmth of the distant and beckoning light, or blend with the whole of the universe. No, here was her destiny, here in this cubicle that was her assigned place in hell where she would endure penance throughout eternity.

What was it she had done in life that had so derailed her destiny? What evil had she perpetrated on others that invoked this revengeful karma?

Immeasurable time again passed as she sought answers to the riddle until at last *They* told her. *They*, the cretins who tortured her daily had given her the clue she sought. Thinking she couldn't hear, *They* had said there had been a crash, that she had been a pilot, that many people--entire families--had died fiery and agonizing deaths at her hands...

She pondered this at length for what may have been minutes, hours, days, weeks, time immeasurable, until fragments of memory gradually joined like pieces of a puzzle. Suddenly the picture appeared with stark clarity, the awful and terrifying moments seared into her mind and she saw the aircraft hurtling down the darkened runway, and then gracefully lifting into the sky as it sought altitude, then...

"Watch out! Watch out! Watch out!"

Again she relived the sickening tumbling of the aircraft, the shrieking and rending of torn metal, the shattering impact. It was then that she discovered that hell was on earth, and worse: She was alive and many others were dead... And the little girl? Was the beautiful little girl with the beguiling eyes also dead?

She could count days now, days filled with intense pain wracking her broken body, and nights awash in guilt and despair. During the days she looked forward to the onslaught of pain as the numbing drugs wore off, making her mind clearer. It was in these agonizing moments that she was at least able to think with some clarity, to focus and remember the events leading up to the crash and try to sort out what had happened. Each time she came to the same dead end: The aircraft had stalled and she was at a loss to know why.

She wanted desperately to communicate, to move her body, to blink her eyes or nod or shake her head, but still she was encapsulated in a lifeless body bereft of motor ability. She tried telepathy of sorts, straining to send mental messages to the darkhaired doctor who tended her wounds with compassion. She sensed that he knew she could hear him, see him, feel his touch, but he would only shake his head sadly and walk away, and she screamed inwardly with bitter frustration.

Gordy Rosenberg slammed his locker shut in the TransCon crew lounge, then sucked in his ample belly as much as he could and buttoned his uniform tunic. It fit poorly as did the trousers that rode high above his shoe tops, but there hadn't been time to take the new uniform and its mate back to the tailor. Too much had happened too fast since TransCon had acquired what remained of Coastal.

He sighed as he unbuttoned the tunic and let his belly sag. "To hell with it," he murmured, then slid his cap over his head. Just then a hand reached and patted his middle.

"Chief pilot's not goin' to like that, Gordo," came the drawling voice.

It was Captain Jimmy Truax, a cretin to most including Anne who had years ago hung the moniker of cracker-shithead upon him. "It's not me, Jimboy, it's the uniform. Doesn't fit right."

Truax nodded. "Nothin' seems to fit right since the merger, includin' us."

"Speak for yourself," Rosenberg answered, peering into the mirror and adjusting his tie. "But that was no merger, it was a dismemberment. They kicked the blocks out from under us then came at us with a chainsaw, took what they wanted then tossed the rest in the bone pile."

Truax shrugged, "We got a better job out of it, more secure anyway, and being based here in San Francisco sure beats the hell out of La Guardia. We've got Ryan to thank for that."

Rosenberg spun around and faced the lanky Oklahoman, "Leave it alone, Jimboy! If she were standing here now you'd be squawking mayday and prying her foot out of your crotch."

"Maybe. But I'm right and you know it, and so does every-body else. Ray Thompson crippled the camel and that twit Ryan broke its fucking back."

Rosenberg's rage suddenly boiled over and he grabbed Truax's lapels and drew him close. "You filthy son of a bitch—"

Large black hands caught him firmly by the shoulders. "Easy now, Mr. Gordy. He ain't worth it, son," said Titus Wofford, tugging him away from a smirking Truax. "Lord knows we got us enough problems without you jes' makin' things worse."

He relaxed his grip and gave Truax a shove. "It should've been you that night, asshole."

"Come on outside with me, Mr. Gordy, les' talk. Come on, now."

It was a mild January morning in San Francisco, and they sat on a baggage cart outside the terminal's north concourse sipping steaming coffee from Titus' thermos. Gordy stared absently into his cup, swirling it. "Thanks, Titus. You saved me from doing something stupid that could have cost me my job."

"Bad enough we lost Miz Annie. Can't lose you too. Did you talk to the hospital this mornin'?"

Gordy nodded and looked up into Titus' huge brown eyes. There was a great sadness there mirroring his. "There's been no change. She's still unconscious."

Titus Wofford eased his bulk off the cart, dumped his coffee, and then screwed the cup onto his thermos. He shook his head slowly. He didn't know the right words, the technical jargon, but the circumstances of Anne Ryan's crash not long after Ray Thompson's troubled him deeply. Something was wrong, very wrong. He kneaded his large hands nervously as he watched a ground crew service a TransCon DC-9 that had once belonged to Coastal. It was a DC-9 like Miz Annie's.

He turned to Gordy, his large and callused hands outstretched, pleading. "Miz Annie," he began, searching for the words, "she...she didn't just 'lose it' that night like they all say, did she?"

It was a question he'd been struggling with himself, yet a question which now, in light of all the media reports, seemed to have no other reasonable answer. Early on he'd believed otherwise, but now he wasn't so sure. And that uncertainty now brought corrosive guilt, guilt that such thoughts were in some measure a betrayal of his unfailing loyalty and friendship to her. Yet the bits and pieces of evidence that the FAA and the NTSB were willing to share with the public seemed damning, and what knowledgeable person, what pilot, could conclude otherwise? Clearly there seemed to have been a stall on takeoff, yet once one occurred even the best of pilots, and Anne Ryan could well be counted among them, couldn't prevent the tragic and inevitable result at such low altitude. But what nagged him most was that from early in flight training, pilots were drilled incessantly on stall avoidance—probably more than any other aspect of flight. Seasoned pilots, especially airline pilots, just didn't stall aircraft. But Anne Ryan apparently had. And so had Ray Thompson. Why? How?

He looked up and saw the stricken expression on the huge black man's face, and he suddenly realized he hadn't answered him. Titus Wofford, he knew, adored her as though she were his daughter, and yet he could offer little comfort short of lying. And that he couldn't do. "I don't know," he said at last. "I just don't know. Only Anne can answer that."

Gordy snapped his coffee stir-stick in half as Titus turned and walked slowly away. In the distance a Boeing 767 thundered down the runway on its takeoff roll and he watched as its blunt nose lifted smoothly and the great ship rose into the morning sky. "There. Right there," he murmured, watching as the aircraft climbed at a steep angle a hundred feet above the runway. A stall could occur right there, right when the aircraft left the invisible cushion of ground effect and became most vulnerable during its quest for altitude. He watched the 767 climb higher over the bay, then turn and speed westward toward the Golden Gate and the ocean beyond.

But the 767 had not stalled, as he knew damned well that it wouldn't, even climbing steeply.

Why? *Why*, because the flight crew knew precisely, within one mile per hour, the speed at which the aircraft would stall, and had factored their climbout speed well above it. All flight crews did it, standard procedure. Even the weekend Piper Cub pilots did it. It was the most basic of training drilled into pilots. And so Anne would certainly have done the same, have provided for the stall margin, yet still...

He glanced at his watch, saw that only fifteen minutes remained until check-in for his flight, and rose slowly to his feet. Twenty-three years they had been best of friends, more like brother and sister, and now she lay broken and comatose in a hospital bed a continent away, unlikely ever to regain consciousness. It tore at his guts like a hot knife each time he remembered their last words in the crew lounge shortly before her tragic flight. She was rushed as usual, but she had been so *up*, so...*Anne*; and there hadn't been the slightest indication that she was stressed or in any other way troubled...

He yanked open the men's room door in the crew lounge, eyed his poorly fitting uniform in the mirror as he passed, then shuffled up to a urinal. He stared at the ceiling as he relieved himself, remembering that night not long ago...

"Hey, Anne, long time no see. How you doin'?"

"Oh! Gordy! Jeez, I'm sorry. Fine. Fine. Look, I've got to go, I'm late."

"Did you get the dose of Far Side *I sent you?"*

"Yeah, thanks. Right now I need a dose of something else."

...dose of something else...dose of something else...dose of...

His eyes suddenly focused as her hollow words crystallized, and he slammed his hand against the tile wall. "Oh no! Oh, Jesus Christ, No!"

John Haviland Williams

SIX

Mitchell Hardison closed the Coastal 193 summary file and tossed it on the stack with those containing the reams of data he and his Go-Team had collected over the past weeks. On the opposite side of his desk stood another stack of files, those that were the post-mortem of the similar accident at La Guardia involving Coastal 288 a month earlier.

He sat drumming his fingers on his desk as he thought about them. The demise of both Coastal 193 and Coastal 288 was remarkably similar in many respects. Both had occurred at night in cold and inclement weather, and both had been DC-9s that had been thoroughly de-iced prior to takeoff. Then both had stalled and crashed on takeoff. Both at La Guardia. Earlier, logic and experience told him that a deadly pattern existed there somewhere and waiting to be found. It was a pattern that seemed to cry out that something was amiss, something well beyond the presumed and technically inescapable conclusion of pilot error.

But now that had all changed. Now it was abundantly clear that the two accidents were similar in appearance only. Oh, they had both inexplicably stalled on takeoff, all right, both had rolled severely right and left while floundering in the sky before crashing onto the icy runway and bursting into flames, but it was now clear that the causes differed.

Captain Ray Thompson in command of Coastal 288, toxicology factors testing negative in the post-mortem, had apparently failed to anticipate and prevent the deadly stall, or had otherwise failed to act in a decisive manner and maintain safe airspeed at a critical moment. He had likely succumbed to human failing. Pilot error.

Scratch 38 lives, including Thompson and the first officer.

But with Captain Anne Ryan of Coastal 193 it had been altogether different, Hardison now knew. Indeed, Ryan had apparently also failed to anticipate and prevent the deadly stall or otherwise failed to act in a decisive manner at a critical moment, but with Ryan there now appeared to be a causal factor not present in the crew of Coastal 288. Ryan had illegal drugs in her bloodstream.

Felony manslaughter. Scratch 47 lives.

Scratch any notion of a deadly pattern.

Scratch an airline.

He shook his head as he read again the lab report on her blood samples taken after the crash. Then he leaned over his desk and punched the intercom. "Westphal, come in here."

Minutes later the younger investigator strode through the doorway. "What's up, Mitch?"

"Get hold of the FAA and the U.S. Attorney's office," he said, handing Westphal the Coastal 193 summary file. "Tell the FAA thanks for their cooperation in waiting, but we aren't going to sit on this any longer."

"And the U.S. Attorney?"

"As far as I'm concerned, they're free to prosecute to the full extent of the law. More, if they can. We're gonna urge them to send an unmistakable message to pilots and the public that this kind of behavior'll provoke a world of hurt on the perpetrator." He spat a flake of tobacco into his wastebasket, then rose from his chair and stared out the window. "As I see it, Ryan murdered 47 people, Doug. This shit's got to quit. We gotta have zero tolerance, nothing less."

At Queens Memorial Hospital Dr. David Levinson also stared out a window, seeing the bleakness that was mid-January in New York City. Anne Ryan was on his mind as well. Still she lay catatonic, and except for her breathing she appeared more dead than alive. He arched his back and pressed his palms firmly against his kidneys, easing his frustration and fatigue, then turned to watch her. Still she breathed slowly, evenly, her chest rising and falling...

An idea borne of utter helplessness nudged him and he shrugged. Well, why not? There was nothing else to try.

He sat again in the small swivel chair and scooted close to her bedside, his heart thumping. Then he reached and placed his palm between her small breasts.

"Anne, if you can hear me, hold your breath for a moment."

Levinson felt foolish as he waited, watching her chest rise and fall, but the beating of her heart beneath his hand had changed. Gone was the slow and easy cadence; it was now thumping like a trip-hammer. His heartbeat now matched hers, but still her chest rose and fell, rose and fell. Maybe she hadn't heard him clearly?

"Anne, hold your breath!" he snapped.

Suddenly her breathing stopped.

Levinson stiffened then quickly pressed his stethoscope to her chest. There was still a strong heartbeat, but it was the beat of an excited heart muscle, as though stricken with fear. Or anticipation. *Anne Ryan was holding her breath!* He looked at her eyes and saw that they were open perhaps an eighth of an inch, but there was no movement of them, no indication that she was aware of his presence.

"Now breathe, Anne," he said, watching her chest closely.

She exhaled through chapped and parted lips and slowly her chest rose and fell again. David Levinson suddenly wanted to leap from his chair, shout for all to come see, yet he restrained himself, uncertain whether it may have been just a fluke.

Again he placed his palm on her chest. "Let's try it again, Anne. If you can hear and understand me, hold your breath— but only for a few moments." His heart beat furiously as he watched, willing her chest to again be still. Then her breathing ceased. "Breathe," he said, and she did.

Quickly he reached for the nurse's call button and punched it several times. In moments Regina Dotzer hurried in followed by two other nurses.

"What is it, doctor? What's hap—"

He raised his hand for quiet. "Watch," he said, quickly counting the number of persons present, then motioned them closer. In a normal voice he said, "Anne, if there are five people in this room, not counting you, please hold your breath for a few moments." She continued breathing normally and Levinson smiled at the nurses' puzzled expressions, his eyes twinkling mischievously, then he turned to Anne again.

"Anne, if there are *four* people in this room, please hold your breath for a few moments."

Regina Dotzer also held her breath, anticipation gripping her as she reached and touched the pitiful young woman's chest as it rose and fell slowly. And then it stopped. "Oh..my..*God*..." she murmured, quickly withdrawing her hand as though burned. "How long...? How long has she been like this, doctor?"

"I have no idea. Maybe a week, maybe more. It was some-thing I just had to try a few minutes ago." He edged the swivel chair closer and took Anne's fingers in his. "We're glad you're with us, Anne. We can help you now, and we'll try to think of other ways to communicate with you."

It was uncanny, Regina thought, and eerie too. From all appearances the young woman seemed dead except for her breathing, and yet she had been watching them for days or more as they went about their duties. She suddenly wondered what the young woman may be thinking, needing. She leaned over Anne's motionless body and spoke quietly, "Anne, I'm Regina Dotzer, a nurse, and I want to ask you something. Same drill, okay?" Gently she placed her hand between Anne's breasts. "Are you in pain?" Instantly Anne's breathing stopped. Regina glanced at David Levinson and raised her eyebrows, saw him nod. "I'll get you something right away, dear."

Lyle Pennington stood quietly at Sylvia Edelbrock's side in her second floor sitting room while she examined the fax sheets he had brought.

"Were you discreet in obtaining these?" she asked.

"Of course, Mrs. Edelbrock. The man is very good with computers. They call his sort *hackers*, I believe, and he said he had little difficulty tapping into the system at Mr. Donnelley's firm."

"It leaves no trace?"

"He assured me there would be none."

Sylvia Edelbrock nodded and looked again at the summary of her husband's and Philip Darcy's transactions in Coastal Airlines stock. It was just as she suspected. The timing of the stock transactions and the trend was obvious to any close observer of the airline industry; they coincided closely with Warner's smearing ad campaigns and fomented union turmoil he had aimed at Coastal. More, was the equally obvious timing of the two aircraft crashes, followed by TransCon's absorption of Coastal. Warner Edelbrock and Philip Darcy had done well for themselves, she saw, nodding and kneading her hands.

She pointed to an unusual symbol on the transaction listing. "Does this mean that the proceeds were transferred to Swiss accounts?"

Lyle Pennington leaned closer and recognized the symbol the hacker had explained. "Yes, Mrs. Edelbrock."

Sylvia nodded again and narrowed her eyes as she stared ahead through the windows. Warner was acting well within his character, profiting on the sly and squirreling it away overseas for a rainy day. Just as she had suspected he would.

She excused Pennington so that she could be alone with her thoughts, then rolled her wheelchair to the windows and stared out at the leafless branches. She reflected over the twenty-eight years of their marriage. It hadn't been love, not in the beginning nor through the years. It had been a marriage of convenience for both of them arranged by her father, C. Gordon Preston, then chairman and founder of TransCon Airlines. He had ordained that the bright young executive was perfect material to later assume command of the airline when he stepped down, but insisted that control should remain in the family. Thus he deemed that his crippled daughter, Sylvia, then thirty-seven and principal heir, should be the partner in the arrangement and provide the needed balance. Upon C. Gordon Preston's passing, Warner Edelbrock would run the day-to-day affairs of the airline and make the executive decisions while Sylvia would retain control and ownership of the voting stock through the Preston Trust.

She remembered that the arrangement had been a blessing of sorts insofar as her loneliness was concerned. She was wheelchair-ridden, her body twisted and deformed, and there had never been an interested suitor. Until Warner Edelbrock there had never been sex, something of which despite her limitations she was quite capable except for childbearing. So Warner had become the after-business-hours husband, companion, and lover for which she yearned; it mattered little that he was bought and paid for. And for several years he had doted upon her, showered her with expensive gifts, taught her secrets of intimacy that she had only read about, whisked her away to exotic and faraway places in the corporate jet, and catered enormous banquets to celebrate her birthdays.

Yes, it had been the time of her life.

But that would all change, she remembered. In a few short years the pendulum would swing from happiness to desolation. A cycle completed. It began shortly after her father's death, as she feared it would. Her eyes misted remembering the great man, the funeral attended by many.

C. Gordon Preston had been a pioneer in the fledgling aviation industry of the thirties, had built TransCon Airlines from little more than a barn-storming mail carrier flying two rattling aircraft held together with little more than baling wire, a thread of hope and a prayer. He, along with Patterson of United, Bob Six of Continental, Frye of TWA, Baker of National, Rickenbacker of Eastern, and Trippe of Pan American had forged an industry against formidable financial odds, conniving bureaucrats, and a wary public. And they had succeeded.

C. Gordon Preston had left her the fruits of his lifelong struggles that dark day many years ago when they lowered his casket into the earth, but she was left with his other legacy as well—Warner Edelbrock, who that day became chairman and chief executive officer of TransCon Airlines.

The ensuing changes in their relationship had been subtle at first, he was home less often, he seemed less doting and genial, and their frequent excursions to favorite ports became fewer until soon there were none. Once again she became the wealthy yet lonely cripple. For conversation those few nights when Warner was home, their only common denominator was the airline and he often resisted discussion of it. When pressed, he became verbally abusive, and thus emerged a vicious temper that had been long suppressed. C. Gordon Preston's passing had cleared the decks.

As months became a year, then two, a sort of truce emerged that she recalled vividly. He had struck her once in a fit of rage when of sheer frustration she demanded to meet with the airline's executive committee to dissuade them from a proposed merger with Continental. The merger made no economic sense, and more, Continental would come out on top.

"It's none of your fucking business, Sylvia," he railed.

"It is *my* money, Warner, *my* father built this airline and I'll not allow you and your hooligans to destroy it! I'll cast all of my voting shares to overturn the merger."

Then shouting obscenities, he had loosed a roundhouse swing with his open palm that struck her aside the head and toppled her from the wheelchair. Her frantic screams had brought Romo the gardener bursting through the door to subdue him.

She would long remember pointing a shaking finger at her enraged husband, his arms pinioned by Romo: "You will live to regret this, Warner Edelbrock. You will pay, and pay dearly."

The turnaround had been immediate, she remembered, stroking her cheek as though the ugly welt of years before still throbbed. His apologies had been profuse, the merger died, and for a time he had again become the Warner Edelbrock she had known before. Lavish gifts arrived unannounced, there had been a cruise to Acapulco, and for her forty-fifth birthday he had given her a luxurious van fitted with hydraulic ramps.

"I'll need a driver," she said, and she advertised and chose carefully from the many applicants. In spite of his frightening appearance, Lyle Pennington had been her choice. He was muscular, subservient, a former pilot retired on disability due to an accident that had sheared the top of his skull away, and he possessed far more intelligence than the others. Armed, he would also serve as her personal bodyguard. Otherwise unemployable, his loyalty would be assured.

But it wasn't many months before Warner Edelbrock regressed from his state of newfound love for his spouse to one of benign civility, the latter assured in part by the presence of Pennington. And so it was that an undeclared state of ceasefire prevailed upon Warner the aggressor. For a time.

Several years later the compassionate Romo, long a member of the Preston and now Edelbrock household, had given her a

114

puppy as a companion. She remembered how he had stood before her that day, grinning, wide-brimmed gardening hat clutched in one hand and a squiggly dachshund in the other. "Un compañero por usted, señora," he said, setting the puppy at her feet.

"Oh, what a darling sweet puppy. Muchas gracias, señor Romo. What shall I call him?"

Romo frowned, settling into deep thought. Then his eyes brightened. "¡Yo se, señora! Se puede llamarse ah...ah...Jocko!"

"Jocko?"

"Si'. Jocko."

Six months later she had found Jocko beneath a bed of roses, his skull crushed...

Sylvia Edelbrock shook away the ugly memory then pressed a button on her control console and spun the wheelchair around. She had long suspected that Warner Edelbrock was capable of murder. That others may think so as well. He had the bad temperament frequently witnessed by others; he was well known in the industry as a vicious infighter, especially where Coastal Airlines was involved; had raised the suspicions of the authorities when Coastal's former president had apparently committed suicide; and then there had been the fare wars and now the devastating crashes coinciding with his secret profits on the sale of Coastal's plummeting stock. It all fit. Warner Edelbrock had the motives and temperament of a killer.

"Pennington," she called.

"Yes, Mrs. Edelbrock?" he answered from the doorway.

"Bring the van around. We're going for a drive."

"To the hospital to visit the young woman?"

Sylvia Edelbrock looked away and stared out the windows. "Yes," she said at last, nodding. "It's time."

It had been frustrating at first, knowing that Anne Ryan could see, hear, feel, yet not communicate other than halting her breathing, but now Dr. David Levinson had gained ground. As each day passed he worked with her frequently, knowing that by talking to her and keeping her focused on recovery he would eventually break through the barrier.

His efforts paid off. Within a week she could blink her eyelids in response. A day later she raised a trembling finger, and still later came a twitch of a toe, and then, at last, her lips moved. It was a gravelly, hoarse whisper at best, and only a word or two that were thick and nearly unintelligible, but they were words, real words, and he clapped and cheered for her.

By the end of the second week he elevated her upper body so that she could see the entire room. He saw that her eyes were open and clear, alert, followed his movements, and he reduced the level of her pain medication. He removed the casts from her fractured arms and the bandages from her skull, but the body cast from her waist down would remain for weeks.

He had been careful to steer their limited conversations away from the cause of her injuries in fear that she would lapse into a void once again. When she spoke they were brief phrases, coherent but whispered, and the effort obviously tired her. As he was about to end their session for the day, Regina Dotzer entered, smiled at Anne, and then motioned him into the hallway.

"She has a visitor waiting. Is it okay?"

David shrugged, "I don't see why not, so long as it's brief. It's not the press or the Feds is it?"

Regina laughed, "Hardly. It's an elderly woman in a wheelchair who claims to be a friend."

David nodded. "Okay, but make it short and stay with them, all right? I don't want her to become agitated or exhausted."

Sylvia Edelbrock disengaged the gears of her wheelchair and allowed the nurse to push her into the room. For a moment she gazed at the young woman lying in the bed with her eyes closed, then slowly she wheeled herself forward. She turned to the nurse and whispered, "May I speak to her?"

Regina Dotzer nodded, "Yes, but only for a few moments, and please...keep it light, cheerful."

Sylvia reached for Anne Ryan's hand lying palm up at her side and clasped it gently in hers. "My dear," she began quietly, "You don't know me, but I feel as though I know you very well. I know this is a very difficult and painful time for you, but I just thought it would help you to know that someone is on your side."

Anne's eyes fluttered open and she slowly turned her head on the pillow and looked at the older woman. "Who are you?" she whispered.

"I am a crippled and meddling old woman who knows well the pain of confinement as well as abandonment by those whom you thought were your allies. I am Sylvia Edelbrock, my dear, and I will help you in any way that I can."

Regina Dotzer placed her hand gently on Sylvia Edelbrock's shoulder signaling that it was time.

The words were still difficult to form, but at last Anne whispered, "Thank you. I...I..."

"Don't try to talk, my dear, just rest now and know that you have a friend, an ally when the time comes. Now I must go."

After two more weeks with Dr. Levinson's help Anne regained most of her motor responses. She was delighted she could at last turn her head at will, raise and lower her arms, wiggle her toes, and speak in brief yet hoarse sentences. Still, her lower body was uncomfortably encased in a cast from her waist to just above her toes, and would be for several more weeks, but now the insidious itching became a torment she would gladly exchange for pain. It felt like an army of fleas crawling over her flesh, and she had amused the conservative Dr. Levinson to the point of laughter when she asked that they call the exterminators.

There had been damage to her larynx and it was painful to talk, but she ignored it as best she could since speaking and communicating was the only way she could gain answers to the dozens of puzzling questions she had concerning the crash. And

Levinson had tried to discourage her but she would have none of it; the key to her mental health lay in learning the facts with which she could defend herself and prove that she hadn't erred, killing all those people.

She was certain she hadn't committed an error, and for days she lay deep in thought, eyes closed, mentally replaying from memory every moment leading to the crash. She read dozens of newspaper accounts of the tragedy, studied quotes from FAA and NTSB officials, but their inferences were clear: It appeared to be a case of pilot error and would be pursued as such. Then a later article disclosed that the FAA had suspended her airline transport pilot's license. She turned back to the paper dated the morning after the crash. Again the headline jumped out at her: *47 Dead in Air Disaster.* Worse was the photograph below it of a family of six who had died in the crash, of an enchanting little girl and her family who would remain etched in her memory forever.

Anne laid back on the pillows and closed her eyes, rolling her head from side to side, trying to shut out the awful memory. Many of the newspaper photographs had been ugly, stark and grisly. Unnecessarily gruesome. With her eyes closed she could still see the photos shot at night; the lumpy body bags lying about in the snow, one of which probably contained Overmeyer—or part of him, another the little girl; the steaming and shattered wreckage lying on its back and dripping with fire retardant foam; and the work crews clustered about the crushed cockpit, metal saws shrieking as they tore through the twisted metal, extricating her own apparently lifeless body... The body of the careless killer who had lived...

But how? How could it have happened? Everything was fine until...until...

Tears streamed from the corners of her eyes and she clenched her fists tightly, pounding them against the mattress, at last venting her frustration in heaving, guttural sobs. Then she felt a stinging jab in her arm and blackness overcame her.

Hours later she awoke from a deep and dreamless sleep, her tongue thick and dry, mouth gummy, tasting of what might have been yesterday's Swiss cheese, her brain clouded with gauzy cobwebs. She lay with her eyes closed for several moments while her mind cleared. Then she sensed that someone was near and opened her eyes.

"Mornin'."

"Gordy!" she rasped, trying to raise her head from the pillow. "Oh God, Gordy, I've missed you so."

He cupped her forehead with his hand and gently eased her back. "Easy, kiddo. Don't get excited or they'll make me leave."

"How...how did you get in? They've kept everyone away except Mrs. Edelbrock."

Gordy frowned. "Mrs. Edelbrock? *The* Mrs. Edelbrock? As in TransCon?"

"Yes," she whispered, "she just wanted to help, if she could. She's crippled too."

Gordy doubted that anyone in the Edelbrock family possessed a whit of human compassion. Since Coastal's absorption into TransCon he'd heard much through the rumor mill about the ruthless and quarrelsome Warner Edelbrock, enough to color his thinking about anyone bearing the name. Then he saw Anne's quizzical expression and decided to let it go.

"I've been here before, only you didn't know it. Leavenworth and I have an understanding."

"Levinson."

"Yeah, Levinson. Nice guy. Listen, Anne, can I get you anything?"

She closed her eyes again and gripped his hand tightly. "I just...I just need your support."

"You've got it, munchkin. Wiener Rosenberg to the rescue. Someone's finger you want broken?"

Her voice cracked painfully as she laughed, then whispered, "Yeah, the fickle finger of fate. Seriously, though, Gordy, Dr. Levinson can't hold them off much longer...I'm getting better...I'm..."

"You mean the FAA? The NTSB?"

She nodded. They were waiting, she knew, waiting as circling vultures with their hundreds of questions and their tape recorders. Waiting for answers she didn't have. And without answers they would draw their own conclusions and label her the same as they had Ray Thompson. Close behind would be the press, grazing the battlefield and goring the wounded. She would be a leper with blood on her hands. She couldn't live with that. She wouldn't.

"They can be pretty rough," he said. "Are you sure you're ready for that?"

In a halting whisper she answered, "I'll never be ready for it, but I'd rather just get it out of the way. Get it over with. Then go away some—"

"No. Don't think that way, Anne. It ain't over 'til it's over. Maybe once we hear the cockpit tapes, see the flight recorder data and study it, we'll find something they didn't. You never know. Maybe something—"

She gripped his hand tightly, "Gordy, I was *there!* It was a normal takeoff, the engines functioned perfectly and we had a solid rate of climb! I remember we were at vee-two plus ten, a speed well above a stall, and then...then...it just *stalled!* It just goddamn fell right out from under me!"

Gordy nodded as her nails sank deeply into his palm. He imagined the scenario, remembered the sickening sensation in his gut when he'd stalled a DC-9 simulator while in training, and later the precautions they had drilled into him and others to avoid one. Yet what Anne described sounded right; it shouldn't have stalled. Not unless...unless she hadn't been thinking clearly.

"...right now I need a dose of something else..."

Her words of that night haunted him, yet he had never known Anne to even experiment with drugs. She seldom even drank! But then he hadn't seen her for nearly two months until they met in the crew lounge the night of the crash. Had she gotten involved with the wrong crowd? Been shacking with some guy who turned her on to some kind of dope? It would be unlike her, but...

"Anne," he began carefully, "have you thought about what went on before the crash, whether you'd had a good night's sleep, were stressed out or something?"

Anne suddenly released his hand and shoved it away. Her throat hurt badly now from talking but she forced the words out anyway. "Goddamn you, Gordy, whose side are on?"

He slumped his shoulders and sighed. "I'm sorry, Anne, but those are questions they're going to ask you. And a hell of a lot more. Better we talk about it first, open, no secrets, just like we always have. Just like years ago when I told you about my...uh, my little problem."

His little problem had been bedwetting, she remembered. He'd been embarrassed but open and honest about it, seeking her help and advice. He had trusted her. Now she felt guilty for her callous remark. She rolled her head to face him, blinking away tears, "I'm sorry, Gordy, I just flew off the handle."

"S'okay. I probably shouldn't have asked."

She took his hand again. "I had a decent night's sleep before the flight and I wasn't stressed. I just had a sore back, that's all."

"A sore back? How'd that happen?"

"I fell, skiing. No big deal."

"Were you...taking anything for it?"

"Just Advil or something, later some aspirin before the flight." Her affair with Warner Edelbrock was the one secret she had kept from him and she was relieved he didn't ask who she was with that day.

Regina Dotzer rapped gently on the door. "Captain Rosenberg? Time to go."

Gordy took Anne's hands in his and squeezed them. "Just let me know if there's anything you need, or anything I can do. Oh, by the way—the pilots association's got a representative lined up for you for the NTSB hearing in three weeks. They say he's good on pilot error cases."

Anne clenched her teeth tightly, seething. "I didn't screw up, dammit!"

"Easy, kiddo, I know you didn't, but that's the way they're going to pitch it. They're playin' hardball and we've gotta step up to the plate, swing at it."

Anne sighed, exhausted, then whispered, "Tell Titus I love him. And Gord? I love you too."

Mitchell Hardison sat on his worn sofa with Dog at his slippered feet while studying the data he'd collected on Anne Ryan and Coastal 193. On the table beside him was an ashtray brimming with dead cigar butts and he poked through them looking for one long enough to relight. There weren't any, but in looking he had counted eleven dead ones; one every half hour. He'd been at it for five and a half hours.

He grunted as he leaned forward and scratched Dog's ears. The sad hound-dog eyes stared back at him dolefully and he saw that the fur around them was wet and streaked with tears. And no wonder, he thought. The small living room was filled with a suffocating haze that would rival Los Angeles on a bad day. He would cut down on his cigars some...maybe, say, limit himself to one every forty-five minutes. Maybe even start tomorrow.

He stretched and yawned then massaged his jowls and eyed the scattered stacks of files, transcripts of interviews with dozens of witnesses, photographs of wreckage, and computer printouts that lay haphazardly on the floor. They were the fruits of his efforts over the past two months, the technology used in the forensics of airline disasters, and there was far more information than necessary to conclude the case of Coastal 193.

And that troubled him.

Unlike many other airline disasters he'd investigated, the demise of Coastal 193 and its related cause seemed cut and dried, so different from other disasters often requiring many months and sometimes years of lengthy and painstaking technical investigations. Disasters like the mysterious crashes of Lockheed Electras in the early sixties; the DC-10s that seemingly exploded in midair in the seventies; and perhaps the most infamous of all—the mysterious crash and later the ghostly apparitions of Eastern Airlines Flight 401. Yet his close analysis of Coastal 193's wreckage and flight data recorder had early on eliminated any notion of mechanical malfunction, a bomb or incendiary device, windshear or microburst, and the cockpit voice recorder gave no indication that there may have been an intruder in the cockpit. Tomorrow, when he would have his first interview with Anne Ryan, he would explore the latter possibility yet he doubted anything would come of it.

And so he kept coming back to pilot error—it could only be pilot error compounded by drugs. There could be no other viable explanation, and tomorrow he'd confront her with it before the authorities made it public, before she knew that they knew.

Still, it all seemed too pat.

Yet for the past five and one-half hours he'd combed the files and data for something he may have missed, a *something* that offered a fork in the investigative road, a faint trail or different avenue to explore leading away from the obvious. He remembered well the DC-10s in the early seventies that appeared to have mysteriously exploded in midair, and the conclusion by some that they were the work of terrorists, of bombs. Only by looking well beyond the obvious did resourceful investigators aided by aircraft design engineers later learn that the latches on outward-opening cargo doors had failed. The doors had blown outward as internal pressure built, causing massive decompression and structural failure. So, yes, the aircraft had indeed exploded, but not for the reasons first thought. But it had taken more than one such incident involving a DC-10 to convince investigators to look further. Nearly 350 lives were to be snuffed out first.

With that in mind he had set out to go the extra mile and pulled the files on every domestic DC-9 takeoff crash since 1968. He shifted his weight uneasily on the sofa and again scanned the listing:

12/27/68: Ozark Airlines, Sioux City, IA
06/26/78: Air Canada, Toronto
02/05/85: Airborne Express, Philadelphia, PA
08/16/87: Northwest Airlines, Romulus, MI
11/15/87: Continental Airlines, Denver, CO
02/17/91: Ryan Airlines, Cleveland, OH
11/10/99: Coastal Airlines, New York, NY (LGA) Flt 288

He shook his head and laid the listing aside. Some of the accidents seemed related in some measure to failure to properly de-ice prior to takeoff. And for that the blame usually rested with the captain of the ship. So with some exceptions there had been a pattern emerging, but a pattern that ended with the crashes of Coastal 288 and 193—both had been properly de-iced. There were witnesses and Westphal had nailed that down tightly.

He reached for Anne Ryan's file, yanked it from under Dog, and flipped it open. He riffled the pages then stared again at the toxicology report. *Methyl morphine*, otherwise known as codeine, present in both urine and blood samples taken within minutes of her admission to the hospital. The drug concentration in her bloodstream was enough to impair her judgment at a critical moment.

He fought back his anger at the obscenity of it. People like Ryan were a scant minority in the industry, yet in recent years the incidence of drug or alcohol use among operators of passenger-carrying transportation equipment was increasing. There had been the commuter airliner that crashed in Colorado in 1988, the captain's blood having been found to contain cocaine. Then there had been the freight train vs. Amtrak passenger train collision on the east coast, killing 16 and injuring 174, the crew of the freight train having tested positive for marijuana. And of course, there had been the notorious *Exxon Valdez* disaster in Alaska, the captain of which was alleged to have been under the influence of alcohol. And now Coastal Airlines, burdened with the undeniable finding that Captain Anne Ryan had been flying under the influence of drugs. Forty-seven dead.

He remembered how pilots, bus drivers, and railroad engineers screamed bitterly that the majority should take the heat for the actions of a few, yet when it came to legislation requiring random testing for illegal substances they were the ones most outspoken against it.

And Anne Ryan had been one of them.

That and an unrelated incident several years before had been the reason her name at first seemed familiar.

But the emotionally-charged ranting of she and her colleagues years ago about the invasions of random drug testing had evoked his memory of the writings of Shakespeare: *Methinks the lady doth protest too much.* Indeed she had, he thought, it seemed a predictable pattern among the guilty.

But it wasn't his job nor the NTSB's to prosecute—that was the domain of the U.S. Attorney and a Federal Grand Jury, and by agreement they would hold off until the gavel came down at the final NTSB hearing and the conclusion of probable cause was entered. Then his role in Coastal 193 would end.

Again he scanned his briefs, his list of witnesses to testify and the nature of their testimony, and of all of the other data he would enter in the record during the hearing that would bring the Board to the inescapable conclusion that Anne Ryan had erred grievously. A conclusion that, with her senses impaired by drugs, her supposed error of omission had become one of commission.

In a detached way he felt sorry for her, sorry for a skilled pilot of many years experience whose professionalism had somehow become eroded by the ills of a society that more and more seemed lacking in ethics, morals, bent upon destroying itself. Already the FAA had lifted her license and at the close of the NTSB hearing it would be permanently revoked. Then the judicial process would commence, a process that would likely result in a jail term for the damned-all Ryan just as it had for the imbibing captain of a 727, who, with an also inebriated crew, had somehow successfully navigated their airliner from Fargo to Minneapolis without incident. Fools.

But Ryan, unlike the intoxicated captain, would suffer far more than just the public pillorying and incarceration; she would carry the guilt for life. She would carry to her grave the rotting chicken judicially hung about her neck and reminding her of her misdeed. Ryan had taken 47 lives.

Tomorrow he would visit the hospital and face her for the first time. It was a task he relished little, except for perhaps gaining some answers.

SEVEN

The NTSB hearing room in Washington, D.C., buzzed with activity and anticipation for most, tension and foreboding for two who sat in the rear. It was a large, theater-like auditorium facing a dais and a long elaborate rostrum upon which rested five microphones, one for each of the presidentially-appointed NTSB board members. Also facing the dais were tables for the NTSB staff and witnesses, much like a courtroom.

As the hearing room filled and video and TV cameras were positioned, microphones tested, lights and tables rearranged, Anne Ryan and Gordy Rosenberg sat in the rear, nervously awaiting the ten o'clock call to order. The wheelchair was painfully uncomfortable for her frail buttocks, and she fidgeted and shifted about in the confining seat while clutching Gordy's equally sweaty hand. Against David Levinson's advice she had jumped ship after the body cast had been removed from her waist and legs, insisting she would fly to Washington and attend what would likely amount to her own funeral. After the devastating interview with Mitchell Hardison only a week ago, she now wished there had already been a funeral. She squeezed her eyes shut, remembering...

It had only been a week ago, yet she had recovered from her injuries to the point where neither she nor the doctors could any longer keep investigating officials at bay, and at last she was interviewed by Mitchell Hardison, and later by the FAA. The fat little man from the NTSB reeked of stale cigars and there was dog hair on the tails of his jacket, but he had been gentle and almost apologetic in his demeanor as he asked probing questions. Then he had placed a tape recorder on her bedside table and inserted a tape.

"What's that?" she asked.

"It's the tape from the cockpit voice recorder, Miss Ryan. I'm going to replay portions of it and ask you to tell me what some of it means."

Anne turned her head away, dreading any replay of the events of that awful night. "I--I don't want to hear it." For moments that seemed minutes she lay there, staring at the opposite wall, her head turned away from him. She could hear the rasping of his labored breathing as he waited patiently. At last she turned toward him again. "Couldn't you just let me read a transcript of it instead?"

He shook his head. "Better that you hear the tape. There might be a noise, a sound of some sort other than the dialogue that you might remember, something that would help us--and yourself."

There was no avoiding it; she would have to listen. "All right. But please...please just play the parts that you have questions about. I--I don't want to hear it all."

He nodded, ran the tape forward and punched it on. For seconds it hissed, no dialogue, only the distant sound of the engines running at ground idle. Then, *"...are you okay, captain?"* It was Overmeyer. Hardison snapped the recorder off. "Is that significant?" he asked. "Care to comment?"

Anne closed her eyes and slowly shook her head. It was an incautious remark by Overmeyer, yet insignificant. "No. I was sitting with my eyes closed for a moment, thinking, staring out the cockpit window, waiting while they de-iced the aircraft. I was just...just thinking. No big deal."

She heard Hardison grunt, then run the tape forward again. When it stopped he cleared his throat and said, "Miss Ryan—"

"Captain," she corrected.

Mitchell Hardison held her steely gaze, saw her steadfast defiance, and slowly shook his head. "Not anymore, I'm afraid," he said quietly. She looked away as he continued. "I want you to listen carefully to this part, try to remember exactly what was happening at the moment, what you were doing at this very instant." He snapped the recorder on and instantly the roar of jet engines at takeoff thrust filled the small hospital room. Then, *"Watch out! Watch out! Watch out!"* and Overmeyer's panicked voice brought the awful events of that night crashing down upon her.

"NOOOOOO!" Anne suddenly shrieked. "Shut it off! Oh, God, SHUT IT OFF!" she screamed, beating the mattress with her fists. Her mind now filled with the visions of shattered and steaming debris, of lumpy body bags lying in the snow, of the beguiling eyes of a child now dead.

Regina Dotzer hurried to her side, restraining her. "I think you'd better leave now," she said to Hardison.

But he had returned the following day, and with Levinson and Regina present, ready to again eject him if she became agitated, he pressed on. "So what was it that Overmeyer saw, Miss Ryan? Why was he shouting `watch out' ?"

Just a reaction, she told him, the reaction of an inexperienced and understandably frightened young man when the aircraft had inexplicably stalled and heeled over on its side before crashing. It was a lie, really a half-truth, but she would never tell otherwise. The truth wouldn't help her case, and worse, it would cause irreparable harm to Overmeyer's family. She would never tell them how Overmeyer had panicked when the aircraft suddenly rolled, how he had screamed and flailed at her like a terrified child as though she had caused the aircraft to go berserk. That she had then backhanded him viciously across the face an instant before the crash. She sensed that Hardison knew she wasn't telling it all.

And then Hardison dropped the other shoe.

It was then that he reached into his briefcase and withdrew a single sheet of paper and handed it to her. She scanned it briefly, saw her name at the top and that it seemed to be some sort of medical report. Then her eyes bulged when she read the conclusion, *"Specimens indicate presence of methyl morphine."*

"Care to comment on that, Miss Ryan?" he asked without emotion.

"Drugs! You—you're saying I took *drugs?*" Anne stared at him incredulously as he nodded, her throat constricting. "This— this can't be mine! There's been some mistake, some foul-up somewhere! I never—"

"Two blood samples drawn a little over an hour after the crash, Miss Ryan. Each sent to separate labs, each concluding the same. In short, there's simply no question. But what I want to know is why you took the risk, and how long you've been doing it. Is that why you trip-traded out of Coastal 288? Because you were on drugs? And if so, why didn't you also trip-trade out of flight 193?"

"No! Oh, God, no! I didn't do this! I swear to God I didn't do this..."

Anne shook away the memory of the shocking confrontation with Hardison when the audience suddenly quieted and NTSB board members began filing in. The presence of all five was unusual for a hearing, her pilot's association representative had explained. Normally there would be one board member present to observe and oversee the process while the hearing was conducted by the investigator-in-charge. But the successive and

130

devastating crashes of Coastal aircraft at La Guardia and that of another carrier months earlier had spawned considerable political pressure from White House staff to assure that the hearing gave all appearances of a gravely concerned government looking out for the public interest and warranting the attention of its full board every step of the way. That such a forum was unusual at this stage of the investigation gave added credence to the administration's hue and cry that the airline industry, in the years since its deregulation, may have bartered safety for economic survival and would be examined closely. The Board, and particularly the FAA, were chosen to send a message. Anne Ryan was the message as well as the messenger.

She squeezed Gordy's hand hard, her nails digging deeply into his palm. There had been little time for her to prepare for the charges of pilot error, but Hardison's revelation about the drugs, later echoed by the FAA, had been a staggering blow she was totally unprepared to fight.

Now as she sat waiting she felt nauseous, alone and utterly defenseless. Like in her recurring dreams, finding herself alone on a busy street corner in Manhattan...naked, frantically trying to cover herself as people laughed and pointed.

The pilot's association representative assigned to her, Gregory Hines, now sitting on Gordy's right, was a pleasant man in his fifties and also an airline pilot. He had seemed eager to help at first, certain that sufficient evidence was lacking to conclude that she had erred, and willing to push for a continuance and further investigation. Yet upon learning of her damning toxicological report he no longer seemed sympathetic; he seemed resigned to her guilt, had become abrupt in their discussions, and now she suspected his support would be minimal at best. She sensed that he saw her as the example of all he and others of The Cloth held repugnant: a cancer on the profession, worthy of swift excision. She sensed that even Gordy didn't believe her. The rats were fleeing the ship.

The gavel came down with a resounding splat, the sudden sound jolting Anne as it ricocheted off the auditorium walls, and the swelling audience settled into hushed whispers. Far down in the front row she saw three men and two women with recorders and steno pads propped on their knees, ballpoints poised at ready. Reporters. Reporters, like jackals smelling blood, eager to feast upon her rotting carcass when the Board finished with her. They would write her obituary; not a sympathetic ear there, nor would there be in the eyes of the tens of thousands who would likely be watching on television.

She saw the rotund figure of Mitchell Hardison seated at the table in front of the reporters, flipping pages in a file, and to his right sat a battery of other men she didn't know. Other NTSB investigators, she guessed. She wondered if they too had dog hair on their jackets.

"The secretary will please call the roll," intoned the board chairman.

A matronly woman seated at the end of the panel leaned toward her microphone. "National Transportation Safety Board hearing in the matter of Coastal Airlines Flight 193, March 9th, 2000. Chairman Lieberman and members Ronsone, Parghetti, O'Hara, and Winfield present. Also present are the investigator-in-charge, Mitchell Hardison, and investigators Westphal, Walker, and..."

For half an hour they listened to the preliminaries and Anne sat riveted in spite of her aching legs, absorbing every word while jotting notes on a pad. As she wrote she heard the auditorium door to her left open and hiss shut, then she heard a faint whirring and glanced up.

"Hello, my dear," Sylvia Edelbrock whispered as she jockeyed her wheelchair in beside Anne's.

Behind Sylvia Edelbrock stood the most frightening man Anne had ever seen. He was the embodiment of the ancient Cro-Magnon man or of Dick Tracy's nemesis, *Flattop*. He gazed without expression into Anne's eyes and at last she looked away.

132

"Mrs. Edelbrock," Anne whispered, "What are you doing here?"

"I called the hospital and they told me you had checked yourself out. Then Dr. Levinson told me that you were coming to the hearing, so I thought I could offer you some moral support." Sylvia Edelbrock pointed a gnarled finger toward the dais, "Besides, they're ganging up on you."

Moral support? Why for her? Surely the woman knew of her affair with her husband—or did she? Still, the woman's presence was unnerving... And that Neanderthal with her— *yukk!* She glanced again at Sylvia Edelbrock who had now taken a bag from beneath the shawl covering her knees and took up her knitting.

Far across the auditorium a man in an expensive suit and alligator shoes sat chin in hand and waiting impatiently for the proceedings to shift into high gear. He scanned the audience, saw his deep-throat from the FAA two rows away, winked, then looked toward the rear and stiffened. There was no mistaking the tall, hulking man standing in the rear, nor of the hunched old woman sitting in a wheelchair before him. And beside her, also in a wheelchair, sat none other than Anne Ryan.

He swore under his breath and quickly his eyes sought an exit. He saw one two rows away and looked back to the rear, saw that Sylvia Edelbrock's head was turned from him and Pennington was gazing ahead at the proceedings. Slowly, avoiding quick movements, he rose and walked straight to the exit.

Lyle Pennington stared ahead and moved only his eyes, watching as Philip Darcy moved toward the side exit. When the door closed he leaned and whispered to Sylvia Edelbrock. She nodded without turning.

Philip Darcy's fingers trembled as he inserted his calling card in the public telephone and punched in the unlisted number of TransCon's corporate offices. "It's me," he said, "Something strange going on."

After a brief recess the hearing continued and focused upon Mitchell Hardison presenting details of the crash, his findings, and the calling and swearing in of witnesses. Later he quoted from the transcript of the cockpit voice recording of the takeoff while Anne sat trembling with her eyes closed. Though voiced by the gravel-throated Hardison, Overmeyer's frantic last words echoed chillingly throughout the auditorium. Then Thomas Walker, a bearded and bespeckled man from the NTSB's aircraft performance group, gave his analysis of the flight data recorder; La Guardia control tower personnel gave their views of the crash; and NTSB investigator Douglas Westphal testified that the aircraft had been properly de-iced only ten minutes before takeoff.

A representative of the manufacturer of the de-icing solution testified as to its freezing-point deterrent value, and that laboratory tests had shown that a proper mixture of Type 1 solution would deter icing for fifteen minutes according to the weather and other conditions existing the night of the crash. When asked whether wing ice could have formed within ten minutes of application, the holdover interval between the de-icing of Coastal 193 and its subsequent takeoff, he said it was highly unlikely unless there was precipitation such as freezing rain or snow. In fact, he said, wing ice couldn't have formed in that interval since the tower controllers had confirmed that the snowfall had ceased by the time of the de-icing and subsequent takeoff.

And finally NTSB's Thomas Walker added that the possibility of wing icing resulting from cold-soaked fuel in the wing tanks had also been ruled out. Fresh, warmer fuel had been boarded shortly before the flight.

A palpable silence settled over the auditorium as the last of the potential causes of the accident seemed eliminated, leaving only one.

Anne Ryan closed her eyes and slowly shook her head. It was all nice and neat, she admitted, and were she sitting as a Board member she too could easily conclude pilot error, right where Hardison and his people were leading them. What else was there for them to believe? When her turn came they would probably listen attentively, respectfully, but already she suspected that the damage had been done. Certainly before the hearing all of the board members had been made privy to the toxicological report; what she was witnessing was but an exercise, the outcome of which was already concluded.

Since Hardison's revelation a week ago that drugs had been found in her blood, she had rebutted the charge as a mistake, an error occurring in the emergency room frenzy of tending many injured. But it was Dr. Levinson who revealed that he had witnessed the samples being taken and Regina Dotzer had personally taken them to the lab.

But it wasn't until early this morning during the flight down from New York that her memory responded. She had been thinking of her last stay with Warner Edelbrock, of his conniving behavior, how he had suckered her into going off *The Leap* and injuring her back. And she thought of his cruel laughter about her spectacular fall, the smoking gun and the dead dog... And then it had come to her as she stared out the aircraft window at the clouds blanketing the coast far below. *"...just an evil concoction of barbiturates for your aching butt..."* Edelbrock had said that, handing her some tablets as he stood by the crackling fire. And she had taken them. Like a naïve fool, she had taken them.

Could he? Would he have done that? Given her controlled substances that he knew were illegal in the cockpit? And if he had, why? And suppose he had, how would she go about proving it? Would she sit at the witness table and tell the world with the cameras focused upon her and the press nearby scribbling furiously as she spoke, that Warner Edelbrock, the chairman and chief executive officer of TransCon Airlines, a cruel and inhuman dog-shooter whom she was screwing on a regular basis, had conned her into some strange pills for her aching butt? That she was but a naive, college-educated, forty-year-old (plus a few) airline captain who didn't even know what drugs looked like? That she had taken them without so much as a question? It would be the equivalent of the President's ridiculous assertions of not inhaling marijuana when he said he had tried it. The laughter would rock the auditorium.

Anne tensed as Mitchell Hardison prepared to deliver what she knew would be the crushing blow. The drugs. She saw him place a cigar butt carefully in an ashtray and rise to address the board. Quickly she leaned across Gordy, ignoring the searing pain in her pelvis as she twisted in the wheelchair, and tapped Gregory Hines's forearm.

"I want to go on *now*," she whispered anxiously, "They've got to hear my side before they get a mind-set."

Hines, the pilot's association representative, shook his head and leaned in front of Gordy. "I wouldn't advise it until you've heard what the other witnesses have to say. Wait until they've had their turn so you'll know what you're dealing with. Whatever you might say now could lock you in to something that you might later regret saying."

"The *truth*? Jesus Christ, I'm not going to go up there and lie! Why—"

"Mr. chairman," Mitchell Hardison began, "the evidence we've examined and presented today leads us to conclude that the crash of Coastal Airlines Flight 193 occurred as the result of pilot error. We believe that the evidence clearly shows that Captain Anne Ryan failed to anticipate and take swift and decisive corrective action at the moment the aircraft approached a stall. We also believe that there are exacerbating circumstances which inhibited or otherwise diminished Captain Ryan's capacity for anticipating and taking such corrective action."

Anne sat rigid, frustrated, her fists tightly clenched, steeling herself for what was to come. She glanced quickly left at Sylvia Edelbrock, saw that she was calmly knitting, her expression pleasant as she stitched, only occasionally looking up at the proceedings as though watching a soap opera. A hint of a frown creased Anne's brow but she looked away quickly as Hardison continued.

"We have a toxicology report from a reputable laboratory which shows that at the time of the crash, Captain Ryan's bloodstream contained methyl morphine, otherwise known as codeine, in amounts sufficient to cause diminished capacity."

Suddenly the audience came alive and a chorus of incredulous comments filled the auditorium. The gavel came down as sharply as pistol shots and Mitchell Hardison continued.

"Mr. chairman, I'd like now to call several other witnesses."

"Proceed."

Hardison, standing, leaned down to his microphone. "Will Mr. William Lorenzo please come to the witness table."

A tall and spare middle-aged man dressed in a dark business suit walked purposely forward, took a seat and was sworn in.

"Please state your name and occupation for the record," Hardison asked.

The man adjusted the microphone and spoke in an articulate voice. "My name is William A. Lorenzo, and I am an assistant U.S. Attorney, United States Department of Justice."

Mitchell Hardison clasped his hands behind his back as he paced. "Mr. Lorenzo, did your office obtain a search warrant to gain access to Captain Ryan's locker in what was then the Coastal Airlines crew lounge at La Guardia airport?"

"We did."

"And did your office exercise that search warrant?"

"Yes, we did."

"Please tell this board, Mr. Lorenzo, the results of that search."

The assistant U.S. Attorney cleared his throat. "Among miscellaneous personal effects not relevant to these proceedings, we found an aspirin bottle containing eleven white tablets."

"And did your office have those eleven white tablets analyzed in a laboratory?"

"We did. The tablets were sent to the Federal Bureau of Investigation's crime laboratory."

"And?"

"They found that the tablets each contained methyl morphine, otherwise known as codeine."

"Thank you, Mr. Lorenzo. Tell me, did the FBI lab also dust the bottle for fingerprints?"

"Yes, they did. There were two sets of prints on the bottle, both different, one of which has been identified."

"Were Captain Ryan's prints on the bottle?"

"Yes, they were."

"Thank you, Mr. Lorenzo, that'll be all."

Anne sat stunned as the U.S. Attorney left the witness table. *Her aspirin bottle!* She had taken three before the flight! No wonder her back pain had lessened so quickly. It hadn't been the tablets she'd swallowed at Warner's after all! Her mind reeled, unhearing as Hardison called the next witness.

"The board calls Captain James Allan Truax."

Gordy sat forward quickly and nudged Anne's elbow. "Look who's here."

Truax! She watched the arrogant Oklahoman swagger toward the witness table, pull out a chair, then flip his uniform coattails like a concert pianist as he sat. She listened closely as Hardison asked his name and occupation, wasting no time in getting to his point.

"Captain Truax, did you speak with Captain Ryan shortly before she boarded Flight 193?"

"I did."

"And did she seem normal? What I mean is, since you've testified that you have known her for many years while employed with Coastal Airlines, did she seem any different that night?"

Truax nodded, "She seemed stressed."

"Was that before or after she went to her locker in the crew lounge?"

"It was before. I had just brought the aircraft in from Cleveland and I joked with her for a few moments. I knew it was the aircraft she'd be taking out as Flight 193 and I told her not to bend it," he said, looking about for reaction.

A twittering of laughter arose from the audience while Anne seethed, wondering how Truax could possibly know that she had not yet been to her locker. What troubled her more was that Truax *knew* that she was to command Flight 193. That was suspicious.

Again the gavel came down and Hardison pressed on. "And what did she say to you?"

"Exactly? Word for word?"

"Word for word," Hardison answered, pacing, his lips pursed as he glanced at the board members.

"She told me to go fuck myself."

The audience howled and Hardison spun around, "Oh, that's quite professional. Has she spoken like that to you often?"

Truax shook his head. "No, not like that night. Like I said, she seemed stressed."

Anne pounded the arms of her wheelchair. "That's a damned lie," she hissed, and heads in the back row quickly turned.

"And did you, Captain Truax, observe or overhear Captain Ryan speaking to anyone else before she went into the locker room?"

"Yes, I did. I was standing a few feet away when she bumped into Captain Rosenberg."

"And?"

"He asked her if she got the dose of *Far Side* cartoons he'd left in her mailbox. She seemed in a hurry, stressed, as I said, and only talked with him for a moment. As she turned to leave I heard her say, `I gotta go, right now I need a dose of something else'."

Anne quickly reached across Gordy and slapped Gregory Hines's shoulder. "Jesus, do something, you dork! They're taking it all out of context!"

Hines raised his hand in abeyance, "We'll deal with that when you take the stand. This isn't a courtroom and I'm not an attorney. I can't play Perry Mason and shout objections."

Anne ground her teeth in anger, yet now she had a thread of hope; it had to have been Truax who had planted the drugs in her aspirin bottle, set her up for long suppressed revenge and—yes! That was it! That was why her lock was on backward! He could easily have gotten her combination!

"Mr. Hardison," the board chairman reminded, "This is not a court of law and the witness you have just questioned has spoken as a matter of hearsay on an issue not germane to our function here. We need not prove how or why Captain Ryan came to be in possession of controlled substances, nor the circumstances leading to her taking of such substances, nor for that matter her demeanor in conversing with her peers. That is beyond our jurisdiction as well as our interest. What *is* relevant is that it is established fact that she had such substances in her bloodstream when acting as pilot in command of an aircraft operating under Part 121 of the Federal Aviation Regulations. I suggest you call your next witness."

Hardison nodded, expecting the admonishment. It was like scolding Dog after he crapped on the floor: Dog may get the point, but the stain remained. "Will Captain Anne Ryan please come to the witness table."

"Good luck, dear," said Sylvia Edelbrock, patting Anne's hand.

The audience buzzed as Gordy wheeled her down the aisle and Gregory Hines followed.

Heart pounding, she set her jaw and avoided the scores of curious eyes following her as though they were the eyes of those who had come to witness a hanging. Yet deep within she couldn't shake a gut-wrenching feeling of guilt. Whatever had

140

happened that night, she felt somehow responsible. *The little girl... Oh, Jesus, the little girl...* If only she'd canceled the flight for want of a couple of lousy burned out ten-cent landing gear indicator bulbs. She could have. It was the captain's pre-rogative, but she'd chosen instead to save Coastal's bacon--a canceled flight meant more lost revenue to the ailing carrier. And lost revenue equated to loss of jobs.

Gordy pushed her before the table and adjusted the micro-phone, then gave her shoulder a squeeze and took a seat behind. Hines settled in beside her and they were both sworn in. Then he spoke first.

"Mr. chairman and members of the board, my name is Greg-ory Hines, and I am Captain Ryan's representative from the pi-lots association. Before Mr. Hardison begins with his questions, I would first like to thank you for recognizing that the testimony of Captain Truax has no bearing on the matter before you.

"Second, I would like to state for the record that Mr. Hardison's tentative conclusion of pilot error on the part of Captain Ryan is circumstantial at best, and by his focusing on the *who* he may be avoiding needed focus on the *why* of the ac-cident. We believe that something other than Captain Ryan had brought that aircraft down, and that Mr. Hardison's conclusion is a *default* conclusion, since neither he nor his technical staff was able to demonstrate any contributory factors of a mechani-cal, procedural or meteorological nature. Thus, their focus is entirely upon the pilot. And we would not necessarily disagree with that focus except that the conclusion drawn in this case has no basis in fact. Mr. Hardison has not presented evidence to support his conclusion that Captain Ryan failed to perceive a crisis, nor has he shown that Captain Ryan failed to act. His conclusion is based purely upon the premise that if it isn't A or B, then it has to be C. It's like saying the sun rises because the rooster crows."

Gordy clapped involuntarily, prompting a searing glare from the chairman.

Hines continued, "The evidence presented shows clearly that the aircraft stalled at an altitude so low that there was virtually no chance that any pilot could recover, but the evidence also shows that during the takeoff climbout the aircraft was operating at a speed sufficient to prevent its stalling, and in accordance with the aircraft operating manual. Furthermore—"

"Mr. Hines," Hardison interrupted, "Are you suggesting that someone tampered with the aircraft in such a way as to modify its stalling speed without the pilot's knowledge?"

"I'm not suggesting that at all, but I certainly wouldn't rule it out. And that in itself is my point: You haven't proven that pilot error is the probable cause."

"Nor, Mr. Hines, have you proven that it isn't," Hardison added, "and I'll remind you that technicians have combed every scrap of that wreckage, examined every flight control and in-strument, and found that all were functioning properly and within manufacturer's specifications."

Hines leaned closer to the microphone. "I'll still submit that you haven't found the probable cause."

"And if you have a better answer, Mr. Hines, we're all ears. We may never pin down the *actual* cause to everyone's satisfac-tion, but we can certainly narrow it down to *probable* after all sources of information are exhausted."

Enough of this bullshit, thought Anne, and raised her hand.

Chairman Lieberman nodded. "Yes, Captain Ryan? Is there something you'd like to share with us?"

Share. God, how she despised that favorite psycho-babble term of the liberal left. It reminded her of kindergarten, of the period set aside for *sharing and caring.* She leaned forward in her wheelchair as Hines adjusted her microphone. She had pre-cious little to *share*, but something had to be said in her defense. "I'd just like to say that in spite of everything you've heard, I'm the only one here who was in the cockpit that night." She waved a hand toward Hardison, "These guys can posture and postulate all they want with their cockpit recorders and flight data record-

142

ers, and their innuendo about what they think happened, but I was there!" Then with an expansive gesture of her arm she indicated the board as well as the investigators and the audience. "No one in this room, or anywhere for that matter, was there but me, so how can they say—"

"We're painfully aware of that, Miss Ryan, I'm sorry to say," the U.S. Attorney interjected.

The chairman tapped his gavel, "Mr. Lorenzo, if you please..."

Anne tensed, chiding herself for the incautious remark, yet as she suspected they were locked and loaded, ready to pounce. She took a deep breath to calm herself and continued. "In twenty-three years of flying airplanes I've never experienced anything like what happened that night."

"Do you *know* what happened, Captain Ryan?" asked Chairman Lieberman.

Anne gripped the armrest with her left hand and pressed on her right knee with the other to still the involuntary muscle spasms in her atrophied leg. "I know that the aircraft stalled. I also know, and the transcript of Overmeyer's takeoff observations on the voice recorder proves, that our speeds during takeoff and climbout were well above stall. The aircraft *shouldn't* have stalled—I guess that's been said enough already, but even Mr. Hardison admits it shouldn't have stalled. I—I've thought about it a lot since I've been conscious, and there's just no way I could have made that kind of mistake. There was something wrong with that airplane; that's the only explanation I can give. The only time I've ever experienced anything at all like what happened that night was during training in the DC-9 simulator. It was a situation where they simulated ice on the wings."

Mitchell Hardison rose from the opposite table, walked slowly around it, then settled a meaty hindquarter on the corner as he glanced first to Anne, then to Hines, and then to the board members seated at the dais. "Mr. chairman, the notion of ice on the wings of Flight 193 during takeoff has been totally discounted through our investigation and the testimony which you've already heard, which leads us back to focusing on the pilot again. With that in mind, I'd like to quote from the transcript of the cockpit voice recording and ask Captain Ryan some questions."

He flipped through his notes, glanced once at Anne, and then looked at the chairman. "What I'm going to read to you is part of a cockpit conversation between Captain Ryan and first officer Overmeyer before Flight 193 pushed back from the terminal." He cleared his throat. "I quote:"

" *'Give me the log.'* said Captain Ryan."

" *'What?'* first officer Overmeyer replied."

" *'The log, goddammit!'* said Captain Ryan."

Hardison peered over his glasses at Anne, then tossed his notes on the table. "Captain Ryan, was there any particular reason why you were so testy with first officer Overmeyer?"

Anne hesitated for moments, remembering. Maintenance. Yes, it had been about maintenance. "I...I guess it was because I was angry about some of the things that went on at Coastal Airlines. About maintenance. I didn't think they did a good enough job in keeping up their aircraft. I remember sitting in my seat when I said that to Don, and I had been sort of glancing around the cockpit while we were waiting for pushback from the gate. The seat fabric was badly frayed, paint was peeling everywhere, the cockpit stunk like a stable, and...oh, yes, I remember, the right main gear indicator bulbs were burned out. I guess if you put it all together it sort of burned me too, even though it was minor, and I asked for the log to see what else they hadn't done. I should have canceled—" She suddenly felt Hines's hand upon her forearm, warning her.

Chairman Lieberman leaned forward and pulled his microphone close. "Captain Ryan, is it your usual cockpit demeanor to ask of a first officer, `give it to me, dammit'?"

"No sir, it is not."

"Then would you say that it was because you were stressed that evening before the flight?"

Stressed? She could see where this was all going, drugs aside. First her conversation with Truax and now this. Yes, considering these tidbits and what had happened with Warner earlier, which they didn't and wouldn't know about, she supposed that she was stressed. But it hadn't affected her performance. And even if she had codeine in her blood as they said, other than relieving her back pain, she still had been clear-headed, cautious.

"No. I wouldn't say I was stressed. Irritated, maybe, but not stressed."

The chairman nodded patiently, examined his notes, and then gazed at her as he spoke again. "Captain Ryan, the lab report shows beyond doubt that there were debilitating controlled substances in your bloodstream at the time you commanded Flight 193. Now, regardless of your motivation for taking them, did you at any time feel affected? Affected in a manner that as a professional pilot you should have removed yourself from the crew list for that flight?"

Anne controlled her breathing, calming her anger. "I'm glad that I at last have a chance to speak to this. First, I did not, nor have I ever taken drugs except when prescribed by a doctor for the flu or an infection or something, and when that was the case I didn't fly if the stuff was in violation of the regulations. But I can tell you that if there were drugs in my bloodstream that night, then someone put them there. Someone substituted the aspirin I keep in my locker for—what was it—codeine? And I don't know who or why, although I've some good ideas," she said, looking directly at Truax. "But to answer your question, no, I felt nothing. My head was clear and I was very cautious."

For moments the entire auditorium was silent, yet still she felt scores of accusing eyes boring into the back of her head. She looked again at Truax seated with other witnesses at the adjacent table, saw him snicker. Saw his hands in his lap, his left hand forming a circle with thumb and forefinger, his right middle finger sliding through it. God, how she longed to shatter it with a two-pound history book, just as she had done to the boy taunting Gordy in high school.

Mitchell Hardison thumbed quickly through the cockpit voice recorder transcript, found what he wanted and rose from his chair. "Captain Ryan, while first officer Overmeyer was reading from the before-start checklist he said to you, `*cockpit voice recorder?*' You were to check that it was activated and respond. Please enlighten us on what you meant when you responded in a hoarse whisper, presumably to first officer Overmeyer, and I quote, `*Halo estatue?*' " He shook his jowls in apparent wonderment, "I presume that was you speaking this nonsense in an exaggerated gravelly voice, Captain Ryan?"

Anne felt her face flush, and yes, it was indeed she. Why hadn't she been more circumspect with her language? Was it the codeine? Had she been affected after all? She sighed heavily. "Yes, it was me. It was just a joke to lighten the mood in the cockpit."

"Or drug-induced silliness," Hardison added with a grunt.

"Captain Ryan," said board member Parghetti, "had you forgotten about the regulation imposing a `sterile cockpit'? The regulation that prohibits exchanges of casual cockpit conversation on matters other than the business at hand until you have reached an altitude of ten thousand feet?"

Anne waved her hand noncommittally. "No sir, I haven't forgotten."

Parghetti smiled, "Well then, for the sake of some levity in this otherwise sober proceeding, would you mind letting us in on the joke and the occasion in the cockpit that prompted it?"

There was a brief twittering in the audience but Anne wasn't laughing. "Like Mr. Hardison said, it's part of the checklist, checking to see that the cockpit voice recorder is operating. So I said something for its benefit, and, apparently, for your humor today. `*Halo estatue*' is back-street Italian for `*hello, is that you?*' Sorry, Mr. Parghetti, I didn't know you'd be listening."

This time the audience roared and Anne glanced at Mitchell Hardison, saw him stifling a laugh betrayed by the quaking of his great belly. The gavel came down with a splat.

"Mr. Hardison," said the chairman, "Are you sufficiently composed now to continue? We are nearing time to adjourn."

"I have one more quote from the voice recorder transcript. This one was recorded while Flight 193 was being de-iced. I quote first officer Overmeyer:"

"`*...Are you okay, captain?*' "

Hardison turned to Anne and raised his bushy eyebrows, waiting.

There it was again, Anne thought. Overmeyer's incautious remark had come back to haunt her and there was little she could do but tell them as she had told an unconvinced Mitchell Hardison before. "I...I was sitting with my eyes closed for a moment, thinking, while we waited for them to de-ice us. I guess he—Don Overmeyer—thought I wasn't feeling well or something." Anne looked up quickly, scanning the impassive faces of the board members peering down at her, realizing she should have phrased it differently. The audience behind was hushed as she glanced to Hardison and saw him staring at her. Just staring without a hint of emotion...

"Mr. Hardison?" asked chairman Lieberman.

"One more question." Hardison slipped his hornrims over his nose and peered at his notes. Then he nodded and inclined his head toward Anne. "Captain Ryan, did you scrape the tail of the aircraft when you rotated Flight 193 for takeoff?"

Anne sat massaging the spasming muscles in her thighs and now the pain from the injuries to her pelvis was becoming un-bearable, but more than the pain she winced at the question. There was only one answer.

"Yes."

"And has that ever happened to you before?"

She stared at the table, unseeing, her face suddenly flushing, blood roaring in her ears, as the room seemed to become a broiling oven. Hardison had done his homework well. He had scraped up every scrap he could to incriminate her, from segments of the voice recorder tape which were explainable yet odd-sounding in the context in which they were used, to elements of her past with the stinging question now hanging in the air. And whoever had done the drugs on her, probably Truax, had sealed her fate inescapably. She was trapped.

"Captain Ryan?" prompted the chairman.

Again she looked at the expectant faces of the board members and she knew it was all over. "Yes," Anne said at last, sensing Gordy's dismay.

Hardison adjusted his glasses and read from his notes. "On 13 June, 1996, Coastal Airlines Flight 1412, also a DC-9, departed Cleveland-Hopkins International Airport with 68 passengers aboard. During the takeoff roll the captain pulled back on the yoke and rotated the aircraft too quickly, causing a tail strike and resulting in separation of the tail cone from the empennage. The aircraft returned for an emergency landing without incident."

He removed his glasses and looked up at the board members. "Captain Anne Ryan was in command of that aircraft."

Hardison turned away and reached for his summary file. It was time to sum it up before they adjourned. Time to compress the scenario of probable cause and do what had to be done. For a moment he scanned the file and organized his thoughts, then he cleared his throat.

"Mr. chairman and members, throughout this hearing today you have heard considerable evidence and testimony on the results of our investigation into the crash of Coastal Airlines flight 193. We have shown that the aircraft and its engines functioned properly, that there had been no bomb, no tampering of the flight controls or instruments, no errors in the procedures prescribed in the aircraft operating manual as it pertains to takeoffs, no cockpit intruder, and that the aircraft had been properly and thoroughly de-iced prior to takeoff. In short, the fatal stall that occurred that day shouldn't have happened unless there had been a failure on the part of the pilot.

"Further, toxicology reports show that the captain, Anne Ryan, was under the influence of controlled substances while in command of the aircraft. Also, segments of the cockpit voice recorder tape as well as testimony of others give strong indications that she was experiencing stress. I refer to her verbal abuse of a peer shortly before she boarded the aircraft, to her behavior toward the first officer while in the cockpit, and to the first officer's apparent concern for her condition when he asked if she was okay. Then there was the tail-strike on take off, which, under the circumstances, would seem to have been sloppy technique at best.

"Absent any other facts relating to the cause of the crash, and we have searched carefully and extensively and found none, the investigating staff concludes that the probable cause is due to the captain having failed to anticipate an incipient stall of the aircraft and failing to act swiftly and decisively in its prevention. We conclude also that such failure was induced in part by the captain's diminished capacity resulting from ingesting controlled substances prior to the flight. This, we believe, is evidenced in part by the captain's uninhibited humor in the cockpit, and by the tail strike on takeoff.

"We recommend that the Board consider and ratify staff's findings and conclusions, and refer the matter to the Federal Aviation Administration for the appropriate actions with recommendation of permanent revocation of Captain Ryan's airline transport certificate."

The audience buzzed with excited voices as the chairman spoke. "Thank you, Mr. Hardison. Captain Ryan, this hearing will resume at ten o'clock tomorrow morning at which time you may address this board with a closing statement or provide additional information or rebuttal which may assist us in formulating a conclusion as to the probable cause of this most unfortunate accident. This will conclude today's hearing."

As the gavel came down and reporters rushed for the exits, Anne sat in hopeless despair, beaten. She felt Gordy's large hands cup her shoulders and she reached and squeezed them desperately as tears suddenly streamed down her cheeks.

At the back of the auditorium Sylvia Edelbrock put away her knitting and twirled her finger at Lyle Pennington. He turned her wheelchair around and pushed her out through the doorway.

Philip Darcy stood in a phone booth in the lobby, a hand held to one ear and shutting out the noise of the departing crowd as he spoke. "It's over," he said, "Ryan's done. Clean deal."

"There was no discussion of animosity between airlines? Nothing implicating us?"

"Not a word," Darcy said. "We're home free."

EIGHT

Gordy threw down the morning edition of the *New York Times* and spun around. "Dammit, Anne, you just can't sit here and do nothing! You could have at least gone to the final hearing and made another statement. Anything. But to just walk away and—"

She slammed her hand on the wheelchair armrest, "I didn't just walk away! As any fool can see, I can't!" There came a vigorous thumping on the ceiling from the apartment above and she jabbed her middle finger at it. "Up yours, Roscoe!" Trembling with anger, she spun the wheelchair around and headed for the tiny kitchen. Her hands shook as she twisted the cap off the bottle of painkillers Levinson had prescribed, then reached and filled a glass.

"You shouldn't take too many of those, Anne. Levinson said you could become addicted and—"

"I don't give a flying fuck what Levinson said. I don't give a fuck what anybody says anymore! I don't give a fuck who—"

"Hey, easy," Gordy said as he came up behind and rested his hands on her frail shoulders.

She pushed his hands away and quickly downed the capsules, then tossed the glass into the sink where it shattered. "Fuck it."

"Fuck it," he repeated. "Fuck the world and everyone in it, including yourself. That's what you're doing, Anne, fucking yourself. It's been a week since the hearing, and all you do is sit around this dingy little apartment feeling sorry for yourself when you could be fighting back. Sure, you've been screwed over, but what I'm seeing isn't the Anne Ryan I know. The Anne Ryan I know wouldn't take any shit from anyone. The Anne Ryan I know would—"

Anne spun the wheelchair around and sped back to the living room. She grabbed the newspaper and flung it at him. "Did you read it?" she shrieked. "Did you read `Pilot Busted for Drugs in Death of 47 Passengers'? Did you read `NTSB Concludes Pilot Error'? Did you read `Federal Grand Jury Indicts Pilot for Felony Manslaughter'? Did you read `Charges to be Filed Against Pilot'? Well, *did* you? Did you? Talk to me, goddammit!" she yelled, ignoring the furious thumping on the floor above.

He nodded weakly and stood helpless as she railed at him.

"And just what the fuck am I supposed to do? Say a thousand times `I didn't do it'? Is that how I continue to defend myself? `The plane stalled, Captain Ryan, why?'," she whined in a mocking sing-song. "How the fuck do I know why it stalled? `There were drugs in your blood and in your locker, Captain Ryan'. Well, I didn't put 'em there, asshole. I don't take fucking drugs and I don't keep fucking drugs in my locker! Jesus, Gordy, I've said all that and it doesn't make any fucking difference to anyone."

"You're taking drugs now, Anne, and if you keep on this way you'll be exactly what they say you are. And shouting *fuck*

152

this and *fuck that* doesn't help. Besides, it doesn't sound like you."

"You son of a bitch, don't pontificate to me. That isn't helping me! If you want to help, go take a chainsaw to that fucking Truax. He did it. I *know* he did it. He's been trying to fuck me over since day one."

Gordy sat heavily on the sofa. "That's what I came to talk to you about," he said wearily.

"So talk. He said he didn't do it, right?"

Gordy nodded. "Right."

"And you believe him."

He tossed his hands. "I...I don't know what to believe. I leaned on him some and he..."

"He what? Spit it out, goddammit!"

"He laughed. He said that if he really wanted to get at you he'd have done it long ago, back when you guys were at each other's throats shortly after you came to Coastal."

"And that's good enough reason why he wouldn't set me up now?"

Gordy leaned forward. "Anne, it's been sixteen years, for God's sake. Sixteen years! Why would he wait sixteen years to get even? It doesn't make sense."

Anne sighed. No, it didn't make sense. Oh, he was capable of it, all right, but other than exchanging biting invective they'd been in a state of cease-fire for a long time. But then he'd come forward at the hearing and twisted things just enough to make matters even more difficult. And before the flight he'd said, *"Don't bend the ship tonight, Ryan. We haven't that many left."* And he'd told the NTSB that he knew that "the ship" she was to command that night was flight 193. She hadn't told him that. That was something he wouldn't have known unless he'd specifically asked. Then there was the matter of her lock on backward. He'd probably nearly been caught meddling in her locker and had hurried. It all fit.

"He did it, Gordy," she said at last. "He set me up."

Gordy nodded, resigned, then sank his face into his hands and rubbed the stubble on his cheeks. "Okay," he murmured. He looked up and saw the dark circles beneath her eyes, her eyelids beginning to sag. Already the drugs were taking effect. Again. She popped them like candy now, he knew, not so much for the pain in her body but for the wrenching pain deep within her soul. The ordeal had taken an excruciating toll upon her; the massive injuries, the guilt he knew she felt even though innocent, and the NTSB hearing that had been a public crucifixion. Then had come the hounding media, the obscene and threatening phone calls, and finally the revelation that the authorities were seeking criminal action.

He had to do something to once again ignite the spark of an Anne Ryan he'd once known before it was too late. For that he would go along with her on the supposition that it was Truax who had set her up. She needed at least a kernel of hope to cling to, some belief that answers lay somewhere and they could be found.

He couldn't blame her for anger, for the uninhibited profanity that was so unlike her. On the surface her outbursts seemed irrational, juvenile. Deep down, though, he knew that her anger was a shield for fear. Anne Ryan, crippled and frightened, would likely go to prison.

He glanced at his watch and saw that it was time to leave. "Anne, I've got to get back to San Francisco. I trip-traded with another captain to come out here and now I've got to pay it back. What do you want me to do?"

"I...wan' you...nail Trooo-ax."

Her slurring speech alarmed him and he regretted having to leave, fearing she would overdose. "C'mon, kiddo," he said, scooping her frail body from the wheelchair. He carried her into the bedroom and laid her gently upon the rumpled bed, then covered her. Kneeling at her side and stroking her forehead he said, "I can probably get back in a week. In the meantime I'll make some calls and see what I can do. Try to stay clear-headed,

Anne, we need two heads on this one." He nudged her chin fondly with his knuckles, "And yours is better than mine. Always has been."

She reached and stroked his cheek. "I trib-traded...once," she whispered groggily. "Wish't I din't."

"Ray Thompson's flight?"

Anne nodded and closed her eyes. "Jus' wishhh I din't, s'all. Shoulda been me. Then th' liddle gurl'd still be alive."

She heard the front door close quietly behind him as her head spun dizzily. But soon she'd be asleep and she could again escape. For a while. *Escape...escape...just escape...* Tears streamed from the corners of her eyes as the veil of drugged sleep overcame her.

Gordy presented his pass at TransCon's La Guardia ticket counter then went quickly to a payphone and called Levinson. He described Anne's condition and David Levinson agreed to look in on her later in the afternoon.

"Why can't you just readmit her, Doc? I'm afraid to leave her alone."

"Gordy, we can't force someone to come in to the hospital. She checked out against my advice and I've tried twice to get her to come back. She just won't. I'm sorry."

"Then do me a favor—cut off her pain medication."

"That I can do, but there are other doctors, you know. She won't have any problem getting it somewhere else."

Now as he stirred his coffee absently while sitting in an airport cafe, he began to feel her frustration.

"I'll make a few calls," he'd told her an hour ago.

He snorted. Oh yeah? Call who? Just what in the hell could he do? Trap Truax in the parking lot some dark night? Chain him to the bumper of his car and drive slowly around, nudging the gas a little now and then until the drawling bastard at last screamed and spilled his guts? The thought held considerable appeal. Stamping hard on the gas held even greater appeal.

Or maybe he could turn Titus loose on him for a few minutes, except that the giant of a man could not be inflamed. Titus was a gentle soul.

Titus...

Maybe Titus had seen something that night. Something that meant nothing at the moment but which now may be vitally important. He would talk to Titus when he got back to San Francisco.

He stared at the grimy countertop before him, searching his mind for fragments of something—anything—that would fit together and give him a lead. Something that would at least be enough to give Anne some hope. He thought of the NTSB hearing, mentally replaying the damning testimony while absently making swirls with his fingers in the oily fingerprints dotting the countertop, left there by countless patrons. The grime annoyed him. Spilled salt, congealed jam some two year-old had gleefully finger-painted, rotting cigarette butts in the ashtray, oily fingerprints... Fingerprints…

He signaled a surly waitress to wipe up the mess. Then it hit him: *"Thank you, Mr. Lorenzo. Tell me, did the FBI also dust the bottle for fingerprints? Yes...there were two sets of prints on the bottle, one of which has been identified..."*

"Yeah? Somethin' wrong? You want more coffee?"

He had to get to a phone, and fast. "The counter's dirty, someone oughta clean it," he said, rising quickly from the stool.

"So call a janitor, a'ready."

He leaned over the counter, reached for a damp rag and wiped his hands on it. Then he took her hands, stuffed the filthy rag in them and tossed a quarter on the counter. "You'll do," he said, hurrying to the door.

Outside he found a telephone booth, dialed Anne's number and waited impatiently while it rang. No answer. She was probably zonked. After ten rings he hung up and glanced at his

watch. Quarter to five. There was still time. He called directory assistance for the number and then dialed.

"Mr. Hardison's office."

"Let me speak to him."

"Who's calling, please?"

"Captain Gordon Rosenberg. It's an emergency." He
drummed his fingers while on hold, saw passengers queuing at
the gate for his flight. *Hurry up, dammit.*

"Hardison," came the gravelly voice.

Anne awakened slowly, her mind a drug-induced fog, and for a
moment she thought she was back in the hospital. There at her
bedside sat Dr. David Levinson, his pleasant face hovering near.

She sat up quickly. "Dr. Levinson! How did—"

"Easy now, just lie back. How do you feel?"

Anne fell back on the pillow and covered her eyes. "Like
shit. How did you get in here?"

"The building super let me in. I showed him my hospital
ID."

"Gordy called you, didn't he?"

"Um-hmm. He cares for you a great deal."

"I know, and I treated him like shit a few minutes ago."

Levinson shook his head. "More like five hours; you've
been out a while. How many of these did you take?" he said,
rattling the bottle of capsules.

"What I needed."

She watched him rise and walk into the bathroom. When
she heard the toilet flush she knew what he'd done. "No! No,
goddammit!" Anne struggled upright, pushed her legs over the
side of the bed and reached for the wheelchair. Her head suddenly spun dizzily as she braced her hands on the armrests and
swung her body over, missing the chair, and her legs crumpled
beneath her as she fell.

"Whoa," he said, rushing out of the bathroom, reaching her
too late. He kneeled beside her and scooped his arms beneath

her body, saw the tears of frustration in her eyes. More, he saw the widely dilated pupils, felt her fragile and undernourished body beneath the threadbare housecoat. "You haven't been eating much either, have you?" he said, settling her on the bed.

"I'm not hungry."

"It's a deadly spiral, Anne. Keep this up and you'll have wasted everything we've worked months for." He reached and pressed his fingers against her upper abdomen just beneath the rib cage, felt the telltale swelling. "Your liver's swollen, Anne. This stuff you're taking metabolizes in the liver. Overdoses have the same effect as alcohol—turns the liver into a brick and you die. And I suspect that's what you want."

She turned quickly from him and buried her face in the pillow. Yes, that's what she wanted, and now he'd taken it from her. Flushed away the only thing that gave her a moment's peace, her only escape.

She felt the warmth of his hand cupping her shoulder, and suddenly she could no longer control the torrent within. Her body shuddered as she felt it coming, the long-suppressed tidal surge of emotions she had so carefully contained now swelled over the mental dikes and spilled in a rush. Not since her father had been killed when she was a child had she so agonized, and now the tears came freely with great guttural sobs.

He held her to him as she wailed in her suffering, rocking her as though a child, helplessly trying to comfort that which he couldn't cure. She had been in death and he'd brought her back, had done his duty, and now he found it repugnant that in so doing he had sentenced her to a life of emotional torture. And given the chance she would probably destroy that which he had given her. Maybe some suicides were justified; he didn't know.

The bedside telephone rang as he held her shuddering body. He ignored it, but still it rang insistently, and he thought of quietly taking it off the cradle. Instead he reached and answered it.

"Yes?" He listened to the caller, then interrupted. "She can't come to the telephone. I'm sorry, this just isn't the time."

He listened impatiently as the caller argued, and then suddenly raised his eyebrows. "Just a minute, I'll put her on."

"It's your friend, Gordy," he said, "I think you should talk to him."

Snuffling and gasping with spent emotion yet still clinging to him, she took the receiver. "What is it, Gord?"

"I've got some news I thought you'd want to hear."

"Where are you? Your voice sounds funny—you can't be back in San Francisco yet."

"Ah...I'm at a payphone 31,000 feet somewhere over Utah, courtesy of my Visa card. Listen, this is costing a bundle so I'll make it quick: Remember that guy Lorenzo and his testimony? The U.S. Attorney? Remember he said there were *two* sets of prints on your aspirin bottle?"

Anne broke away from David Levinson and sat up quickly. "Yes, yes I remember."

"Well, I called Hardison and found out that the FBI never ID'd the other set. They didn't bother; they didn't have to. Yours were all Lorenzo needed to show that you'd used the stuff in the bottle."

Anne's heart raced. "So are they—"

"Yep. Hardison said he'd ask 'em to run a make on the other set. Take about a week, but he said he couldn't promise anything. The FBI's got 180 million prints on file, but not everybody's."

"Oh, God, Gordy, we're going to get him. I just know we are."

"Anne? Don't take any more of that painkiller crap, okay? Hang in there and we'll fight this damn thing, or I'm not Wiener Rosenberg. I'll see you in a week."

It was dark in San Francisco when Gordy's flight landed, and he eased forward in the crush of deplaning passengers, thanked the flight attendant at the cabin door and quickly took the stairs to the ramp beneath.

"Titus! Yo! Titus! Wait up!" he yelled, waving to the huge black man driving away on a baggage tractor.

Titus grinned broadly and braked. "Mr. Gordy! Hop on, my man." Gordy climbed on and pressed his uniform cap to his head as the tractor shot forward. "You been to see Miz Annie? How she takin' all this mumbledy-jumbo about drugs an' all that stuff?"

"Not good," Gordy hollered above the roar of the tractor as they sped into the baggage vestibule and braked to a stop. He climbed off as Titus began slinging bags onto a conveyor. "She didn't do it, Titus, but we're going to have one hell of a time proving it. Can you remember anything about that night? Did you see anything out of the ordinary? Maybe someone near her locker?"

Titus's thick arms surrounded four huge suitcases and he effortlessly spun and dropped them on the conveyor. "Can't rightly recall anything, nothing special, anyways. I saw Miz Annie walkin' roun' 'neath the plane, lookin' and pokin' like she always does, bein' careful, you know." He heaved another armload on the conveyor then stopped and mopped his brow. "I recollect that I said, *'you don't trust nobody, does you, Miz Annie'*, and she said sumpin' like *'not in this rinky-dink outfit'*."

"Did she find anything wrong with the aircraft? Anything that bothered her?"

Titus rubbed the sparse stubble atop his head as he thought about it. "No, can't say that she did. Wait...wait now, I 'member. I axed her if the bird looked okay and she said it did. Yep, that was it. She said it looked okay."

Gordy didn't want to ask the next question but he knew he had to. "Titus...did *she* look okay? Seem okay?"

Titus stared at him for seconds, his expression suddenly contorted. "Aww, Mr. Gordy, you not thinkin' that way too, are ya? Not about Miz Annie?"

He sighed, "No, you know me better than that, but they did prove that she had drugs in her, and you know and I know and

160

Anne knows that somebody put them in her locker and she took them by accident. What we're trying to find out is who, and I only asked the question wondering whether she seemed affected by them, that's all."

"She seem fine enough to me. Miz Annie didn't seem no different at all," he whined.

"Titus, did you see anybody near her locker that night?"

He stood resolute, slowly shaking his head. "Uh-uh. Nope. Can't go in there, Mr. Gordy. They don't let no one but flight crews and the janitors go in there. Thas' off limits to us folks."

Gordy nodded. He knew that, but now he would grab for anything; he was that desperate. Anne would likely be arraigned soon. "You've been around La Guardia for a long time, Titus, was *anything* different that night? Like the way they refueled the aircraft, or—"

Titus again shook his head. "Every night's different, you know, weather and all, people out sick, sometimes we short-handed, or a plane comes in late and we got delays. Hard to say anything's really different—shoo, man, it's always different. Ain't no two nights alike."

"Were there different crews servicing the aircraft? Anybody you didn't recognize."

"Naw, I know 'em all. Same folks. Some was out sick, but I knew their reliefs. 'Cept maybe the de-ice crew. When the tanker went rollin' by to do Miz Annie's plane I waved to Willie in the cherrypicker, but it weren't him. Lotta people out sick, I guess. God knows, it be awful weather."

Gordy rode the shuttle to the employee parking lot, chewing the inside of his cheek as they bounced and swayed along the cir-cuitous route. He hadn't hoped to gain much from Titus, yet there was a slim chance that he or someone may have seen somebody fumbling with her locker and pleading that they thought it was their own. If an eyewitness could be found, and the prints on her aspirin bottle identified as the person witnessed, Anne's pleading would take on credibility. She would stand a chance before a jury; at least a chance to cast a shadow of doubt that she'd willfully taken drugs. Still, that left the issue of pilot error to deal with. Even if exonerated on the drug issue, Anne would likely never fly again unless that too was overcome.

Her problems were monumental, he knew, and there were more to come. Already relatives of the deceased passengers were filing civil suits for wrongful death and claiming mind-boggling amounts for damages.

Take it a step at a time, he decided, and he would have to convince her of such. Convince her to shut out the frightening and apparently insurmountable big picture and focus on chipping away at the foundations of her troubles as best they could. The prints on the bottle were the first step. But at the moment they were the only step, and if that didn't pan out there was little else to go on. Anne would lose what little momentum he had instilled with his airborne telephone call.

Deputy U.S. Marshal James Gratz stood by the side door of the courtroom, clipping his nails as the charges were read, occasionally glancing at the defendant seated in the wheelchair beside her attorney.

Times were changing, he thought.

For the past thirty-two years he'd issued subpoenas and escorted criminals of all sorts and descriptions to the federal bench. He'd handled mobsters, drug kingpins, arsonists, skyjackers, Soviet spies, Manuel Noriega, even some of the Watergate bunch. Now the mix of the accused was taking on a new flavor. Two years ago he'd hauled in a twelve-year-old kid, a computer hacker who'd electronically busted into the Pentagon's cryptic files just to see if he could. Then there'd been that airline captain and his crew who'd gotten juiced, and in a state of inebriation flew their passenger-laden 727 to Minneapolis, luckily without incident.

They let the computer kid go with a slap on the wrist, he remembered, snipping away a hangnail, didn't even take away his number-cruncher. But *His Royal Sogginess*, the drunken airline captain? Oh, they nailed him good, they did. And fast. They put him in the slammer and took away his airplane. Funny how things go, he thought as the proceedings droned on. Take Noriega, for example. Now there was a really bad one. But he'd gotten special treatment. He'd languished in the so-called "Dictator's Suite" at one of the federal country clubs for a long time before he was convicted.

Bucks--simple green. Or influence. Or politics. That's what it took to do that and stretch out the legal process.

James Gratz looked up again as the U.S. Attorney finished his arraignment summation. This one would go fast too, he knew, just like it had for the airline captain who'd had a few. Due process and a speedy trial, then the slammer. He wondered if jail cells were structured for wheelchairs. If not, they probably would be before long; the bleeding-heart liberals would see to that.

Yep, times were changing.

He snipped another nail as the judge made his closing remarks.

"This court orders that trial be set in three weeks on the charge of felony manslaughter. The defendant is released on her own recognizance until that time. Court adjourned."

The gavel came down and James Gratz opened the side door as the judge brushed past, then closed it and watched as the young woman's attorney wheeled her from the courtroom. The hounds of the press were waiting, he saw, barking and braying as though they'd treed a friggin' coon. He saw the young woman sink her face into her hands as her attorney wheeled her past the noisy throng.

Too bad, he thought, folding his nailclipper and slipping it into his pocket. She'd seemed a decent sort, but then so had the other airline captain—the bottle-to-throttle guy. Jeez, what was it with pilots, anyway? It'd be a cold day in hell before he, James Gratz, Deputy U.S. Marshal, would ever again accept an assignment as a sky marshal. You just never knew anymore what went on in the cockpit. And now they put women up there. Split-tails. Beaver-pelts. Pussy Pilots. Sheez-Louise, a guy could get himself killed in airplanes.

"Time for your exercises, Miss Ryan."

Anne looked up from the stack of NTSB hearing transcripts she was reading and shook her head at the healthcare aide Levinson had arranged for her. "Later, Dorine, I'm busy. Go watch a soap or something."

"Ten minutes and counting."

"Okay, ten minutes." She hated the exercises. They were painful and tiring, so painful that she could no longer sit in the wheelchair afterward, and Levinson had taken away all pain medications except aspirin. He was a sadist. He was forcing her to endure more pain and strengthen her atrophied muscles so she could care for herself and eventually walk again. Yeah, right. It made a lot of sense to be able to walk unassisted into a federal penitentiary where the steel doors would clang shut and she would sit and rot.

Levinson had shrugged. "So don't do it. Go ahead and remain an invalid so everyone else can feel sorry for you too."

The arraignment a day later had been humiliating as well as frightening but she hadn't expected less. It was the precursor to the end and the culmination of all that had gone before. But what she hadn't expected—or had forgotten—was the effect it would later have upon her. For two days afterward she had sat isolated in her apartment, ignoring the telephone, again swirling in a backwash of corrosive self-pity and hopelessness while the clock subtracted the minutes and hours and days until the trial and sentencing. Her mind unwound to her younger years, years that had also been filled with pain and suffering as well as anger and frustration. Years when time and again those she loved and the goals she sought were wrenched from her grasp. Gone were her mother, wherever she'd disappeared to; her father killed; and later her godparents lost to cancer and heart disease. Gone when she needed each of them most. Then in early adulthood she fought and failed and fought again to convince the male fiefdom that women too could pilot aircraft for the nation's airlines. Only through clenching her teeth and constantly butting her head against an unyielding wall did she at last wedge her way in.

She now realized the *why* of her successes and overturned failures. Each had taken a crisis spawned of gross inequity, first sounding the bugle for retreat to despair and hopelessness, later igniting rage as realization dawned, until at last emerged strength of will, calculation, and dogged determination. Such was her cycle. She won by fighting back no matter what the odds.

She won by getting her nose bloodied and losing and fighting back again.

She won because deep within, Anne Ryan loved a good down-and-dirty streetfight. But more than anything else, she won because she wanted to please her father, even in death.

Now with the toughest challenge ever before her, her freedom, her dignity and self respect, her very life at stake, she realized that already had come the predictable cycles of despair and rage. On deck and waiting was the calculating and dogged determination to win; she need only grasp for it once again. The judicial clock was ticking and time was growing short.

It was time to seek a weapon and fight back.

"Ten minutes is up, Miss Ryan."

"Ten more, Dorine. Promise."

For three days she had scoured the transcripts of NTSB testimony and reams of technical data that had been Hardison's case, searching for inconsistencies or a fleck of vital information that had been overlooked or maybe misinterpreted. Ironically, she admired how thorough he'd been, wishing only that the case hadn't been hers. But Hines, her pilot's association representative, had been right: the NTSB's conclusion of pilot error was of a default nature; if it wasn't mechanical, meteorological, or procedural it naturally had to focus upon the pilot. Yet they hadn't actually proven pilot error, only that something had gone wrong that could only have been an act of omission or commission by her. Just exactly *what* remained to be seen, but would probably never be known. She didn't know, they didn't know. But it had been the drugs that sealed the case and forced the inevitable conclusion.

So, she thought as she chewed on a pencil, remove the presumption of willfully taking drugs and that left only pilot error.

Only pilot error? *Only* pilot error had left 47 dead and her career and reputation damned-all.

Well, then maybe she should try turning it around: Suppose there had been no pilot error, only the drugs—which for the moment let's suppose she couldn't disprove. But suppose she *could* prove that the *actual* cause of the crash was none of her doing—wouldn't the presence of drugs be academic? Bzzzt. Bzzzt. Sorry. Remember the airline captain caught drinking on the job, smart girl? Booze but no accident, and still he was sentenced to breaking rocks. Next question.

What next question? What others were there? Answers only came with questions. No, that's not right. On *Jeopardy* they gave you the answer and you had to come up with the correct question. Answers like: *General Grant.* The question: *Who was buried in Grant's tomb?* Uh-huh. Or like, *Truax: Who set up Anne Ryan?*

Okay, enough of this silliness, Anne-girl, look at the questions you already know: Just who was it that set you up with the drugs, and what in God's name was wrong with that aircraft?

So, Anne, what other questions do you need?

She shook her head at the silly mind-game, yet there really were only Two Questions and somewhere out there were Two Answers... They simply hadn't been found.

"Ten minutes plus ten minutes is up, Miss Ryan, ready or not here I come."

"Dorine, Jeez, just when I had an idea—"

"And I've got a better one."

Half an hour later, body aching, muscles cramping and spasming, Anne lay on her bed, spent, trying to refocus her thoughts on Two Questions and Two Answers when the telephone rang.

"Miss Ryan, this is Mitchell Hardison."

She could almost smell his reeking cigars through the telephone, but her heart raced with anticipation. It had been eight days since the request for ID of the second set of prints on her aspirin bottle was relayed to the FBI lab. Now might come the answer she'd been waiting to hear, the answer to one of the Two Questions. *Truax. Please let it be Truax.*

"Yes, Mr. Hardison. Ah, have you...did you find out anything about the prints?"

"That depends on how you want to look at it, Miss Ryan."

There's a choice? "Okay, I'll bite. Whose are they?" She heard his heavy sigh through the telephone and knew he was stalling. "Tell me, Mr. Hardison, I have to know."

"They are...Christ, I don't know what to make of this. Miss Ryan, they are the prints of a dead man."

"They're *what*?"

"They're the fingerprints of a man, a navy fighter pilot, listed as killed in action over Laos in 1969. His name is—was—Lieutenant Robert A. Nash. No next of kin."

Anne sat stunned for a moment, dismay flooding her senses. "Are they sure there were no other prints on the bottle?"

"None that could ever be identified. There were some fragments, but they're likely yours, they think. Or maybe this guy Nash's."

"But how--?" Anne's mind reeled absorbing it all. Any other prints, even if they weren't Truax's would have helped, would have at least given her a lead. But the prints of a dead

167

man? How in the--? "What...what do you think about this, Mr. Hardison? What—?"

"It doesn't matter what I think as far as you're concerned, Miss Ryan, this is a criminal matter out of the NTSB's hands. It's what the Justice Department thinks that matters."

"But what do *you* think?"

She heard a lighter flick as he hesitated, heard him exhale. "What do I think? For what it's worth, I think somebody screwed you over on the drugs. Obviously, whoever Robert Nash was has been resurrected, somehow. That he's still around raises a lot of questions about his identity. It also raises the questions of *how* he's still around when he's been listed as a killed-in-action, and why he was fiddling around in your locker. But one thing's for certain—"

"What? Tell me!"

"He sure as hell isn't Jesus Christ."

"A *dead man*?" Gordy echoed.

Anne nodded, "He's supposed to be taking a dirt-nap some-where in Southeast Asia, according to Hardison. There's a cross with his name on it in Arlington, but the FBI says it's an empty grave. There's a lot of 'em like that, he said."

Gordy sat heavily on her sofa, bewildered. "What's your attorney doing about it?"

Anne tossed her hands. "I thought this dead-man's-prints business would raise a lot of questions, and it has, but my attor-ney says the Navy's stonewalling it. Classified, they say, something to do with the MIA thing and negotiations with Viet Nam. But he's filing a motion for a continuance to set back the trial date while we, he, anybody, gathers more evidence."

"Well, that's a ray of hope. Maybe—"

"Not really. The feds and the prosecutor say the presence of other prints doesn't change the face of the case. *My* prints were on the bottle, and there were drugs in *my* blood at the time of the crash. They call it primma donna evidence."

"Prima facie."

"Whatever. It could be enough to convict."

Gordy looked at her oddly. "You said that as though it were happening to someone else. Sort of...detached."

Anne shrugged. She wasn't detached, but if she forced herself to look at it clinically it allowed her to focus, get out of her self, avoid backsliding once again into a pit of despair.

"Anne?"

"What?"

He reached and took her hands. "I'm glad you've got your head screwed on straight again, and—"

"Miss Ryan, time for your exercises."

Anne spun her chair around, "Dorine, buzz off, will you?"

"Who's that?" Gordy asked, watching the plump woman stalk out of Anne's living room.

"That, is the result of your phone call to Dr. Levinson, thank you very much. Look, Gord, I asked you to come because I need somebody to help me brainstorm some ideas. It's less than three weeks to the trial and somewhere in that pile of crap stacked on the table are some answers. And if not there, somewhere."

Gordy nodded and nibbled his thumbnail, thinking. "Okay, let's take on the aspirin bottle, then. How long's it been in your locker?"

"I've already thought about that. I bought it on my way to the airport about three weeks before the crash. It went right from the store to my locker. Nobody touched it, so it had to have been tampered with while it was in my locker."

"And nobody's allowed in the crew locker area except pilots and janitors. Titus says they were pretty tight about that," Gordy added.

Anne nodded. "He's got that right. I remember the day the chief pilot ran Ray Thompson's ten year-old daughter out of there and—"

Gordy quickly raised his hands. "Whoa, Anne, don't go there."

169

He was right, she knew. Already her throat was constricting as she thought of Ray. She sighed heavily and made an offhand gesture, "Okay, so it's got to have been a Coastal pilot. That fits. This Nash guy was a navy pilot and a lot of Coastal people came from the military services, including Jimmy Truax."

"He was air force. So what are you saying? Nash wasn't killed after all, crawled out of Laos, took on a new identity and later came to fly for Coastal?"

"That's the idea."

Gordy shook his head. "It doesn't wash. I mean the idea's okay, but if it wasn't Truax then why would anybody else want to set you up? All the others liked you, Anne."

"Maybe. Gord, grab that pencil and pad over there. Write this down. Point one: Call attorney—request cross-check of all Coastal pilot's fingerprints against those of the dead dude."

"Tall order," he said, scribbling quickly.

"Tall problem."

For an hour they shot questions and rebuttal at one another, and the point-list grew to two pages. He quizzed her repeatedly on everything that happened before and during the flight, and they speculated about every enemy she could have had since childhood. Nobody was sacrosanct, he'd said, including Titus, to which she'd bristled and kicked him in the shins.

Exhausted, he leaned back against the sofa cushions and massaged his eyes. Still nothing of substance was coming of this.

"Gordy?"

"What?" he said with a heavy sigh, his forearm draped over his eyes.

"Matthew and Corinthians. Remember?"

He nodded. "I remember you asked; they didn't work for Coastal."

Anne reached and slapped him with a magazine. "It's biblical, you idiot. What's it mean?"

"How would I know? I haven't been in synagogue since my Bar Mitzvah."

Anne wheeled herself quickly across the room, reached into the closet and grabbed her airline flight bag. "Here," she said, withdrawing a scrap of paper. "It says, `Matthew 15:19 / Corinthians 6:9`. It was in my mailbox when I checked in for the flight that night."

Gordy peered at the neatly typed print and shrugged. "So?"

"So go down the hall to Mrs. Pillsbury's apartment and ask her what it means. She reads the good book all the time."

He groaned but did her bidding. When he came back he stood by her window, looking out. Troubled.

"Well?" Anne asked.

At last he turned and stared at her, puzzled. "You say someone put that note in your box at work?"

Anne nodded.

"Well, it means...it's about...it's about screwing around. Fornication. Adultery."

Anne froze, her heart suddenly racing. "Titus?" she said weakly. "You think Titus put it there?"

"Could be. He's very religious. But that's beside the point. You've been holding out on me, haven't you?"

Anne looked away. "You don't have to know everything."

"Dammit, Anne, if I'm going to help you I've got to know as much as you do."

"All right. I had an affair. But it's over."

"Maybe for you. Who was it? A Coastal pilot?"

"No."

"Who, dammit! It could be important."

Maybe it was. Until now it hadn't seemed important, so much had been her focus on Truax. But with Truax presumably out of the picture, things were wide open. "Sit down, Gordy."

"No. I want to know who it was."

"I said, sit down!" She lowered her voice. "We've got a lot to talk about."

171

He sat and scowled at her. "Start talking."

"Warncr Edelbrock."

Gordy shot to his feet. "Oh, Jesus Christ! Oh, God damn, Anne. Tell me you're putting me on."

"I'm not putting you on. It happened and it's over."

"And so is Coastal. I wouldn't put anything past that son of a bitch. So who dumped who?"

"Whom. I dumped him."

Gordy paced the room, fuming. "Perfect. Ego-driven jilted lover, cannibal of the industry, he wanted Coastal so he set you up and by God he gets it." Suddenly he spun around. "Why in God's name didn't you think of this before?"

Anne slammed her hand on the armrest. "I *did* think of it before! He was the one I thought was responsible until Truax testified at the hearing, twisting his testimony to make things look worse for me, then I was certain it wasn't Edelbrock. Until Truax, it all fit. He tricked me on the ski slope and I hurt my back, he shot the dog, gave me some kind of pills for my back, tried to convince me to come to TransCon because Coastal seemed to be going under, and—"

"What pills?"

She told him the entire story, leaving out no detail, and as she described her affair with Warner Edelbrock it refocused her earlier conviction that it had to have been him. Truax had been a convenient focus because of his skewed testimony, their long-standing vicious battles, and of course, he had the opportunity as well as access to her locker.

"His old lady probably sent you the note."

"Sylvia? I don't think so. I don't think she thinks any more of him than I do. Besides, she's trying to help. She came and visited me in the hospital, told me how she understood the pain of confinement in a wheelchair and abandonment by someone she trusted. Then she came and sat with me at the hearing for moral support... No, if anything, she's an ally. Or at least someone who cares, understands."

"Or a Trojan Horse," he added. "Still, this resurrected navy pilot poses a weird question."

"And an answer." Suddenly a flood of thoughts crowded her mind, and her words gushed as it all came together. "He probably works for Warner, or at least did his dirtywork. Once we find out who he is we can probably link him easily enough. And the pills Warner gave me at his retreat? They were probably harmless—he said they were Advil, or something, and they probably were. But it was probably a ruse to throw off suspicion later if I survived. He knew I was hurting from the fall—he set that up too—and that I probably would need more aspirin or something before the flight. Then this Nash guy was probably already cued to make the codeine switch in my locker, and disguised as a pilot anyone could do it easily enough if they really wanted."

Breathless, her mind spinning, she thought of one more possibility. "I'll bet you ten to one the Feds were tipped to be waiting for me in Detroit when I landed so they could do a drug test and have me arrested for flying under the influence."

"Except that you didn't get to Detroit."

"Which made it that much easier for him—Warner, that is. Either way, the notoriety would have been enough to drive Coastal under."

And it had, Gordy thought, chewing his lip. "So you think he had nothing to do with the accident? Just the drugs?"

"Oh yes I do. At least now I do. Something was wrong with that aircraft, and whatever it was I'm sure he had a hand in it. The Feds waiting in Detroit, if they were, was a backup in case I didn't crash."

Gordy shook his head. "I don't get the connection. How you link Edelbrock to the crash."

Anne leaned forward eagerly. "I'll tell you. I remember some of the things he said to me that day driving to the airport— the day of my crash. He was asking dumb questions, saying inane things like the weather looked bad, that I'd probably be de-icing at La Guardia, was I worried about the weather, that sort of thing. Then he suggested that maybe I should trip-trade and let someone else fly the trip to Detroit, as if he really cared." Anne shook her head, "Bullshit, every word of it. He was covering his tracks in case I lived."

Gordy frowned. "But if you'd followed his suggestion and trip-traded, it would have screwed up his plan. If he had one. I'm sorry, Anne, but it doesn't make sense."

She reached for his hands and gripped them. "Oh yes it does. He *knew* I wouldn't do it. He knew that I was feeling guilty for trip-trading with Ray Thompson during bad weather. This time he knew he had me. He knew I wouldn't trip-trade again after that.

Gordy sat again, his face in his hands. Then he looked up, trailing his fingers down his cheeks. "We got a real problem proving all that."

Anne tilted her wheelchair back, balancing on the main wheels only, grinning. "Didn't know I could do this, did you?" she said, pirouetting the machine.

"Showoff."

"You ain't seen nothin' yet. I'm going to win this case."

Gordy drew out his wallet, thumbing the few bills within. "How many investigators do I have to hire?"

"None. Zip. *We're* going to do it. You and me. I've got an idea."

He tossed his wallet in the air. "Anne, I've got to fly. I have a job, you know."

"And I've got to fly too. You're coming with me to Denver."

NINE

The TransCon 727 landed with a jolting *thud* on the runway at Denver's International Airport, rebounded as though it had changed its mind, then settled in hard again. The three engines far to the rear suddenly thundered in reverse thrust as the brakes howled and ground, quickly decelerating the aircraft as though a solid wall lay directly in its path.

Seated in the passenger cabin, Anne tensed and gripped the armrests of her seat while Gordy braced his hand against the seat ahead, certain their captain was a former aircraft carrier pilot. "Jesus," she said, "there's 12,000 feet of runway out there. Is he myopic? What's he think it is, the USS Enterprise?"

Gordy chuckled, "And his name's probably Captain Tail-hook. Look at the expression on the stew's face."

Anne looked ahead in the first class cabin and saw the flight attendant sitting eyes-wide on her jumpseat outside the cockpit door. "She looks like she peed her pants."

Sheer terror, Gordy thought. Some never got used to it, yet "firm" landings were pretty much standard at Denver, regardless

175

of who was flying. He cocked his head and looked out the window at the bright mid-day sun high above the Front Range of the snow-capped Rockies. Nice, he thought as they taxied toward the terminal, even if it was still winter here. Someday he should learn to ski. Cross-country variety, of course, well-suited to his shuffling gait. Well, snowshoeing, maybe. He glanced at Anne's incapacitated legs, suddenly felt guilty, and decided not to mention it.

"Hardison's going to meet us at the gate?" he asked.

Anne shook her head as she also absorbed the magnificent view, longing for the slopes. "He'll meet us at the simulator," she said absently, kneading the atrophied muscles of her thighs and looking once again at the lofty peaks, wishing...

Gordy looked away, sensing what she was feeling, and thought instead of the afternoon that lay ahead. It had taken Anne much wheedling and cajoling to pull this one off, he knew. But she had done it. And why not? Hell, she always got what she wanted—sooner or later. But to convince Mitchell Hardison and the NTSB to release the cockpit and flight data recorder information from Coastal Flights 193 and 288 for purposes of making DC-9 simulator runs had taken more than just arm-twisting. She had to agree to allow the simulator results recreating the two flights to stand in evidence, whatever the outcome. It was a great risk and he'd tried to talk her out of it. If she flubbed it, the obscure probable cause handed down earlier could well become clarified, further damning any chance she had of later overcoming it. But when Anne had her mind set on something...

He squeezed her hand as the 727 nosed into the jetway gate. "You sure you want to go through with this?"

"Surer than I've ever been about anything. I know what was wrong with that airplane now, and I owe it to Ray Thompson's widow as well as to myself to prove it. Today I will."

"And you're going to keep me in the dark about it?"

"You'll see soon enough. If I tell you, it'll jinx it."

The heavy steel door to the huge chamber housing the simulators clanged shut behind them and Anne braked her wheelchair to a stop. For a moment she stared at the curious electronic creatures she knew well, as though again measuring their capabilities for the contest to come. The simulator room was a sterile and cavernous echo chamber, larger than a basketball court beneath a ceiling three stories high. Three gigantic aircraft simulators stood before her perched high upon gangly spider-like legs anchored to the concrete floor; they looked nothing at all like aircraft, yet inside each of the box-like cubicles atop the hydraulically actuated support legs was the cockpit of an aircraft equally as real as that which it was programmed to simulate. They cost upwards of $12 million or more apiece, Anne knew, but for that price the computer-driven chambers of horrors could reproduce with frightening realism any aspect of flight, including emergencies of every hand-wringing description to test the spectrum of a pilot's skill as well as the effectiveness of his deodorant.

Today she would give the one on the left a run for its worth as well as her own. She hoped she was right—that some answers would come with what she was about to do. She had gambled much on it.

"Let's do it," she said at last, her voice echoing. Gordy and Mitchell Hardison followed as she wheeled herself toward the elevator that would take them to the mezzanine level and the gangwalks into the simulators.

The simulator operator stood waiting at the gangwalk and greeted them. "Good afternoon, Captain Ryan, it's good to see you again. Been close to a year, hasn't it?"

She knew that Walt Miklaszewski, better known as "Zooski," was well aware of her much-publicized circumstances, but she was grateful that he greeted her respectfully as though this were just another of the routine training checkrides all airline pilots were subjected to, and that he had called her *captain*.

Some gentlemen still remained in a society that seemed to have forgotten the basics.

"About that. Good to see you too, Zooski. Are we all set?"

"Whenever you're ready. The program's set to simulate Ray Thompson's flight 288 first."

Gordy helped her from the wheelchair and she slung an arm about his shoulder as she hobbled across the gangwalk and into the cockpit.

"Anne, I don't see how you're—"

"I can do it, dammit. I've got enough strength in my legs to work the rudder pedals and brakes, just get me into the left seat." She settled herself into the captain's seat while Gordy slid into the copilot's seat to her right. Hardison unfolded the jumpseat behind her where he would sit as observer. At right angles behind him sat Zooski at the computer console that controlled the programs to simulate the conditions for their flights to nowhere.

Anne kicked off her loafers and flexed her toes, then positioned her feet on the rudder pedals. She gripped the control wheel in her left hand, savoring its familiarity as she glanced about the cockpit of the DC-9 simulator. It was one of few remaining in the country, so aged had its real-life brethren become. Ahead of the windshield was nothing but blackness, but when she gave the word for the "trip" to begin, the runway lights of La Guardia would appear as well as the nighttime panorama of the airport as seen from the cockpit. She closed her eyes and reached blindly left, right, above, down, touching switches and levers from memory. Gratified that she had not fumbled once, she knew that she was still in full possession of her long-acquired skills. In a few minutes she would need them.

As she fastened her seatbelt and shoulder harness she knew without looking that Hardison sitting behind was watching her every move carefully. Maybe she would prime his pump some, give him something to chew on.

"The system's up, Captain Ryan," said Zooski. "Just give the word."

Anne turned in her seat and called back, "Zooski, I need a warm-up first. Switch to a program for a night takeoff out of Dulles, then throw me an emergency."

"Okay, what kind?"

"Whatever turns you on."

Minutes later he was ready and Anne reached for the before-start checklist and together she and Gordy went through it. Then came engine start and from a cockpit speaker came the low moan of turbines spooling up, a *thud* as they ignited, and Anne watched the instrument panel as the mock engines stabilized.

"What's our call sign, Zooski?" she called over the inter-com.

"Let's make it...how about Coastal 596?"

"Whatever." The simulator bounced and swayed realistically as she taxied the DC-9 "aircraft" out to runway one-nine-left. This one would be a takeoff in the clear, she saw. Stars were twinkling like diamonds on the video-taped horizon, there was no fog haloing the taxiway lights passing by the cockpit windows, and it was...Jesus, it was cold. Zooski was simulating an honest-to-god, dead-of-winter night at Dulles by blasting them with the air conditioning.

"Put a log on the fire, Gordy," she ordered, pointing to the heater controls.

"Thanks," Hardison muttered.

Left hand gripping the steering tiller, she swung the nose in a wide arc, the stalk-like Dulles control tower passing from view. Then she set the brakes and methodically went through the challenge and response of the before-takeoff checklist with Gordy. Satisfied, she was ready to go and nodded to him. "Call 'em, Gord."

"Dulles tower, Coastal 596 holding short of one-niner-left, ready to go," Gordy said.

"Coastal 596, taxi into position on one-niner-left and hold for traffic crossing the runway," came the mock tower control-ler's voice through her headphones.

179

Gordy repeated the clearance and Anne released the brakes and gripped the thrust levers, inching them forward. The simulated turbines whined in response and the aircraft began to move onto the runway. She lined the nose up with the runway centerline and held her toes on the brakes, right hand resting on the thrust levers as the turbines idled patiently. Her heart began to thud as the moment neared, and she mentally prepared herself for whatever emergency Zooski was about to concoct. It was grandstanding, she knew, asking for a practice run first and giving Zooski carte blanche to try to do her in, yet she felt that she needed to impress the seemingly unimpressible Hardison. She needed to prove that she was a capable pilot when the chips were down before embarking upon the simulator runs of ill-fated Coastal flights 288 and 193, the results of which would either reopen the NTSB cases or nail the lid on them so tightly they would never again be pried open. If that happened, her Petition for Reconsideration would amount to no more than a fart in the wind.

Her nerves tightened as they waited. It had been many months since she'd last flown, and only now, at the moment of launch, did she worry that her skills might fail her for lack of practice. She dug at the control wheel with her thumbnail, chipping away a fleck of paint. Then she shrugged imperceptibly. Too late now, girl.

Through the windshield she watched the realistic shadow of a DC-10 move across the runway ahead of them, taxiing toward the terminal area. A wave of nausea suddenly swept over her as she realized that the last time she had waited at a runway threshold like this she was but seconds from real disaster. She glanced at Gordy quickly, as if assuring herself that he was not Overmeyer.

"Coastal 596, cleared for takeoff, one-nine-left," came the controller's voice.

Gordy repeated the clearance and glanced at Anne, saw her take a deep breath and let it out slowly, and then she pushed the thrust levers forward. "Five ninety-six, rolling," she murmured as the DC-9 surged forward.

Mitchell Hardison shifted his bulk uneasily on the cramped jumpseat as the DC-9's engines thundered and the nose began to swallow the runway centerline. A former pilot, it had been years since he'd sat in one of these things, forgetting how incredibly realistic they were. As they gathered speed he looked over Ryan's shoulder at the instruments, watching the airspeed indicator in particular. He tensed his buttocks as they hurtled down the runway, the simulator vibrating and rattling realistically as the runway lights flashed past.

"One hundred knots," Gordy called.

"Checks," Anne answered, glancing at the airspeed indicator on her side. She felt the ship coming alive in her hands, the pressures of increasing speed making the control wheel become responsive. In seconds they would be airborne and she sensed that any moment Zooski would throw her a curve. Then she saw it. The DC-10 that had earlier crossed the runway had inexplicably turned around, its fat nose now barging into their path little more than a quarter-mile ahead.

"Abort! Abort!" Anne shouted. "Runway incursion!"

In a blur of practiced motion she jerked the thrust levers to idle, deployed the spoilers, then yanked the thrust reverser levers up and aft and stood on the brakes. The turbines thundered in protest and she and Gordy and Hardison were thrown against their harnesses as the "wheels" beneath chattered and bounced over the concrete, simulating the stripping away of the tire casings as the mammoth and shadowy bulk of the errant DC-10 grew in the simulator's windshield.

The muscles in Anne's atrophied legs ached and spasmed as she stood on the brakes, and she saw they weren't going to make it; they would torpedo a hole through the side of the DC-10. She felt Hardison's meaty hand gripping her seatback to steady himself. There was only one thing to do—head for the boonies. She released the left brake long enough to swerve the nose to the

181

right, then stood on both again as the aircraft lurched from the runway. A jarring thud shot up her spine as they plowed through a ditch, shearing away the landing gear, and suddenly they pancaked onto the frozen earth and skidded sideways as the shadow of the DC-10 flashed past not a hundred feet away.

"Shut 'em down!" she cried, closing the thrust reverser buckets and fighting the shuddering and uncontrollable beast. Gordy's hands flew across the switches, shutting down the engines and the fuel systems to avoid a fire.

Too late. A shrill clanging suddenly filled the cockpit. "Fire in number two!" Gordy shouted, and Anne quickly reached for the red fire handle controlling the CO_2 bottles, yanked and twisted it right, extinguishing the engine fire. With a final lurch the cockpit was suddenly still except for the humming of the instrument gyros as they spun down.

"Evacuate the aircraft," she said, then let her breath out in a rush and massaged her aching thighs. She had busted the ship, but it was all anyone could do. At least she had missed the DC-10. If the situation had been real and there had been passengers aboard they would all still be alive.

"Well done," said Zooski, clapping. "Soon as I change the tires, we'll be ready to go again."

Hardison chuckled and rose from his jumpseat. "Not before I change my underwear."

Anne turned in her seat and looked up at him, scowling. "Why bother, you're going to shit bricks when we do Coastal 288 and 193."

"That's not funny, Ryan."

"Who's laughing?" she shot back. "Sit down and I'll show you how it's done."

Minutes later Zooski pronounced the simulator program ready to replicate the conditions for the takeoff of Ray Thompson's fatal flight 288. Anne nodded and clipped her takeoff notes to the control yoke. Gordy and Hardison each had copies of the detailed notes describing the parameters for Ray Thompson's takeoff. From them, she would duplicate every move and maneuver that Ray had made from the moment of pushback from the La Guardia terminal to the instant of his fatal stall that had been remarkably similar to hers. She'd had weeks to study the data and now was the moment of truth—her turn to prove that what had happened in both cases had been unavoidable.

Minutes passed as they began the choreographed replay and "taxied" out to La Guardia's runway 31, she and Gordy reading and responding to the cockpit checklists, pausing to simulate de-icing in the disconsolate weather that plagued La Guardia that night months ago. Then Anne aligned the nose with the runway centerline and held her stockinged toes on the brakes, waiting.

"Coastal 288, cleared for takeoff, runway three-one," the tower instructed.

Anne glanced one last time at her notes to be certain she followed all aspects of Ray Thompson's takeoff exactly as they happened. Behind, Hardison was watching closely. And well he should, she thought, for before the afternoon was over Mitchell Hardison, NTSB, as well as Gordy was in for one hell of a surprise. If her theory was right.

"Two eighty-eight, rolling," she answered, and pushed the thrust levers forward. Again the simulator's mock engines thundered in the cleverly hidden cockpit speakers, and the DC-9 now known as Coastal 288 surged forward to its destiny.

"One hundred knots," Gordy called, tensed, watching the runway lights flash past, knowing that in a few moments Anne would lose it just as Ray had.

"Checks," Anne answered.

"Vee-one," he called, watching his airspeed indicator wind past 130. He glanced again at his copy of the notes, confirming that Ray's copilot had called for rotation at 135 knots. His eyes flicked to the airspeed indicator and there it was. "Rotate," he called, watching the nose rise smoothly from the runway as Anne eased the wheel back.

Hardison also sat tensed, glancing from Ryan to Rosenberg to Ryan as though watching a ping-pong game, assuring himself that they were following the script of Ray Thompson's fatal flight.

Then came the familiar *thump* as the wheels broke free of the runway, and Gordy saw that the airspeed indicators on both sides of the panel had wound past 140. "Vee-two," he said. Then: "plus ten...positive rate of climb." Any second now it would happen, he knew, gripping his armrest tightly, listening for the telltale surging of the engines that would begin at any moment, signaling the onset of the fatal stall. He tensed for the sharp and sickening roll to the left that would follow, and the beginning of the death throes of Coastal 288.

Anne held the control column back toward her lap as the simulator continued climbing and the runway dropped away beneath. *If my theory is wrong it will happen any second now,* she thought. *The shit should hit the fan right...about...NOW!*

Still the simulator climbed normally.

Nothing had happened. No sinking sensation, no engine surging...nothing. She waited five more seconds, watching the altimeter carefully as it measured more altitude, her buttocks tensed as sensors, alert to the minutest signal from the bowels of the ship that something was awry. At last she knew without doubt that her theory had been right. The takeoff had been perfectly normal. And she knew why.

"Gear up," she called, grinning and easing back on the wheel, increasing their angle of climb. *Three bars,* she thought. Silver dollars should come spewing out of the instrument panel.

Frowning, puzzled, Gordy tugged the gear handle to the *up* position, watching incredulously as the altimeter quickly wound past a thousand feet. But he should *not* be surprised, he reminded himself. Flown according to the book, as they had just done, Ray's flight *shouldn't* have crashed. Anne had proved nothing that would help her case. He shot a glance at her and saw that she was thoroughly enjoying herself. Then he looked

184

over his shoulder at Hardison, saw that he appeared unmoved, unimpressed. Not good, he thought.

Hardison leaned over her shoulder and barked in her ear, "Gear up and climbout's not in the script, Ryan."

His tobacco-breath was nauseating but she was euphoric, beyond caring. "And neither is an uneventful takeoff, Mr. Hardison. But we did it, didn't we? We flew it just as Ray did, to the letter, all the speeds and control movements were the same and you saw it. And not a damn thing happened."

Hardison scowled. "No, nothing happened, and frankly I don't find that surprising. I think you and I both know that something's missing here."

The simulator was still climbing and Gordy watched the altimeter wind uneventfully past 2,000 feet. And now he thought he knew why. It was incredible, yet there couldn't be any other reason. But still, if Anne was right, she'd have a difficult time proving it.

"Something's missing all right," Anne agreed, "but you aren't going to find it in the notes. Now relax while I 'land' this thing. Call the flight attendant for coffee if you like."

Minutes later and enjoying Hardison's waste-of-time and patronizing expression, she greased the simulator in for a perfect landing and shut the engines down. Ten minutes later Zooski had it set up for Anne's Coastal flight 193 and again they took off and climbed high into the fake skies above La Guardia without incident. Just as she knew they would.

Once again they "landed" and Hardison rose from his jump-seat and prepared to leave. "The only thing you've proved to me, Miss Ryan, is that both Coastal 288 and 193 could have been flown without incident, and that certainly doesn't help your case any."

Anne spun in her seat. "And that's exactly what I wanted to prove. So now you agree that flown exactly according to the book, neither aircraft could have stalled and crashed? Is that a fair assessment, Mr. Hardison?"

"It is," he admitted.

"And yet they did," she added, "and you'd like to know why."

Hardison sighed patronizingly. "I would. Suppose you enlighten me to something I don't already know and quit the games."

Anne nodded, holding his gaze, satisfied that she'd baited him enough. "All right, then sit down. And this time watch me even more closely. We're going for another ride." She nodded to Zooski sitting at the computer console.

Sweat soiled her armpits and her temples pounded as she prepared for another takeoff. This would be the acid test of her theory, and it had better be right. During the short break they had taken, she had quietly told Zooski what to do. Now as she sat staring down La Guardia's darkened runway again and waiting for the preprogrammed takeoff clearance, reality set in. Fifteen minutes ago she had "flown" flight 193 in precisely the same circumstances as the night of her fatal crash, but without incident; now it would be different. This time they would suddenly plummet from the sky and crash onto the runway in a resounding shattering of metal and bone, soon to be consumed in a fiery holocaust. She could never forget the sickening, terrifying moments of months ago, and the agonizing pain afterward. Now Gordy became Overmeyer and behind sat two flight attendants and fifty-four passengers, including a charming little girl, enroute to Detroit. Forty-six of them would soon perish, as would Overmeyer.

Even though a simulated run, she now agonized over commanding the instant replay of how it had been; how it had happened. She felt nausea again in her churning stomach, bile rising in her throat, her breathing becoming shallow, labored. Her fingers were clammy where they rested on the thrust levers, and for a moment she thought she couldn't endure the frightening reality the simulator would soon duplicate. It would be as though it happened all over again.

186

Are you okay, captain?

Overmeyer's words echoed in her mind and she remembered again why he'd asked. She had been stewing about Warner Edelbrock and all that was wrong with her life with him in it. Now she forced up more ugly memories of the cunning bastard, a mental vomit of sorts, re-igniting her rage and the fury of her determination to overcome what she was certain he had somehow arranged. Now she would show Hardison how it was done.

"Coastal 193, cleared for takeoff," came the voice in her headphones.

Time. Time to come charging out of the gates and let it happen. She sensed Mitchell Hardison near, breathing down her neck, watching, waiting... She needed no notes with which to replay this one; now she was four months younger, the calendar was rolled back and it was again December 11th, the wings were dripping with de-icing fluid, a tow truck had just cleared the stalled de-icing tanker from the runway... In the back sat fifty-four passengers, many impatient, some nervous, a few terrified. To her right sat Overmeyer; he seemed nervous as well...

Be careful tonight, Miz Annie, you hear...?

As though disembodied she watched her hand shove the thrust levers forward, and she sensed the surge of power as the mock engines thundered and the aircraft began to roll. "One ninety-three, rolling," she answered at last. The ordeal had begun.

Gordy shifted nervously in his seat, watching his airspeed indicator as they accelerated. "One hundred knots," he called seconds later.

"Checks," she answered, glancing at hers. Her jaw set, Anne flexed her stockinged toes on the rudder pedals, felt pressure there as the speed increased. Suddenly her eyes ached and she realized she'd been holding her breath. She breathed deeply and scanned the instruments quickly as the runway lights flashed past.

"Vee-one," Gordy said, watching the airspeed indicator.

Anne gripped the wheel tighter as the control surfaces on the wings and tail began to respond, the engines thundering at full thrust, the cockpit vibrating and shaking as they hurtled over the uneven pavement.

Get ready... Do it exactly as before...

"Rotate," Gordy called.

She eased back on the wheel and the nose quickly came up. Two seconds later the main gear wheels broke free of the runway and the vibrating stopped. They were climbing. Then she felt the momentary sinking sensation of four months ago and knew with certainty that her theory was about to become reality. "Feel that?" she called over her shoulder to Hardison. And just as happened four months ago she gave the control wheel an extra tug to overcome the sinking. A thump followed.

"Tailscrape," came Hardison's rasping comment.

"Vee-two," Gordy called seconds later. Then, "...plus ten...okay, positive rate of climb."

Then they all heard it—the thundering engines far to the rear began surging. They were but a hundred feet above the runway and Anne instantly lowered the nose as much as she dared, just as before, when suddenly the left wing dipped and the cockpit tilted precariously.

On cue, Gordy shouted Overmeyer's words: "Watch out! Watch out! Watch out!"

The control column shook and vibrated in her hands as though someone were throttling it, and she fought as she had before to control an aircraft that was beyond control. With sickening lurches the cockpit heaved left to right, then left again, and ahead the lights of New York City suddenly tilted perpendicular in the windshield. The left wing struck the runway with terrible force, separating from the aircraft, and Anne relived again the terrifying sensation of tumbling, cartwheeling... Suddenly the heaving cockpit stopped abruptly and became silent.

Lights came on.

"Good God in heaven," Hardison breathed.

Anne slowly unsnapped her shoulder harness and leaned her head forward, resting it against the control wheel. For a moment she thought she would vomit as the adrenaline reaction set in, her muscles trembling from the awful emotion within. But she had done it—accomplished what she set out to prove. Then she felt a heavy hand on her shoulder. Choking back a sob, she sat upright and turned.

"I'm sorry," Mitchell Hardison said quietly, "It took a lot of guts for you to do that."

Anne's voice broke in her throat. "It...it was the only way. You're a difficult man to persuade."

He nodded and held her gaze. "And that's how it should be."

Gordy unsnapped his harness and slid out of the copilot's seat. "C'mon, let's go home, Anne."

"Wait." She held his arms away as he reached for her, looking up at Hardison. "Now do you understand? You just now watched me use exactly the same control inputs as I used the night of the crash, you know that from your analysis of the flight data recorder. You know now that I didn't just fly it into the ground, that I didn't do something I shouldn't have done. You know now that the cause of the crash was not me, but what? Say it. *What,* Mr. Hardison?"

"Ice," he said, nodding. "Wing ice. You told Miklaszewski to set it up that way."

With tears now streaming down her cheeks, Anne clenched her fists and pounded the armrest. "Yes, ICE! And *yes,* I told him to set it up that way, because somebody set me up that way four months ago. Somebody watered down the glycol de-icing solution so that clear ice would freeze on the wings like glaze on a doughnut. Someone tried to kill me!"

"As well as trying and succeeding to kill Ray Thompson and a hell of a lot of his passengers, too," Gordy added.

Again she slammed her fist down. "NO! Don't you *see*? I trip-traded with Ray Thompson at the last minute. I was supposed to fly that trip!"

A flight attendant set coffee on their trays and Gordy watched the gentle sway of her hips as she pushed the serving cart up the aisle. TransCon stews weren't so bad after all, he observed. Better than Coastal's had been, with butts like Weber barbecue kettles. He settled back in his seat and sipped the steaming coffee, thinking of what lay ahead. Things had changed a great deal since Anne's encore in the simulator only hours ago, yet as someone once said, the more things change the more they remain the same. And much still remained the same. Still there was no evidence to prove that Warner Edelbrock had a hand in Anne and Ray Thompson's fate, nor was there a means to prove that Anne hadn't intentionally taken drugs. All that had happened was Hardison's assurance that the pilot error case would be reopened. Well that was something, anyway.

In two more hours they would land in New York. He turned to Anne: "How did you figure out that there had to have been ice on the wings? You'd been de-iced and you made a visual check before takeoff. What gave you the clue?"

Anne reclined her seat and laid back, her frail body weary from the ordeal in the simulator, yet her mind refused to relax. "Actually it was Hardison himself, weeks ago. During one of our interviews before the hearing I told him the plane acted like it was iced. He said that couldn't be, because I'd been de-iced just ten minutes before takeoff, and of course I agreed. Then he kind of rambled on and talked about the crew of an Air Florida 737 back in '82 who also thought they'd been de-iced with glycol when in fact somebody screwed up and sprayed the aircraft and engines with a weak solution, mostly plain water instead. It froze on the engines and wings and they crashed shortly after takeoff. That's what got me to thinking in the first place."

Gordy frowned. "So why didn't you keep believing it? That you were iced? Why didn't you say something more at the hearing?"

Anne sat forward quickly, clutching his wrist. "Because, I *watched* the de-icing. I *saw* the spray from the nozzle in the lights. It was *pink*, just like it's supposed to be. But when that NTSB guy testified—Westphal, I think it was—that he checked the de-icing tanker afterward and found that it contained the glycol solution, I dropped the idea. And then they dropped the bomb about the drugs and I had to focus on that."

"So what you did today in the simulator was a shot in the dark?"

Anne laid her head back against the seat and stared at the overhead compartments. "I guess you could call it that. But when you think about it, there just wasn't any other answer for why the aircraft stalled. All of the numbers were right, the speeds, rotation and liftoff, the winds and temperature taken into consideration, it had to have been ice on the wings. Nothing else would have changed the flight characteristics like that. You know that as well as I do."

"But the glycol...you said you saw it. And you said the wings looked clean, wet, just before takeoff. Westphal testified that—"

"It wasn't glycol, it was Kool Aid." She sat up quickly and leaned on his arm. "Look, once I finally figured out that someone was setting me up, I knew they also had to be pretty damn smart about it. They knew that knowledgeable people would be watching the de-icing, would be checking the wings before takeoff, and they had to also realize that the NTSB might look in the tanker afterward. Colored water, Gord, that's all it could have been. Whoever set all this up knew a lot about airplanes and de-icing procedures, and that *whoever* has got to be Warner Edelbrock, or someone working for him. Like his assistant, Philip Darcy, maybe. Rumor is he's a flake, and he's Edelbrock's right-hand man. They--or he, whoever, knew that a spray with-

191

out glycol would freeze quickly, that what would appear to be clean, wet wings, was in fact a glaze of clear ice, and—"

"Wait a minute," Gordy interrupted, "Hardison's no dummy, why didn't he think of this?"

A shiver passed through her and she reached and shut off the blast of frigid air from the eyeball outlet above. "Because, don't you see? The *drugs*. Oh, he thought about icing too, he said so, but Westphal's inspection of the tanker blew that one away as far as he was concerned. Besides, it had stopped snowing. So he turned his attention to the more obvious—the drugs, convinced that I did something wacko in the cockpit when the poop hit the fan."

Gordy squeezed his eyes shut and massaged his face. At last he looked up. "I dunno, Anne, we got somewhere today—you did, but still we're nowhere. It's pretty clear now that both yours and Ray's ships were iced, but finding evidence and proving that somebody set it up that way with colored water and put drugs in your locker, which you took, is just almost impossible. Hell, that was more than four months ago." He plucked a sausage-like finger, "For one, the phony glycol, if that's what it was, is long gone; and two, the prints on the aspirin bottle belong to a stiff who's supposed to be rotting in Laos; and three, even if you *could* identify the prints as someone living, even a Coastal pilot, they don't prove squat. How're you going to prove you didn't take the stuff intentionally? Suppose they find the guy and he's a Coastal pilot. All he's got to say is that he opened your locker by mistake, and in doing so he touched the aspirin bottle. Maybe he had a headache."

"Mistake, my butt. I had a combination lock, remember?" Anne slumped in her seat, irritated. "You're a bright glow on the horizon. I'm two weeks from trial and you sound like the prosecutor. Jesus, Gord, get positive for once." She turned away, staring out the window at ominous thunder clouds threatening Missouri far below. His devil's-advocacy wasn't getting them anywhere except to raise more questions, yet he was right, she knew. But somehow, some way, she would prove that Warner Edelbrock was behind it all; somewhere there would be a clue, a lead to follow. There had to be.

She closed her eyes, massaging her aching temples. Something had been niggling at the edge of her mind moments ago before Gordy had interrupted her... It was something about the deicing... She'd been talking about the appearance of clean, wet wings, in reality a glaze of clear ice, then the delay while they cleared the runway obstruction... Enough time for the fake glycol to freeze over and then... *Yes*!

Suddenly she jerked upright in her seat, bumping Gordy's elbow and spilling his coffee. "That's it! Runway obstruction!"

He wiped his dripping chin. "What runway obstruction? The DC-10 on the simulator screen?"

"No! The de-icing tanker!" She grabbed his hands and held them tightly. "Listen to me. The de-icing tanker stalled on the runway, delaying my takeoff. Long enough for the water on the wings to freeze into a clear glaze. It didn't really stall, though, I'll bet. Oh, that's what they told the tower, but they just sat there, waiting, blocking the runway. That's how they set it up! I'll bet the same thing happened the night of Ray's flight."

Quickly she reached beneath the seat ahead and yanked out her overnight bag, unzipped it, and withdrew a sheet of paper. "Here, look at this. Hardison gave it to me."

Gordy scanned it, saw that it was a list of icing-related airline accidents involving DC-9s as well as other types of aircraft. He handed it back. "So?"

"So who was the de-icing contractor? Doesn't it make you wonder?"

He nodded toward the list. "Are you suggesting that all of those were set-ups like yours?"

"No, but I'll bet a year's supply of tampons, if I ever get my period back, that one contractor does most of the de-icing at major airports on the east coast. I want to know who it is."

193

Gordy nodded, "That's easy. It's PAE—Preston Aero-service Enterprises."

"Who told you that?"

"Titus. He knows a guy who works for them at La Guardia."

Anne stared blankly at the seat ahead, nibbling a thumbnail as she thought. There were bits and pieces at best, little things that meant little, but then that's how you construct a puzzle; you lay out meaningless little odd-shaped pieces while trying to find the corners matching the picture on the box... In her mind's eye she had the picture; a picture of Edelbrock lusting for Coastal at any cost, setting her up as the scapegoat for pilot error and thus driving the ailing airline to its knees, ripe for takeover. But the question was, why her? Why not just any Coastal pilot? Oh, but wait, she thought. She had dumped him, slashed his monolithic ego, and he probably sensed it was coming. It probably *was* just going to be any Coastal pilot until she had figuratively kicked him in the balls... But there was still something wrong here... Something...

A flight attendant interrupted her thoughts, quickly slapping meal trays before them. It was typical airline fare, uninspired and unappetizing as well as unhealthy, and she picked her way through it, distracted, mentally struggling with some amorphous idea just out of reach.

She dropped her fork in the mess, then turned and inclined her head thoughtfully. "Gordy, play with me for a few minutes."

"Here? Now? I thought we agreed years ago we weren't going to do that?"

She shook her head. "Huh-uh, let's play *suppose*. You're damn good at being the devil's advocate, so I'm going to toss you some supposes and you're going to give me your reactions."

"Shoot."

"Suppose Edelbrock set this whole thing up for the one purpose of gaining control of Coastal."

194

"I'll buy that, it fits well enough. Coastal went down the tubes after your accident and Edelbrock grabbed for it and got it. No argument there. He could've helped it along some."

"And I think he did. A lot. Look at all the damaging ads he ran, the fare wars, the union problems, all the crap he gave the media about Coastal's former president being a queer and an alleged child molester. All of that drove passengers away and put us deep in the red."

"And then came the two crashes."

"And then came the two crashes, of which there probably would have been only one if I hadn't trip-traded with Ray. The crashes knocked the last block of support from beneath us, and now Coastal is history."

Gordy nodded. "I'm with you. And the question is?"

"The question is still *why me?* Why did he try twice to kill me?"

"If it *was* him. But I thought we already answered that. You kicked him in the gonads and it pissed him off. He gets two birds with one stone—you, and Coastal."

Anne shook her head. "Gordy, I didn't kick him in the balls until a month *after* Ray's crash. I broke up with him the afternoon of my crash."

"Okay, so it's coincidence. Your foot in his crotch had nothing to do with it. Maybe we can assume that he arranged the first crash to suit his purpose of gaining control of Coastal and he didn't give a damn who was flying it. You, Ray, whoever. So flight 288 crashes, Coastal slips further into the red, and he sees that it really works. Yippee-skippee. So he waits until the next storm when La Guardia's iced-in and does it again. Just so happened you were flying that trip too. He probably doesn't care who gets in the way."

"Then why the drugs?"

"Maybe because two crashes was too risky without a determinable cause for one of them."

Anne slumped in her seat, confused. "So what did he stand to gain?"

Gordy shrugged. "Power. Knock out the competition and his company makes more money."

"So?"

He laughed and shook his head. "That's *my* game. Now you're playing my role, Anne. What do you mean, *so*?"

"So what did he *personally* stand to gain? In money, I mean. The guy loves money. Other than a bump in pay and perks for carrying out a coup on Coastal, what did *he* get out of it? I mean it isn't as though he owns the company lock, stock and barrel. He may be the CEO, but he's still just an employee."

He saw her point and thought about it for a moment, then shrugged. "I don't know, maybe he bought a lot of TransCon stock before he started all this crap, then as he drove Coastal to the mats TransCon's earnings shot up and he sold his stock at a tidy profit. I know for a fact that TransCon stock went up quite a bit while all that shit was going on. Hell, a lot of TransCon pilots saw it happening and jumped on the bandwagon. Some of them made out pretty good, I heard. Then TransCon stock really shot up after the two crashes."

Anne thought a minute. "Isn't that what they call insider trading? Buying up stock in the company you run and using inside information to make a profit?"

"Is that illegal?"

Anne sighed, "I don't know, but I'm going to find out, and if it is, I'm going to nail him for it."

"That still doesn't solve your problem."

"It's a start," she said as a flight attendant quickly snatched away their meal trays. A stale roll tumbled from hers onto Gordy's lap, and for a moment she thought the young woman would make a grab for it. Anne reached for it instead and underhanded it onto the serving cart. "I'm going to the Securities and Exchange Commission as soon as we get back. If nothing else, it might open up some other ideas. With only two weeks until my trial, I've got nothing to lose. Also, I'm going to find out who owns Preston Aeroservice."

"Anne?"

"What?"

"You should have let her reach for it."

By late the next afternoon Anne had things in high gear. She had met with her attorney, Earl Christopher, and described the overall picture involving Warner Edelbrock as she saw it. Her attorney had been particularly interested in the insider-trading notion she had, and together they went to the Securities and Exchange Commission and met with a senior investigator who seemed noncommittal at first, but she had been prepared for that. Already she had been to the public library and photocopied dozens of Coastal-damaging TransCon ads and slurring articles that appeared in major east coast newspapers over the past year. From her attorney's computer she had extracted reams of financial data from the Internet showing the corresponding upward trends of TransCon stock, especially those which occurred in the wake of the crashes of Coastal flights 288 and 193.

All of this she spread on the table before the SEC investigator, watching his unremarkable eyes with anticipation, searching their apparent void for a hint of interest. At last the investigator rose from his chair and paced the room while offering a droning discourse on federal securities laws.

"It's not illegal," he said at last. "That he is president of the company in whose stock he might be trading is irrelevant. Anyone can do that. You, me, John Q. Public, whoever. But it could be at variance with the law if he were doing so through the exercise of bargain-priced company stock options, and if he had controlled or otherwise exercised a major role in disseminating the information contained in these ads and articles which may have affected the company's earnings as well as the market price of his company's stock in which he was trading. It's SEC Rule number...ah, I forget... Anyway, it's the Rule requiring that such trading by insiders be disclosed to us, whereupon we have the power to render stiff penalties and void the transactions."

"So maybe that happened," Anne offered. She saw by the investigator's eyes focusing elsewhere that he probably hadn't considered that, the myopic bastard. He, like most bureaucrats, probably sat on their collective asses and counting time until retirement unless something virtually dropped into their lap. Then they called it *shit happens*.

"In which case we will find out," the SEC investigator said at last. "And so the IRS." Then had come the nonsense about don't call us, we'll call you, but at least she had tweaked their numbed senses and sparked a flicker of interest.

The afternoon had been more productive. After a brief lunch she and her attorney drove to the offices of the New York Department of Corporations, filled out a request form and waited while the squeaking wheels of yet another bureaucracy were set in motion.

"Yes, here it is," said a clerk at last, peering into a file. "Preston Aeroservice Enterprises is a Delaware corporation headquartered in Chicago. They are also registered and franchised to do business in the state of New York and elsewhere." The clerk then looked up at Anne. "Was there anything else?"

Was? This is the present, lady. "Yes, who owns it?"

"Who owns it?"

God, lady, is there an echo in here? Anne took a deep breath to calm her temper, to control what was becoming flash-pan testiness. Already she had skewered her health aide, Dorine, earlier in the day, and for no apparent reason. She had better get a grip before she said something she'd regret. "Yes, please. Who or what company controls it?"

The clerk flipped the pages of the file then spun it around, pointing.

Anne leaned forward and peered at the line of print beneath a chipped fingernail. Then her heart leaped. It read, *Preston*

Aeroservice Enterprises, a subsidiary corporation of Trans Continental Airways Express, Incorporated.

It was the early name of TransCon.

John Haviland Williams

TEN

Warner Edelbrock sat at the small conference table in his office, discussing at length his expansion plans with Philip Darcy and TransCon's legal counsel, Edmond Burns. Then he stood and walked to the large chart showing TransCon's route structure and pointed. "We own the northeast corridor all the way to Florida, then westward for the southern routes into California, then north to Seattle and Anchorage. A sort of horseshoe with an obvious void in the middle. Then with Coastal's routes we gained the north and mid-central states and linked them to Atlanta. But," he said, pausing and knuckling the western states, "a TransCon passenger can't get from Chicago to San Francisco without going first to Atlanta. That's where the competition's beating us, and it's one hell of a lucrative route."

"United country," Darcy observed. "Fly the friendly skies."

Edelbrock nodded. "It's also Delta, American, and PCA."

Edmond Burns raised his brows. "You want to open up a route there? That'll make five majors flying Chicago to Frisco—"

"Ed," Edelbrock interrupted, "Have you ever been to 'Frisco?" Burns shook his head. "Then don't ever use that term if you do. Californians hate it, and they'll hate us if they hear one of our kind using it. We don't need that. Now, repeat after me: San Francisco. Got it?"

"Right," Burns said. "But five majors flying the Chicago to San Francisco corridor makes for stiff competition. You'll have to do the fare war bit all over again, and I think you'll lose in the long run. United, Delta, and American have both the passenger loyalty and the resources to withstand anything you throw at them. PCA's a wild card, anybody's guess. Maybe they can bite us, maybe not."

Edelbrock grinned, turning to Darcy. "Are there enough seat miles on that route to profitably sustain five carriers, Phil?"

"Nope."

"Four?"

"Yep."

"Then there's our answer."

Burns suddenly removed his glasses and stared at his superior incredulously. "You're going after one of *them*?"

Edelbrock smiled, rocking on his heels and glancing at Darcy. "Perhaps." The intercom buzzed and he reached for it. "I said, I didn't want to be disturbed, Helen." He listened for a moment, then the color drained from his face. "Tell him to hold."

Darcy sensed trouble and looked at Burns who shrugged.

"See you later, Ed," Edelbrock said, pointing to the door.

Miffed, the legal counsel left and Edelbrock motioned Darcy to a seat by his desk. "I'm going to put this call on the box. It's Donnelley, and I think you'd better listen in. Ready?" Edelbrock cleared his throat. "Good morning, Milton. How are things on Wall Street?"

"Warner, as far as I'm concerned it's Black Monday. We're in trouble."

202

He sensed the tension if not outright fear in the broker's usually placid demeanor. "Don't panic, for Christ's sake, what's going on? And what's this *we* business?"

Darcy rose quickly and got a tape recorder.

"Warner, I—I'll begin at the beginning, so far as I know it's the beginning. I should have told you earlier, but I thought nothing of it at the time—"

"Get to the point, Milton. I'm a busy man."

"Your...wife was here in my office several months ago and she... Oh, my, this is so difficult... She asked about your accounts, Warner. Naturally, I said that you had no accounts with us, but now with things the way they are I doubt that she believed me."

"The way *what* things are? What the hell are you talking about?"

"The SEC and IRS. They were here yesterday afternoon, and they're probing your—our accounts. Warner, I'm the broker of record! What are we—"

Edelbrock rocked forward in his chair. "They're *what?*"

It fits, Darcy thought. First the old bitch starts prodding Donnelley, then she's at the hearing with Ryan, and now this. Donnelley would have to be muzzled, and quickly. But he hoped Edelbrock would have the guts to take care of the other end. Sylvia. Donnelley had likely caved to her. And if Sylvia had drawn Ryan in...well, they would deal with her too.

Moments later Warner Edelbrock slammed the telephone down. "Greasy motherfucker! Goddamned gutless piss-ant!" He kicked a wastebasket across the office, then stood and stared out the window. Sylvia's words of long ago, when he had struck her, now haunted him. *"You will pay for this, Warner, and pay dearly..."*

He turned from the window. "Stay here, Phil, there's something I've got to do." He walked quickly to the double doors and stepped out, leaving one ajar.

Philip Darcy sat drumming his fingers on Edelbrock's desk while nibbling the cuticle of another. Things were beginning to unravel, and the call he'd had earlier from his deep throat at the FAA had been equally unsettling. Anne Ryan suspected something and she seemed focused in their direction, he'd said.

The time to act was near.

He rose and stepped quietly to the office doors, peered through to the foyer and saw that Edelbrock was nowhere in sight. The secretaries were absorbed in their typing. Quickly he crossed to the opposite wall of the office, slid the Reubens aside, then spun the dial left, right, left, and opened Edelbrock's personal safe. He glanced quickly over his shoulder then peered in, searching for the slender leather wallet containing the Swiss account code. There.

Edmond Burns stepped out of the elevator and strode across the thickly carpeted foyer to Helen McElroy's desk, Edelbrock's personal secretary. He raised his brows and inclined his head toward Warner's office door, now ajar.

"He's gone for a few minutes, but I'm sure it's all right if you go on in, Ed," she said.

Burns nodded and thumbed through a file as he walked absently toward the door. He reached to push it open and stopped abruptly. Through the narrow doorway he saw Darcy reaching into the sacred safe. Quietly, Burns backed away and turned. "I'll be back later," he said to Helen McElroy. *He must find Edelbrock, and quickly!*

Anne's tension mounted as her trial date neared with only ten days remaining. Still she had no proof of anything; much innuendo, yes, but nothing concrete beyond what seemed circumstantial at best, her attorney had said. And there had been no word yet from Hardison about the reopening date of her pilot error case, nor had there been any contact from the SEC. Twice she had called the SEC investigator to learn what progress they were making, or if they had even initiated an investigation, but he had not returned her calls. And the matter of the mysterious fingerprints on her aspirin bottle remained unresolved as well, the U.S. Attorney's office claiming it needed more time to complete the cross-check of all eleven hundred former Coastal pilots.

She was grasping at straws and she knew it, hurrying what couldn't be hurried, yet there seemed little else to do. That Preston Aeroservice was a subsidiary of TransCon also proved nothing. Short of a confession by Edelbrock or a willing accessory, the case against her still seemed tightly bound. The prosecution had evidence, lab reports on her blood samples, and forty-seven bodies. Felony manslaughter. She remained a pariah.

And her rebuttal? She didn't take drugs, never has. Warner Edelbrock had set her up.

Yeah, right. Even without the issue of pilot error, which she at least now stood a solid chance of overcoming, the matter of the drugs seemed irrefutable. Even had there been no deaths, no crash, the end result would be the same just as it had been for that airline captain that'd been drinking: Jailed and damned-all. And still loomed the matter of the civil suits, the bereaved seeking tens of millions for the wrongful deaths of loved ones.

Now as she sat in her wheelchair in her tiny apartment she thought of how it would be, of a six by eight cell probably shared with another female inmate, or several; of a single stinking commode with no seat. And at night after the lights went out they would come for her, the pretty one, crippled and relatively defenseless, unable to thwart the groping hands and the unspeakable obscenities that would follow... When released, if she survived, she would never be the same. And what pittance she might earn as day wages (doing what?) when at last released into society, would be quickly sucked away by the civil judgments on behalf of those awarded damages...

She was torn by her emotions, torn by rage in contest with utter despair. She needed evidence and there seemed none to be had. The cruel bastard whose bed she had shared had chosen and planned her demise carefully, and for his efforts had been awarded the prize he sought. God, what a fouled-up world.

"Shit!" Anne yelled, throwing her coffee cup across the living room and shattering it against the wall. Then the telephone rang and she snatched it from the cradle. "What!"

"Miss Ryan? Earl Christopher. How are you?"

She ground her teeth at her attorney's usual platitude. She suspected that his meter was already running, that her responses to his inanities usually assured him of at least two or possibly three more equally uncaring inquiries and tsk-tsks, lasting perhaps a minute or two, but equating to about eight dollars of additional chargeable fee even before he got down to issues. Well today she would deny him that.

"Ducky. Why are you calling?"

"Why, Anne, I wanted to know how you're getting along, of course, and express my admiration for how well you're handling these very difficult matters. Tell me, are you still having pain?"

There went another four dollars. "In the rectum, Earl, and you're it unless you've got some news for me."

"Yes, well...some difficulties have arisen and we must rethink our strategy, somewhat."

We? *WE?* Now there was a novel approach. "What difficulties?"

"Miss Ryan, I've just spoken with the U.S. Attorney's office and I'm sorry to report that the FBI was unable to match the fingerprint belonging to the allegedly deceased Lt. Robert Nash, to that of a Coastal Airlines pilot. I'm afraid that for the moment we're—"

"Screwed!" she yelled, and slammed the receiver down.

A. Milton Donnelley could no longer concentrate and he paced his office restlessly long after the closing bell on the New York Stock Exchange. Through the glass separating his office from the bullpen of lesser brokers, he saw the three young men and two women from the SEC and IRS, auditors they were, sitting at a table and carefully examining stock transaction records executed by the firm of Pickard, Wilmott, and DeLeury, A. Milton Donnelley, broker of record. They were the records of Warner Edelbrock and Philip Darcy, also known fictitiously as World-Wide Investors, Ltd., of which he was a partner, but also stacked high upon the table were the records of every client that had traded in TransCon as well as Coastal Airlines stock. There were scores of them, and each seemed to pique their youthful yet professional interest.

He watched helplessly as the auditors sifted the records, stiffening when one would look closely at a document then hand it to the others. Then all would huddle in hushed conversation.

At five o'clock they left, but they would return again tomorrow, he knew. And the day after as well. Their questions had been probing, penetrating, yet also revealing. They knew what they were after, no witch-hunt here. A. Milton Donnelley saw no way out; the phony partnership they had concocted as a tax dodge through Swiss accounts, his complicity in the Coastal short-sales that had obviously been manipulated—all would explode in their collective faces. Oh, Edelbrock and Darcy would take a fall, all right, but after their telephone conversation it was abundantly clear that he would go with them. Risk-capital, Edelbrock had called it. Welcome aboard a sinking ship, Milton.

He kneaded his Phi Beta Kappa key as he paced, considering his options, which were few, one of which was to play the role of innocence, hoodwinked by a cunning client. Or he could turn evidence in exchange for a plea, revealing also the unrelated transactions of Worthington, or Copenhaver, Fortensky... Still, there was Edelbrock to deal with if he turned on him. The man's power and influence was far-reaching, and during their telephone conversation his tone had been menacing, implying—no, *asserting*—that he, A. Milton Donnelley, had already collaborated with the other side. With Sylvia. But more than Edelbrock he feared Darcy. An unstable man, he guessed, a corrupt and vile creature whose greed was exceeded only by his penchant for inflicting pain.

Donnelley remembered well the several occasions when Darcy had been in his office to carry out Edelbrock's bidding. From their first meeting he had established the pecking order of who was master and who the servant. The bone-crushing hand-shake closing the first of the Coastal transactions had been primeval, painfully macho and ritualistic, and the expression conveyed in those chilling eyes unmistakable; you are *mine*, they said. And when later he had suggested to Darcy however obliquely that he be given a larger share in the fruits of their ventures, for which he had put his reputation as well as his broker's license at risk, the man had reached and grabbed his testicles, leading him squealing about his office while casually explaining why it couldn't be.

A. Milton Donnelley watched the secretaries leave and turn out all lights but his. Yes, goodnight to you too, he mumbled, waving. Deeply troubled, he packed his briefcase and prepared to leave. He decided the Empire Club with its quiet and private atmosphere would be a good place to sort things out. He would have his favorite leather chair in the corner by the fireplace in the Library Room, and Parsons would serve his martinis. There was a way out of this, somehow, he reasoned, or at least an avenue by which to minimize any damage he might sustain. He just needed to concentrate. After all, he was Phi Beta Kappa, wasn't he? Indeed, it had taken far more than genes to attain his successes.

He rode the elevator to the first floor, nodded to the security guard, and pushed through the revolving door to the street. Already it was after six and dusk had settled over the city, yet Wall Street was a honking melee' of those still fleeing the financial canyons of Manhattan. He turned left and strode purposefully up the busy sidewalk toward the prestigious Empire Club three blocks away. A. Milton Donnelley loved this part of the city and the economic dynamics that fueled the engine that was Wall Street, center of the universe. He belonged here and no one, *no one*, would take it from him. There had been others in far worse situations than his. It went with the territory, and they had survived just as surely he would. He need only formulate a plan, and already one was germinating.

He brushed past a covey of chattering secretaries, attractive they were, and he smiled wistfully, then stood aside in an alleyway entrance as four men moving office furniture on dollies crowded the busy sidewalk. He jerked and gasped when a sudden pain stabbed in his left kidney, certain it was another attack of kidney stones. Suddenly his body stiffened, and he felt strong hands grasp him about the shoulders and drag him into the alley as a veil of blackness quickly overcame him.

The seeds of A. Milton Donnelley's germinating plan for survival expired. So had A. Milton Donnelley.

The thought struck Gordy while piloting his TransCon 727 on final approach to San Francisco airport. *God, why hadn't he thought of it before?*

"Captain, you're below the glideslope," warned his first officer.

Momentarily distracted, Gordy quickly added power and pulled back on the wheel, his stomach and those of his crew and the 112 passengers seated in the cabin suddenly plunging earthward from the abrupt maneuver. He quietly chastised himself for letting his mind wander at a critical moment, knowing that he would hear more of it later from the flight attendants. Seconds later he flared too high over the approach end of the runway, and his 727 dropped in hard, bounced, then settled in again. He planted the nosegear on firmly, assuring that the aircraft could not choose to go aloft once again, then quickly jerked the thrust reverser levers to their detents and braked hard.

Never again would he chide other pilots for carrier landings. He was now one of them.

Ignoring his first officer's speculative glance, he taxied without delay to the north terminal satellite, followed the guideman's lighted wands and nosed into the jetway. The turbines were still spooling down when he quickly unfastened his harnesses and arose from his seat. "I gotta go, Sam," he said to the first officer. "Clean up the cockpit and put 'er to bed."

"And take the crap from the passengers, too. Thanks, skipper, you owe me."

He walked quickly up the jetway, tipping his hat as he brushed past deplaning passengers, some scowling, and took an elevator to the bowels of baggage operations.

Then he saw him. "Titus! Yo, Titus!"

"Hey-hey, Mr. Gordy. How you be, my man?"

"Out of breath and out of shape, and I just qualified for carrier duty. Listen, did you get a good look at the guy on the de-icing tanker the night of Anne's crash? The one you thought was your friend but wasn't?"

Titus pursed his lips and rubbed his woolly scalp. "Umm, sort of, I guess you could say. It be dark, you know."

"Can you describe him?"

"Oh...tall, sort of, yeah, pretty tall."

"Old, young? What?"

"Mebbe late forties. Mebbe older. He be wearin' a slicker and one of them rainhats, you know. Like they all do when they's out in God's own weather squirtin' juice on airplanes."

"Did he have a beard, a mustache, or anything you'd remember?"

Titus worked his lips, sucking at his cheek, and then shook his head. "Nope. Clean cut, he be. Ugly and mean lookin' fella, though."

"Was he black or white?"

"Oh, he be white, okay."

Tall, Caucasian, ugly and mean-looking. Well, swell. It could fit tens of thousands of New Yorkers. Probably a hell of a lot more. Gordy kneaded the corners of his eyes with his fingers, discouraged. He sighed and clapped Titus' shoulder. "What's your friend's name again? The one you thought was on the rig that night?"

"Willie. Willie Washington."

"Is Willie...black or white?"

"Oh, he be black, okay. Mmm-hm."

After Gordy's urgent call Anne felt re-energized even though his suggestion offered only a glimmer of hope. The next morning with her attorney Earl Christopher in tow, Anne sought and found Willie Washington at La Guardia airport.

"Yes ma'am, I remember that night. Sure sorry about what happened to you," said the young black.

"I—I don't understand," Anne said, "Titus told us you weren't on the rig that night."

"Oh, I wasn't, ma'am. Not then, anyway. Dispatch let me and my partner go at eight-thirty. Said they were overstaffed since not many planes was leavin'."

"Then who filled in for you? Who de-iced my aircraft?"

The young man shrugged. "Dunno. You'll have to ask Dispatch."

She did, and without letting on that she knew Willie had been off duty. Preston Aeroservice Enterprises' records showed that William A. Washington as well as his partner had worked a full shift that night, leaving duty at ten, a full forty-five minutes after her crash. Someone was lying.

Anne raised an eyebrow and looked at Christopher sitting at her side across the desk from the dispatcher, Wayne Paulson. She drummed her fingers nervously on her armrest, pondering her next question while Earl Christopher sat mute, having decided she seemed to be carrying the ball nicely. To Anne, he had become little more than a two hundred-fifty dollar an hour chauffeur.

Paulson caught her look at Christopher and his eyes narrowed. "Something wrong?"

211

Oooh yah, she thought, holding his wary gaze, then took a shot in the dark. "Does the boss come around once in a while?"

"Mr. Wetzel? He's here most of the time," Paulson said. "During the day, anyway."

"No, I mean Mr. Edelbrock."

"Oh *that* boss. Mr. Big. No, I've never even met him. I don't think anybody around here has."

She hadn't expected anything to come of that, Warner was too high a profile to be hanging out here. What she really needed was as much information about who was doing what in the PAE dispatch office the night of her crash. So she opened Paulson's tap to see just how much would flow before he tossed her out. "How many people are in the dispatch office on the night shift?"

"After eight o'clock there's usually just one."

Ah. Now she was getting somewhere. "So if someone on the rigs was to be released early from duty it would be by that someone, the sole person manning the dispatch office?"

Paulson nodded, an arrogant smirk tugging a corner of his mouth. "It would, and that person would note it in the records for payroll purposes. Our guys are paid hourly. Anything else? I've got work to do."

She could see by his expression that he thought her a wise-ass broad, but she had long been accustomed to such people, and immune to their baiting remarks. In a few minutes he would see just how much of a wise-ass she could be. A faint image was forming in her mind of how things could have happened here the night of her crash. Her mind raced as she considered variations of a scenario that was coming together, and the questions that would need to be asked to nail it down. And this would be the pivotal one. "Well, couldn't that person, the dispatcher, release a crew early but show them on the records as having worked a full shift, then substitute an off-duty crew that were his buddies so they could make extra money?"

That startled him. He suddenly leaned back in his chair and narrowed his eyes, studying her for a few moments. "Maybe," he said at last. "But then you got two crews being paid, 'cause they're both on the payroll records then." He shook his head, "That's twice what's needed unless we're swamped, and the payroll department'd get in an uproar. They'd know something was wrong and they'd tell the company controller."

Not quite, not if-- This was going to sound stupid but she had nothing to lose. "But suppose the substitute crew wasn't shown on the records, didn't care if they weren't paid?"

Paulson rocked back again and laughed. "Nobody works for nothing, lady. That's nonsense. Anyway, it sure as hell didn't happen that night."

"And how do you know?"

"Because, I was the dispatcher."

Oh? Now what? Willie clearly wasn't on duty that night, unless he was lying, but being a close friend of Titus's she doubted it. And if he wasn't lying, wasn't on duty, Paulson wasn't letting on that he knew it. So it was Paulson who was lying. Un-less-- "One more question, Mr. Paulson. How do you keep in contact with the de-icing rigs? Two-way radio?"

Paulson swiveled and pointed to the Motorola transmitter on the table behind him. "Right there. They've got 'em in the tankers and they also carry hand-helds."

"And if you're alone and out of the office, say you're out checking a rig or something, you talk to them with a hand-held and they can contact you too?"

"I thought you said one more question."

"Did I? Sorry."

Paulson sighed heavily and tossed a hand. "What the hell. Okay, look. We're never out of contact, okay? We're always on the radio. If we miss de-icing a ship, you airline people'd be all over us like flies to shit."

You got that right, she thought. On impulse Anne wheeled herself around his desk, reached and picked up one of several hand-held radios lying next to the main transmitter and offered it to Paulson. "Do me a favor? Call Willie Washington on this and tell him I'd like to talk to him?"

"Why?"

"Please?"

"Look, lady. I got shit all over my desk, work to do, and I'm tired of your goddamned questions, okay? Now suppose you take what's-his-name there with you, roll out that door there, and go fly an airplane, or something, okay?"

Anne shook her head, still holding the radio out to him. "Do it and I'll leave."

"Shit," he muttered, snatching the radio from her. He keyed the mike, "Washington, come back."

The radio hissed and crackled for a second. Then, "Yo, boss, Willie by."

"Got someone wants to talk to you," he said, glancing at Anne. "Make it quick."

Anne took the hand-held. "Willie? This is Captain Ryan. Was the voice you just heard the same one that released you from duty the night of my crash?" She glanced at Paulson, saw his puzzled expression.

"No ma'am. It was a deep voice, real throaty-like. Said he was some kinda manager filling in while Mr. Paulson went for a late dinner. I know Mr. Paulson's voice real good, and it wasn't him."

Anne looked at Wayne Paulson as she laid the hand-held down, and saw that he was obviously shaken. She tapped the small radio with a fingernail. "How many of these things have you got lying around?"

"I see what you mean. But it wouldn't have to be one of these. Anybody who has a hand-held and knows our frequency could've tapped in."

Anne leaned forward. "Isn't it possible that somebody did just that and released Willie and his partner? Then substituted somebody else?"

He shook his head. "Absolutely not. I'd have heard it."

214

Anne pressed further. "Would you hear or pay attention to every transmission between crews? Every one?"

"I'd hear it, but I may not pay much attention unless it was an emergency of some kind or they were using four-letter words. I've got other work to do around here too, you know. I'm a busy man and we're understaffed."

Even though defensive, she saw that Paulson was running scared now; she had all the information she needed to make life difficult for him. Now that he knew Willie had been released, that something had slipped by him that night, he had at last realized that he could be held accountable. Yet something had also slipped from her grasp. Paulson most likely wasn't the culpable party. Then a thought struck her. "Well, suppose somebody called Willie on the hand-held and told him to switch frequencies. Would you hear that?"

"I might, then again I might not. They chatter back and forth a lot."

"Okay, then try this: somebody with a hand-held that knew your frequency could call Willie, tell him to change frequencies so you wouldn't hear it, then order him released from duty, couldn't they?"

Paulson laughed. "Sure, anything's possible. But why would they do that? Who would de-ice your plane?" Suddenly realization dawned and the color drained from his face. Someone unauthorized had gone out on the tanker that night.

Anne held his gaze. "The guys who don't care if they're paid or not, that's who." *See, you dork? I really am a wise-ass broad.*

Eight days remained before her trial and still she had not a shred of proof. She had thought of having all of PAE's hand-held radios tested for fingerprints, hoping for a match with that found on her aspirin bottle, but Christopher convinced her it would be a costly dead end. He argued that in a span of four months since the crash hundreds of hands had probably operated the radios. Anne agreed and could think of nothing else upon which the perpetrator, assuming one was involved with PAE, may have left his prints that would survive four months of weather and much handling by others.

So at last it was time to confront and quit skirting the perimeter of the enemy. If Edelbrock and his assistant, Philip Darcy, were responsible—and she was certain they were—then she no longer had anything to lose by saying so to their faces. It would be risky, she knew, for until now she presumed they had no notion she suspected them. When confronted they would likely deny it, but the danger lay in threat of exposure and they might later come for her again, certainly before the trial, if they believed she possessed damaging evidence. It was a risk she was willing to take; a risk that may well result in baiting a trap for them. But how to set and spring the trap was something of which she had not the slightest idea.

She would think of something, test the waters first.

She wanted desperately for Gordy to be with her when she challenged Edelbrock on his own turf, but since he now flew for TransCon she couldn't put his job in jeopardy. Hardison was out of the picture as well since it was a criminal matter and out of his jurisdiction. That left Earl Christopher. Expensive as he was for what little help he'd been, her attorney at last seemed to be taking an interest, and his presence in front of Warner might lend credibility to the charges she was about to level. She had no plan of substance for the confrontation, choosing instead to play things by ear and see how they reacted. But Darcy would be the one she would focus upon. Certainly he was Edelbrock's bag-man controlling the mysterious missing Lt. Nash. Or maybe…yes, just maybe *Darcy* was the missing navy lieutenant.

It was early afternoon when Earl Christopher picked her up at her apartment and they headed for TransCon headquarters at JFK. She intended to surprise Warner by not calling ahead for an appointment, instead having called and spoken with a secretary on the pretense of representing some charity, to learn whether Darcy, in charge of public relations, had an appointment with him that afternoon. She reasoned that as Edelbrock's assistant they met often, and she had been right. They were meeting at two o'clock.

Christopher took an expressway offramp at Anne's direction well before reaching the airport complex, and he saw that she seemed to be looking for something.

"Stop here!" she ordered, and Christopher pulled into a parking area in front of an electronics store. She gave him a hundred dollars and told him what she wanted. Moments later he returned with the package.

Ten minutes later they turned into the long curved driveway leading to the glass monolith that was TransCon headquarters, and parked in a visitor's slot. He helped her out and they entered a large lobby where a guard sat behind a counter, reading a magazine. She hadn't expected this, although she should have. Getting past the guard would be the first hurdle.

"Can I help you folks?" said the guard, eyeing her wheelchair.

"Uh...yes. We're here to see Mr. Edelbrock," Anne answered.

"Do you have an appointment?"

"Not for a specific time. I told him we'd be by sometime this afternoon, and he said fine, so long as we didn't mind waiting. We're from the Pilot's Benevolent Association. TransCon's been so helpful in contributing and supporting us over the years, and this afternoon we're going to discuss arrangements to give TransCon a national award."

"Say, that's swell. TransCon's a fine airline, you know. I know Mr. Edelbrock will be pleased. Here, sign the register and then take the elevator to the seventh floor. Oh, and I need to check your package, ma'am." He did, frowned at the instrument as he turned it over in his hands, then shrugged and gave it back. In the elevator she carefully wiped the instrument, her bait, clean.

The elevator doors opened to an elegant and expansive foyer suitable for a Kuwaiti Emir. It fit Edelbrock's ego only too well, she saw. Two attractive and well-groomed secretaries sat at opposite desks near huge paneled double doors with ornate brass fixtures. Behind lay the den of the carnivore, yet the atmosphere seemed so orderly, professional, in spite of its overblown elegance, and, well...benign. It was now difficult to believe that such heinous crimes had been launched from behind those doors.

A secretary rose and walked toward them. "Good afternoon, may I help you?"

Her heart thumped wildly. "My name is Anne Ryan. We're here to see Warner Edelbrock." Anne saw not a flicker of reaction in the lovely dark eyes that seemed even friendly.

"I'm sorry, Mr. Edelbrock is in conference. Do you have an appointment, ah...Miss Ryan?"

"No, but I'm sure if you told him I'm here, he'd want to see me."

"I'm afraid I can't interrupt his conference, Miss Ryan. Perhaps another time. Would you like to make an appointment?"

"Just tell him I'm here and let him decide." She saw a hint of caution, wariness, cloud the secretary's eyes.

Then, "All right, please wait."

Anne's hands were moist and clammy clutching the package from the electronics store on her lap while they waited, watching as the secretary spoke quietly into a telephone. The secretary glanced at her once then spoke into the telephone again, nodding. Suddenly the double doors swung open.

"Anne!" Warner Edelbrock boomed. "How good to see you. You're looking well after your trying ordeal. Come in, come in."

Anne wheeled herself through the doorway and Christopher followed. Edelbrock's office was everything the elegant foyer had promised and more. Rare and expensive oil paintings, Persian rugs, and groupings of tastefully upholstered mahogany and teak furniture lent an atmosphere of an exquisite home. She had never seen his office, but she assumed it was in keeping with the courtly estate on which he lived on Long Island. It certainly fit with the lavish mountain retreat in which she had often been an intimate visitor.

Slouched comfortably in a chair near the expansive desk was a tall, nattily-dressed man whose ferret eyes appraised her cautiously as she approached. He rose with obvious annoyance to greet them.

Tall-ish, Caucasian, ugly and mean-looking. Titus's description of Willie's stand-in could fit millions and this was one of them, Anne observed, yet he wasn't particularly ugly. At least not in a physical sense.

"Anne, let me introduce our vice-president of marketing and public relations, Philip Darcy. Phil, this is Anne Ryan—*Captain* Anne Ryan."

She took the offered hand briefly, staring into darting, hostile eyes. Clever eyes. Only once had she seen eyes like that, the eyes of a pit bull that had cornered her as a child and bitten her painfully before fleeing. Eyes reflected the soul, her godfather had said. And here before her stood a person lacking. A person that may well be the missing navy lieutenant. The age seemed about right, considering that Nash had disappeared in `69.

Warner Edelbrock settled into the chair behind his desk, leaned back and steepled his fingers and focused on Christopher. "I don't believe I've had the pleasure, sir, are you also a pilot?"

Christopher cleared his throat as he seated himself. "I am Earl Christopher, Miss Ryan's attorney."

"Ah," said Edelbrock, raising his eyebrows. He turned to Anne, "You're looking well, considering the terrible ordeal you've been through. I've been worried about you, Anne, I've attempted twice to call you, first at the hospital, later at your apartment, but we never seemed able to connect. But then, I'm sure that with all that's been happening you're very busy. Tell me, is there some way I can help—considering that we're old friends?"

Darcy was to her right and she felt him watching her closely. Too closely, and she sensed his unease. Then her right leg began to tremble as the atrophied muscles suddenly spasmed, and she jammed her hand on her knee to still it. "That's why I'm here, Warner. I do need your help, considering we're old friends."

He smiled and spread his arms expansively. "Anything. You have only to ask."

Anne's heart thudded so heavily she was certain that Darcy could hear it. And she knew that in seconds Christopher would come unglued from what she was about to say. "That's kind of you, Warner. Who did you have leave the glycol out of the de-icing fluid so that the wings of my aircraft would ice-over and I'd crash? And which of your skulking minions put dope in my aspirin bottle? Was it this dork?" she said, jabbing her thumb toward Darcy. "A simple request for help, Warner, you said anything."

Earl Christopher suddenly became apoplectic, Darcy's crossed leg fell from his knee, and Edelbrock's smile drained, his eyes narrowing as he leaned forward on his elbows. "Do you really believe that? Is that what this is all about?"

Anne clenched her teeth, "I'm dead serious, Warner, and I speak not only for myself but for eighty-five others who can't. You're it, Warner; I should have seen it coming. You killed Ray Thompson and thirty-seven others trying to get me, and then you tried again, killing another forty-seven and you won. You got Coastal and you nailed me. Now it's my turn, and when I'm finished I'm going to watch while they give you the lethal injection."

Edelbrock's expression was a mask of shock, incredulousness, and the large office became silent except for the ticking of a grandfather clock. His eyes darted to Darcy, then back. Suddenly he slapped his palms on the desk and barked a laugh that

220

shattered the stillness. "It does look that way, doesn't it?" he said, shaking his head and laughing, glancing first to Darcy then to Anne, and finally to Christopher. "Christ Almighty, put it all together and it *does* look that way. You think *we* did this to you. No *wonder* you're upset."

Anne held his incredulous gaze, unfooled. "It *is* that way, and you know it."

Edelbrock stood quickly and walked around his massive desk, "Oh, for Christ's sake, Anne, what are you trying to do, put the squeeze on me? You dump our relationship, concoct an outrageous story, and now you want money? Is that it? Extortion? Money or a scapegoat for your fuckup in the cockpit that night? Trick or treat?"

Her rage suddenly boiled over. "I didn't fuck up, Warner, you fucked me up! You fucked-up both airplanes killing a total of eighty-five people, and you had a shit named Nash fuck me up with drugs, you son of a bitch!" She felt Christopher's hand gripping her forearm and quickly brushed it away. The horses were now out of the gates and there was no stopping them. "And I've got the just the evidence to prove it!"

Edelbrock shook his head as though she were demented, and walked calmly around behind his desk again, glancing quickly at Darcy as he eased into his chair. He leaned back and rested his chin on his fists. "So prove it," he said mildly. "I suppose darling Sylvia put you up to this?"

Anne caught his eye contact with Darcy and went for the opening. "She's given me all I need to know and I've got a lot more, too. And so do the Feds."

"So why haven't I been arrested?"

She ignored his question for which she had no answer and reached into the paper sack on her lap and withdrew a hand-held two-way radio. She thrust it at Darcy. "Remember this?"

He took it, turned it over in his hands, shrugged, and then gave it back. "What is it, some kind of walkie-talkie?"

Anne carefully slipped the hand-held back into the sack, her eyes boring into Edelbrock's. "The NTSB is reopening the case, we have witnesses who will testify about the drugs in my locker and who put them there, and..." She let the silence hang for a moment, "...we have an eyewitness who'll testify to what you and this bastard did about the de-icing. You're dead meat, Warner. Both of you."

Edelbrock was unfazed. "So why are you telling us all of this?"

"Because we're such good friends, Warner. You're going to need some time to prepare your defense."

Edelbrock leaned forward again, his expression now murderous. "Get out."

Earl Christopher unlocked the passenger door to his car. "That was a foolish thing to do," he said, helping her in.

"What was?"

"Everything, not the least of which was that trumped-up business of saying that you had an eyewitness and that Sylvia Edelbrock had given you evidence against him." He slammed her door, walked around and slid into the driver's seat. "I should never have let you do this. If he's guilty, you may have put Mrs. Edelbrock's life at risk and obliterated any chance you may have of proving what you believe. If he's not guilty, you may have set yourself up for a libel suit."

Anne leaned back in the seat, massaging her throbbing temples. "Earl, I've got so many suits against me I could fill a wardrobe. One more won't matter. Besides, I think we'll have him before he tries to harm Sylvia. As for proof, we have this now. I know I'm right." She reached into the paper sack and grasped the hand-held radio between two fingers. "Darcy's prints."

Earl Christopher sighed and leaned his forehead against the steering wheel.

"What's wrong?"

222

Christopher leaned back against the seat and turned to her, trying to retain his composure. "Darcy's prints, that's what's wrong. If I'd known that's what you were going to do, I'd have saved you the price of that radio. Listen to this, Anne, and tell me how it sounds: Philip Darcy, the highly-visible vice-president of marketing and public relations for TransCon Airlines, walks into Coastal's crew lounge, busts into your locker, plants the drugs, then goes out on a de-icing tanker in subarctic weather while wearing his spiffy alligator shoes and squirts water instead of glycol on your airplane." He shook his head as he gripped the steering wheel. "Anne, it's just plain silly, Darcy doesn't even fit Titus's description of the man he saw on the tanker. It's—" He saw her lower lip tremble, her sapphire eyes suddenly flooding.

"I—I have to try," she said in a choking voice. "I can't just...just let all of this happen to me, Earl. I'm going to go to prison."

"I'm sorry," Christopher said, taking her hand, "No one can blame you for trying. I'll have the prints checked."

He started the car and dropped it into gear. *Never, ever, let a client take the lead,* he reminded himself. They screw it up every time. Now the enemy, if in fact they had faced the enemy, had more than adequate warning to prepare a defense. And it would likely be a solid one. For not only had she laid her entire poker hand face up on the table, a pair of fours at best, but she had reached for a bogus deck from which to deal. It wasn't so long ago when such acts provoked a bullet. *Stupid!*

John Haviland Williams

ELEVEN

Mitchell Hardison hung up the telephone and pushed away from his desk. He stood by the window absently lateraling a cigar butt from one corner of his mouth to the other, reflecting on Anne Ryan's call, when Westphal walked in.

"You wanted to see me, Mitch?"

Hardison turned, "Yeah. You get a good look at the guys on the de-icing tanker the night of Ryan's crash?"

"Not too. It was dark, and except for headlights all I had was a flashlight. Besides, they were all bundled up in weather gear and rainhats. Why?"

"Ryan thinks they weren't the real crew, and I'm inclined to believe her."

"You think the stuff I saw in the tanker was bogus?"

"Could be." Hardison leaned over his desk and reread the notes he'd taken while talking to Ryan. *Tall-ish, Caucasian, ugly and mean-looking.* He drum-rolled his fingers on the desk-top and looked up at the young investigator. "Describe what you can remember of those guys."

Westphal thought a moment then shook his head. "Not enough to do any good, Mitch. I could barely see their faces. They were both white, I think. One was, anyway."

"Tall? Short? Fat?"

"One was pretty tall—taller than me, and I'm six-two. The other was average height, I'd say."

"The tall one—pleasant-looking fellow, was he?"

"About as pleasant-looking as a Raiders linebacker with the score tied and ten seconds left in the fourth quarter. He was the white guy. That close enough?"

"It'll do. You get their names?"

"Yeah, let's see..." Westphal drew out his notepad and skimmed the pages. "Yeah, here. Philip Darcy and Lou Esposito."

Hardison reached into his drawer and slid a photograph across his desk. "This Darcy?"

Westphal examined the face closely, trying to remember. At last he shook his head. "I'm sure it isn't. The Darcy I saw wasn't dapper looking like this dude. Who is this, anyway?"

Hardison retrieved the photograph and grunted, "Philip Darcy, a vice president of TransCon. Let's take a ride, Doug."

As Westphal drove them toward La Guardia and the Preston Aeroservice office, Hardison studied the Coastal 193 summary file. The Board had agreed to reopen the case as well as that of Coastal 288, but not for at least a month because of other active cases, giving him time to poke around some. Time to play spook and look for Darcys who weren't Darcy. Something weird was going on, making Ryan's persistence all the more credible.

The eye-opener had been Ryan's simulator runs. He no longer doubted that hers and Thompson's ships had been iced at takeoff, yet her notion that someone had deliberately left the diethylene glycol out of the de-icing solution and substituted some sort of coloring to the water base seemed over-dramatic and far-fetched; a concocted cause borne of desperation. And Ryan was indeed desperate. But now this Darcy thing. Someone on the de-icing rig that night had passed himself off to Westphal as Philip Darcy. Why?

"So what do you expect to find at Preston Aeroservice, Mitch?" Westphal asked.

A good question. Hardison shrugged, "Maybe a Raiders linebacker." He really didn't know what he expected to find, and if Ryan was right—that someone had patched in to PAE's frequency and substituted crews that night—there was little or no chance that *someone* was a regular employee. And he certainly didn't expect to find a tanker still parked in the bays and filled with colored water. But sometimes a little poking and prodding paid off. An answer waiting for a question. You just never knew.

Tomorrow he would talk to Darcy, ask why someone would want to use his name at the Coastal crash scene, see how he reacted. And get his own ass in a sling for doing so, stepping on someone else's turf. Screw it, he'd do it anyway.

PAE dispatcher Paulson swiveled quickly in his chair and stood up, incensed. "So you guys think we had something to do with those crashes? Goddamn, I knew I shouldn't have talked to that broad without the company attorney here. Son of a *bitch!*"

Hardison waved the man back into his chair. "Now settle down, Paulson, nobody's accusing you or your company of anything."

"You got a search warrant? Lemme see a search warrant."

"We haven't got one, and get it through your goddamned head that you're not being accused of anything. But if I have to, someone from the Justice Department will get one and you won't like it any better if they do." Hardison leaned over the dispatcher's desk and spoke in a mild tone. "We also have to cooperate with the press, Paulson, and sure as hell it'll tweak their interest if you want to stiff-arm a little looking around. You want us, or the FBI? Take your pick."

Paulson took a deep breath and let it out in a rush. "So what do you want to do?"

"Just look around, ask a few questions, that's all."

"I don't know about it, okay? I never seen you guys."

"If you say so. Oh—one more thing..." Hardison reached into his coat pocket and slid a photo over the desk. "You ever see this guy around here?"

Paulson took the photo and recognized it instantly. "Why, that's Mr. Darcy."

"Do tell. He ever come around here?"

Paulson shook his head. "No, thank god. Maybe once or twice in the last couple of years."

"How about around the time of the Coastal crashes? Ever see him then?"

"Nope. The less he comes around, the better. Never's too soon for me."

Hardison raised his eyebrows. "You guys don't get along?"

Paulson snorted and shook his head again. "Not since he tried to get us to water down the glycol de-icing solutions about a year ago to save a few bucks, the crazy son of a bitch. He figured we could dilute the solution a bit and still have an adequate freezing point deterrent value, while saving about a hundred bucks per application. Big deal. But when Mrs. Edelbrock found out about it, she reamed his ass out but good."

"You tell her?"

"Hell yes, I told her. She might be crippled, but she sure as hell can throw her weight around. She practically owns TransCon, which owns PAE, you know. Shit, we start watering down that stuff even a little just to save a few lousy bucks, and one day someone's gonna crash and blame it on us! On me! So fuckin' right, I told her."

Hardison held Paulson's agitated gaze without expression. "So how was he going to cover for it? Diluting changes the color."

"Food coloring. Can you believe it? Fucking food coloring."

They began their probe in the tanker bays located about a half mile from the dispatch office, and Hardison saw the location as a window of opportunity for switching crews without the dispatcher's knowledge. The steel building was isolated. Three ten-wheeled de-icing tankers now slept in the deserted bays and Westphal climbed up on one, checked the tank and found it full of glycol solution. He wedged himself into the cherrypicker platform and swung the cannon-like nozzle around. "Stick 'em up, Mitch."

Hardison raised his hands. "You lose; I got eleven cents."

"So what else is new?"

While Westphal checked the other tankers Hardison strolled around the deserted bays with mild interest. Against the back wall was a row of lockers and he opened one. Inside were rubber boots, yellow slicker, rainhat, flashlight, and a centerfold from a skin magazine taped to the door, showing the splayed crotch of a hook-nosed bleached blonde sporting a bristling overgrowth of black, springy pubic curls well in need of mowing. Not of his taste. He opened another and found the same accouterments but no centerfold; instead, a crucifix. Odd crew. A third locker was empty and he slammed the metal door with a crash that made Westphal jump. A waste of time, he thought. A dumb and knee-jerk capitulation to an agitated woman's pleading. Admittedly he felt sorry for Ryan, but now he felt foolish. Yet, still...

He walked around the side of the building and found two large cylinders lying horizontally, each about four feet in diameter and at least thirty feet long, braced shoulder-high on concrete piers. Stenciled on the side of each was *Diethylene Glycol Type 1*. The juice. At the end of the tanks a large flanged pipe emerged vertically from the ground and made a ninety-degree L. It looked like a large water faucet used for mixing the solutions.

He grabbed the spoked wheel and grunted as he turned it. Suddenly a gout of water shot forth, soaking Westphal from the knees down. He quickly shut it off. "Sorry, Doug."

With great effort he hoisted his bulk and climbed the steel ladder attached to the tanks. When he reached the top he swung a latch aside and opened the hatch. The tank was full. He dipped his fingers into the liquid, rubbed them together and sniffed. It was glycol, all right, slippery and full-strength. He checked the other tank and found the same. Should he have expected otherwise? He glanced down at a shivering Westphal standing on the grating of a storm drain.

"Well?" asked the young investigator, wringing his soaking pants legs.

"Hundred proof." He sighed and wiped his fingers on a handkerchief. They weren't going to prove anything today, nor had he expected to. "Get in the car, Doug, and dry off while I climb down and take a walk around in back. Then we'll go." He saw that Westphal was staring at the drain grating beneath his feet. "What're you looking at?"

"This storm drain. I remember something odd that night."

Hardison grunted as he climbed gingerly down the ladder. Westphal always kept him in suspense, offering an announcement of something to come and then leaving it hanging. Continued next week. High drama. He was an intelligent young man and a solid investigator, curious, persistent, even tenacious, but his manner was sometimes a pain in the ass.

He swung off the bottom rung, laid a heavy hand on Westphal's shoulder and faced him, his expression fatherly. "Suppose you share it with me, son."

"They were dumping what was left of the tanker load in here when I drove up," he said, shivering and pointing to the drain.

"And?"

"Well, if the stuff's so expensive, then why would they dump it?"

230

Hardison arched his bushy brows. *Why indeed?* "Go dry off; I'll see you in a few."

A TransCon 737 thundered past on the runway and Hardison pressed his fingers into his ears as he walked around behind the building. There was nothing. Nothing but weeds and trash. He poked around amid stacks of wooden pallets, scattered paint containers, and empty drums of motor oil. There were several five-gallon plastic containers that appeared full and he opened one. Used motor oil. Beer and soda cans cluttered the area as well as soiled rags and discarded rubber boots amid knee-high weeds. Also a tampon and a couple of used condoms. They hadn't cleaned up back here in a long while, he observed. He kicked an empty gallon paint can aside and was about to kick another when he frowned, staring at the faded label.

Well, son of a bitch.

He reached into his pocket for a ballpoint pen, then stooped and hooked the wire handle and lifted the faded can from the weeds. *Food Coloring - Red #2,* it read.

"Doug! Hey, Doug! Bring the car around!"

Westphal stopped the car beside the building as Hardison came around the corner. "What's that?"

Hardison held the can high. "Maybe the murder weapon. I think it's time the U.S. Attorney had a talk with our frugal Mr. Darcy."

Philip Darcy took another satisfying sip of a bone-dry martini while sitting alone in a booth at O'Hara's Grille, tallying his fortune on a cocktail napkin. Three blocks away and deep in a vault at Citibank was well over $1.9 million in cash, his and Edelbrock's profits on short sales of Coastal stock. He'd wired it in from Switzerland, and now it was his alone.

It was time to get out of Dodge. Call it quits.

He'd been lucky, but now it wouldn't last. Ryan was too close, and her evidence—if she had any, even if circumstantial, could be sufficient to bring the hounds running, maybe warrant indictment.   What Ryan had asserted was ironic and far-reaching, but coupled with what Donnelley may have already spilled and what the SEC and IRS would soon find could turn indictment to conviction.   Edelbrock's plan had backfired and he, Darcy, was caught standing too close to the breech, but not so close he couldn't escape.   Ryan's fury seemed focused on Edelbrock and he would sustain most of the damage—Ryan and Edelbrock's calculating wife would see to that.   But when they came looking for him, he, Philip Andrew Darcy, would be long gone. Gone to a country where $1.9 mil would support him comfortably, without fear of extradition or of retaliation by an avenging Warner Edelbrock. He'd heard that Chile and Argentina had no such treaties with the United States, nor were they likely to in the future, and Edelbrock might well be locked safely away.   If not jailed, Sylvia would surely neuter him financially and he would need bus fare to pick up the chase to South America.

Tuffus dartus, Warner my man.

It had been risky gaining Edelbrock's Swiss account code from his office safe, but he had seen days ago that things were beginning to go awry.   Until then the much-publicized circumstances of Ryan's crash had seemed sealed tightly, a dead issue, but his contact at the FAA had revealed otherwise.   Ryan had somehow disproved the obvious and the NTSB case was likely to be reopened, a fact he had considered carefully, and one—if only by innuendo—which could eventually lead directly to TransCon headquarters with inescapable questions echoing Warner's remarks to Ryan: *"It does look that way, doesn't it?"*

Darcy nodded to himself.   Yes, it did in fact look that way. Thus his decision to keep what he knew to himself and reach for his as well as Edelbrock's marbles before it was too late.   As a child he'd never received a check mark in the box, *plays well with others*, and that wasn't about to change now.   Besides, Edelbrock had plenty of money. He had Sylvia. Darcy chuckled to himself, then looked at his watch and decided to dally no onger; the bank would close in twenty minutes. He savored the freedom and safe haven that lay only hours away, and with that 1e paid his check and left.

Fifteen minutes later, bearing a smug and satisfied expression and lugging a valise stuffed with $1.9 million in cash, he 1ailed a cab and headed for JFK. He had decided upon Santiago, Chile, as his first stop until he had more time to carefully consider where to seek his final safe haven. He worried that he should have had the money wired directly to Santiago instead of New York, but he wanted to see it, feel it first, assuring that it existed before he ran.

His life had quickly changed forever, the resources to acquire much of what he had ever wanted was in the valise now clutched securely to his chest. As the tall buildings of Manhattan swept past he bid them goodbye one by one, unaware of the driver's watchful eyes in the mirror.

Thirty minutes later the tall, heavy-set cab driver drove slowly into the darkened landfill adjacent to the airport, braked and got out. He walked quickly around to the right rear door, reached in and dragged out the lifeless body of Philip Darcy. Then he reached back in and grabbed Darcy's valise, shook out the thick packets of bills, then peeled away the genuine hundreds from the top of each and cast the remaining plain paper cuttings to the wind. He knelt and turned the dead man's right hand palm up and laid a small object in it, then carefully curled the lifeless fingers around it.

Still kneeling over the body, he clenched his right fist and slammed it against Darcy's left cheek, feeling the satisfying crunch of bone beneath. Then he struck him with an equally powerful left, shattering the jaw. He shined his flashlight on the now disfigured face, satisfied that it appeared that a violent struggle had preceded the bullet to the heart.

For a long moment he stood over the body, saw that the arrangement looked okay, then got in the stolen taxi and slammed the door. He grimaced as he yanked away the false beard and mustache, then wadded them up in his rolled sea cap and tossed it out the window.

He glanced again at the mutilated and lifeless body of Philip Darcy, searching his mind for an appropriate remark. He could think of only one, and sighed as he spoke.

"Ah, Philip. What price loyalty?"

It was late in the evening when Anne at last convinced herself that she should call Sylvia Edelbrock. She owed her that much. Christopher had been right; she had been foolish to shoot off her mouth to Warner about Sylvia. She hadn't intended it that way, only to imply it obliquely, yet her rage had gotten the better of her judgment and now she was certain that Sylvia was in danger because of her foolishness.

She reached for the telephone and dialed the number she had gotten from directory assistance. By the fourth ring she quickly hung up, realizing that Warner may answer.

God, get a grip! Her nerves were frayed; she wasn't tracking straight. Too much was happening and yet nothing was happening, not quickly enough, and still she was grasping at straws, groveling for anything she could to defend herself at the trial now only seven days away.

Her hand still rested on the telephone when suddenly it rang and she jerked from it as though shocked. Had Warner sensed her call? Was he calling now to threaten her? Slowly she reached for it again, steeling herself. "Hello?"

"Anne? Earl Christopher."

Relief flooded her senses. Suddenly she sat erect, remembering. "What? What did you find out?"

"I'm sorry, Anne, Darcy's prints on the hand-held radio are just that: Philip Andrew Darcy. He's got a couple of minor convictions and suspendeds from years ago for assault and battery, but other than that he's clean. He's not the missing Lt. Robert Nash, I'm sorry to say, but—"

234

She slowly lowered the phone and sank her face into her hands. She had expected as much, but again she had set her hopes on a breakthrough, however far-reaching.

"Hello? Hello? Anne?"

Her left leg began spasming as she raised the receiver. "I—I'm sorry, what were you going to say?"

"I was about to say he's still around."

"Who's still around? What do you mean?"

"Nash. Have you talked to Mitchell Hardison today?"

"Not since this morning when I told him about our meeting with Paulson, the PAE dispatcher. Why?"

"Apparently he believes you because he and his assistant took a ride out to La Guardia and had a look around PAE. I've just been talking with Lorenzo at the U.S. Attorney's office and he said that Hardison brought in an empty gallon can of red food coloring he'd found near where they park those de-icing rigs."

"Oh...my...god..."

"Hold on, it gets better. The FBI dusted it a few hours ago and found a fully intact left index of a Lt. Robert Nash, U.S. Navy, deceased. The print has the same deep scar as that found on your aspirin bottle."

Anne spun her wheelchair as she gripped the receiver, "Holy jumpin' Jesus, oh god damn, we're going to win! That's it! The drugs, the food coloring in place of glycol, the crash, and now Nash's fingerprints again! It all ties—"

"No, Anne, it doesn't. It still doesn't prove anything. It's still circumstantial. The empty can of food coloring Hardison found doesn't prove that someone used it to color water that was supposed to be glycol, and the fact that Nash's prints were on it as well as your aspirin bottle doesn't prove that someone set you up for drugs. Until we can produce this guy Nash and prove that he did these things and who was behind him, if anybody, we don't have a defense. Your only solid hope for the moment is that when the NTSB reconvenes they'll recognize that your aircraft was iced-over when it shouldn't have been, and you've pretty well demonstrated that, and that preventing the crash was beyond your control. But you've still got to overcome the presumption that you willingly took drugs, the felony manslaughter issue. That's the key to the whole thing, Anne. Unless we can prove that someone substituted codeine for aspirin and sprayed your aircraft with only water..."

So there it was. Right back to square one. Without Nash or Darcy or Edelbrock they were nowhere...except nearer to her trial.

"Anne," he continued, "have you ever heard of a guy named A. Milton Donnelley? A broker with Pickard, Wilmott, and DeLeury?"

She slouched in her wheelchair, massaging her eyes. "I wouldn't know an A. Milton Donnelley if I found him in my soup. Who's he?"

"This guy wound up as beef stock in Manhattan's soup. They found him this morning floating in the East River with a puncture wound in his left kidney and heart. The coroner thinks it was an ice pick, or something. Killed him almost instantly."

"So?"

"So A. Milton Donnelley was Edelbrock's stockbroker. You apparently got the SEC guys pretty excited after all, because they're investigating not only Edelbrock and Darcy, but Donnelley as well. Looks like there was more than a broker-client relationship there."

She sat up quickly. "They think Edelbrock killed him?"

"Who knows? It'll take some time to find out, but the motive is there, according to the information you gave to the SEC. It looks like someone killed him to shut him up. The SEC's meeting with the DA and the U.S. Attorney as we speak."

Anne's heart suddenly raced. "Do you think they'll postpone my trial? Jesus, with all this happening, the crashes timed with the stock transactions, Nash's prints, the food coloring, Edelbrock's stock broker taking a swim in the river, and motive—Jesus Christ, does Edelbrock have motive, how can they not—"

"They're not saying, Anne, but we can hope. If they don't postpone the trial by day after tomorrow I'll file a motion myself. But remember, in spite of all of this, even the dead stock broker, all we've got is—"

"I know. Circumstantial."

"I'm afraid that's right. Until we find Nash, or Edelbrock and Darcy drop the ball."

"Or we knock it out of their hands. We've got to think of something, Earl. A setup of some kind, maybe. I can be a really devious bitch when..."

Earl Christopher closed his eyes as she railed on, praying that something would break in the case before his client led him into the fires of hell and disbarment.

At that moment far out on Long Island Warner Edelbrock stood leaning against the mantle in his study, staring morosely into the crackling fire. He swirled his brandy and slugged it down, then poured and quickly knocked down another—his sixth, but the much-needed buzz wasn't coming. Nothing eased the tension building within. The past two days had been unnerving and he felt his mind as well as his careful planning unraveling, his empire crumbling about him. First had been Donnelley's revelation about the SEC and IRS probes of his accounts and learning that Sylvia had also been snooping. Then had come the unnerving confrontation with Ryan and her assertion that Sylvia had fed her the evidence, that there were witnesses. And then Burns had tipped him that Darcy, his most trusted, had turned on him and reached for the money. He ground his teeth, thinking of Ryan and how she had scared the gutless son of a bitch witless.

Rage seethed within him, knowing that at the root of it all lay the conniving of a demented and vengeful bitch. Sylvia.

"You will pay for this, Warner, and pay dearly."

237

The memory of her haunting vow had fomented for years. Now it was reality. "Bitch! Motherfucking bitch!" He slung the contents of the snifter into the fire where it exploded with a *whooff.* Quickly he poured another, downed it, then grabbed a fireplace poker and staggered into the hallway.

"Sylvia!" he hollered, his voice echoing in the cavernous hallway. "Sylvia, you fucking female Judas, where are you?"

Swaying drunkenly, he slashed the poker at a hallway chandelier, ducking as a shower of splintered glass fell about him, a shard slicing his cheek. Enraged, blood dripping from his chin, he swung wildly at a vase and missed. "Sylvia! I'm going to fucking *kill* you, Sylvia!"

He stumbled along the hallway, throwing open doors, cursing, then stood trembling with fury before the door to her suite. He reached for the knob and turned it. Locked.

"You can't hide from me, Sylvia dear! I'll show you who's going to pay dearly!" He stepped back and slammed his foot against the door and it shot inward.

Sylvia sat hunched in her wheelchair, gnarled hands clasped upon her lap, a faint smile creasing her wrinkled face. "Are we having another marital spat, Warner dear? You seem terribly upset."

Warner Edelbrock swayed unsteadily in the doorway, the poker hanging at his side. "You've ruined me," he said in a hoarse voice, "You fucking bitch, you've been planning this for years."

"Have I, now," Sylvia said, now kneading her arthritic hands, "Let's say I began planning this when I learned what an evil, conniving, murderous bastard you are. I've suspected you since the day that first airplane of Coastal's crashed five months ago. Then when that young woman's airplane crashed, the woman you carried on with and later hoodwinked, and poor Milton Donnelley was found dead in the river, I was certain. You are filth, Warner Edelbrock, you have brazenly taken the lives of eighty-five innocent people, as well as Milton's, to feed your unrelenting greed, and you've ruined that young woman's life with the outrageous scheme you and that hoodlum Darcy cooked up. I shall see to it that you hang for all you've done."

"Lies. LIES!"

"You are scum, Warner. *Filth!* With your silver tongue you eased your way into the Preston fortune by deceiving first my father and later me. C. Gordon Preston's body was still warm in the grave when you turned on me, and from that day forward you have connived and amassed your little secret fortunes and still you wanted more. And, oh yes, I saw long ago that you possessed the capacity to kill in that deranged mind of yours."

Edelbrock gripped the poker tightly, tapping it against the side of his knee, "So they were right. You *are* insane. You've cooked all this up in your twisted little mind and planned it carefully, but you can't prove a word of it."

Sylvia smiled condescendingly, "I won't have to, Warner dear, others will do it for me. And if they don't execute you, then you shall certainly be a very old man when at last they turn you loose on the streets to grovel in garbage cans and beg for quarters. The Preston fortune as well as the airline shall long survive you, and you will share in none of it. Do you hear? You are finished, Warner Edelbrock! *Finished!"*

Suddenly he unleashed a guttural howl and lunged for her, slashing wildly with the poker as she quickly reversed and he stumbled to his knees. Pennington leaped from where he had hidden behind the door and hooked his arms under Edelbrock's, clasping his powerful hands in a hammerlock at the base of his neck. In spite of his drunkenness Edelbrock also possessed a great deal of strength and rose quickly to his feet, right hand still gripping the poker, then reached behind with his left and grabbed the back of Pennington's head. Gargling like an enraged animal, he ducked forward, lifting the big man from the floor, then suddenly rolled left and pounced on top of him. The heavy fall broke Pennington's grip about his neck, and Edelbrock

239

quickly rolled away and leaped to a crouch then lunged for his face with the poker.

"Lyle, look out!" Sylvia screamed.

Pennington deflected the thrust and sliced the side of his hand down in a crushing blow on Edelbrock's wrist. Off balance and roaring in pain, Edelbrock dropped the poker and kicked for Pennington's head, striking a glancing blow that momentarily stunned the big man. Sylvia's terrified shrieking echoed in the hallway as Edelbrock dove for the poker and grabbed it with his left hand. He quickly pinned Pennington's throat to the floor with his foot and raised the poker high overhead.

"No! No! Oh God, Warner, no!" Sylvia screamed.

Edelbrock began his murderous swing but a massive blow struck him from behind and he crumpled to the floor, the pointed end of a pick-ax buried in his skull.

Sylvia sat stunned, terrified as she stared at the grisly wound. Then she looked to the figure looming over him. "Romo!"

"Sí, señora. Romo. Por ustedes, por la señora. Por Jocko."

Dorine walked slowly beside Anne, her face just inches away, urging her on. "That's it, come on, you can do it. Do it! Do it! That's good, keep going. Come on, girl."

Anne struggled between the parallel bars, her shoulders aching from the strain of supporting her weight, concentrating on dragging first one foot forward then the other while her health aide cheered her on. "My shoulders, they're gonna give out...I can't..."

"Yes, you can. Three more steps and you're there. That's it. Two...one. There!" Dorine reached for her as she sagged and nearly fell. "Goo-ood girl, come on, you can rest for a moment. Here, sit down."

"You sound like my mother," Anne groaned as Dorine eased her onto a bench.

"I *am* your mother, until you're through this. Those are my orders, and in five minutes you're going to do it again."

"I want to go home."

"See? Now you sound like my daughter."

Anne kneaded her aching shoulders as she watched the others struggling through their routines in the physical therapy room at Queens Hospital. She supposed most were facing odds greater than hers, yet at the moment it didn't seem so. Still she had little control over her spasming legs, her muscles lacking the strength to support even her diminished body weight.

But she felt guilt nevertheless. All of her limbs were attached, while many she saw in the room were not so fortunate. Across the room was a man at least twenty years her senior also struggling at parallel bars, his face contorted with effort as he fought his way. His legs were those of a scarecrow; they weren't even legs, they were odd-looking prosthetics, but he showed no shame, only dogged determination. Grit, she supposed, wishing she could summon some. He and the others were perhaps worse for wear than she, at least physically, yet all were probably drawn by an invisible carrot before their noses, a carrot signifying *purpose* as reward for their agonizing efforts. Freedom to be gained and the fulfillment of another lease on a useful life.

But none would face condemnation, trial and a jury of their peers in less than a week. Prison. Life had dealt them a blow from which through their own efforts and perseverance they could strive to overcome; such rewards were squarely within their reach and not tugged away by the influence, greed, and corruption of others. Here before her was the essence of the human spirit fighting limitations imposed only by the physical self.

It was a struggle she envied.

She brushed ringlets of hair from her sweaty brow and sighed heavily. Much hope had crumbled last night after the unsettling call from Christopher. Hope that deflated as quickly as it had ballooned with the revelation of Hardison's find at PAE.

Oh, the evidence on her side was there all right: her ship that could only have crashed due to criminally-induced icing; Nash's prints on the aspirin bottle containing the codeine she had unwittingly ingested; the food coloring can Hardison found near the de-icing tankers—again Nash's prints; and the *someone* posing as Darcy on the de-icing tanker the night of her crash. All of it was useful, encouraging, *but*...

But the evidence that could clear her needed a link, a common denominator. Christopher was right: the evidence pointed in the right direction, but until Nash would surface or a definite link well beyond innuendo could be established clearly implicating Darcy and Edelbrock, it was all purely a matter of circumstance. Her only hope now for establishing the needed link lay with the SEC and IRS investigations of Darcy's and Edelbrock's accounts, and that one of them, probably Darcy, would turn evidence and testify to save his own skin. On the other hand, Donnelley's murder may now sweeten the investigative pot and draw even more focus upon them. They would have much answering to do, and maybe, just maybe in doing so Edelbrock would step on his corrupt dick.

"Okay, Anne. Time to have another go at it," Dorine announced, lifting her easily and positioning her hands on the parallel bars.

"Dorine, I—I'm just too tired. I can't do any more today."

Dorine gave her a nudge, "Yes, you can. What would you do if your apartment caught fire? You're making progress and you've got to build your strength, you never know when you might need it."

Strength? For what? To stand up at the defense table and soberly accept her sentence? To fight off the dykes in prison?

"Just do it, Anne. If nothing else, your mind needs an uplift. Don't you feel a sense of accomplishment when you reach the end of the bars?"

The bars. Anne dragged a foot forward, then the other, snickering at Dorine's innocent metaphor. Yes, it would be a great feeling of accomplishment dragging herself along the front of her cell until at last she reached the end of the bars.

Head hanging low, she steeled herself against the grinding pain in her shoulders as she struggled, watching the toes of her fresh white running shoes that wouldn't run, willing each foot forward until at last she reached the end. Gasping, she stared dizzily at the floor near her feet, unable to focus on a pair of men's shoes, the toes of which were nearly touching hers. Slowly she looked up.

"Good morning!" chirped Dr. David Levinson. "Now take a break and then let's see you do it again."

An hour later Anne lay soaking in a steaming tub in her apartment, eyes closed, her head resting on a folded towel while Dorine sat in the living room reading a magazine. If for nothing else, she kept doggedly at the painful exercises to gain strength enough to care for herself. It was embarrassing to have to be assisted on and off the toilet in a bathroom too small to admit a wheelchair, or to be helped from the tub like a child...

Suddenly there came a sharp rap on the bathroom door and Anne jerked awake from drowsiness. "What do you want, Dorine?"

"Anne, I need to come in. Right now!"

"So come in."

The expression on the stocky woman's face sent a chill through Anne's languid body and she quickly sat upright. "What is it? What's happened?"

Dorine quickly closed the bathroom door behind her. "Two men are here!" she hissed. "I opened the door and they pushed their way in. I told them to leave but they won't. They insist on talking to you."

Goosebumps suddenly prickled her body above the waterline, and instinctively she crossed her arms over her breasts. Had Edelbrock sent them? Was one of them Nash? "Is one of them tall, ugly?" she stammered, her teeth beginning to chatter.

Dorine quickly shook her head. "They're *suits*. Know what I mean? Suits? Federal cops? Anne, they've got badges."

Stunned, she looked up at Dorine incredulously. "You...you're sure?"

"They're not wearing uniforms but their IDs look real enough, and one has his coat open. He's wearing a gun."

Anne snagged a towel from the hook above. "Help me out of here." Dripping, she toweled herself quickly while Dorine supported her. Something's connected, she was certain, they were here for a statement or something, or maybe they've found Nash. Dorine helped her into a robe and into her chair, and she wheeled her way down the narrow hallway to the living room.

One was a young college-type, well-dressed and athletically built, the other was considerably older and also wearing a suit, but atop his head was a Stetson and his pants hung over a pair of pointed cowboy boots. Roach-kickers, she remembered someone saying.

They turned as she entered the room and the younger one stepped toward her. "Miss Ryan? I'm special agent Rossi, FBI, and this is James Gratz from the U.S. Marshal's office. I'm sorry, but I'll have to ask you to dress and come with us, please."

She stared at agent Rossi's ID held before her, then to Gratz who held only his jacket open, displaying a badge pinned inside and a large revolver tucked beneath his armpit. Something was wrong.

"Come with you? Can't you just ask your questions here?"

"I'm sorry, ma'am, I'm afraid there's much more to it than that," said agent Rossi, reaching inside his jacket. He removed a folded sheet of official paper and handed it to her. "We have a warrant for your arrest, Miss Ryan. Gratz, Mirandize her."

The cowboy-cop stepped forward as though reciting a proclamation. "Miss Ryan, you have the right to remain silent, anything you say can and will be used against you in a court of law," he drawled. "You have the right to an attorney, and if you cannot afford—"

"Stop it!" she shouted, then lowered her voice. "Just wait a minute. "What's happening? What is this? My trial's not until next week!"

"This has nothing to do with your trial, Miss Ryan, we're arresting you for conspiracy to commit murder," said agent Rossi, as Marshal Gratz reached for his cuffs.

Anne sat alone and fidgeting in the small musty room deep in the bowels of the Federal Courthouse, a guard posted outside. Her mind seemed snarled with perplexing questions, so quickly had it happened. There had been a brief arraignment before a federal magistrate while the charges were read, and she had been allowed to call Christopher before being remanded into custody.

Now as she waited for him she couldn't comprehend it all. Conspiracy to commit murder of Captain Ray Thompson and his thirty-seven passengers and crew aboard Coastal Airlines flight 288, a chilling charge somehow tied to a TransCon stock deal of some sort of which she knew nothing. Edelbrock had scored again somehow, a final slug below the belt for her incautious confrontation with him...

The door opened and Christopher walked in. "Earl! Am I ever glad to see you. What is all this? What's going on?"

He laid his briefcase on the table and drew up a chair. "Trouble, and plenty of it, I'm afraid."

"No kidding, tell me something I don't know at two hundred-fifty dollars an hour. What's this murder conspiracy thing? I don't understand it! What's it have to do with Ray's crash?"

Christopher drew out a legal pad and uncapped his pen, jotted a quick note and then looked at her. "I was hoping you could fill me in. I find it a bit confusing too, but here's the way the U.S. Attorney sees it. They now know you had a long-standing and intimate relationship with Edelbrock, much of which occurred during the time when he was profiting from Coastal's demise, profiting in a way much different from what we thought. He wasn't buying up TransCon stock; he was buying *down* on Coastal. Short sales, they call them. More about that later. Anyway, the SEC and IRS gave the prosecutor all the stuff you gave them, and more—"

"Wait a minute! Just because I was his bed partner doesn't also mean that I was involved with him in all this financial mumbo-jumbo. His accounts ought to show that. You won't see my name anywhere in that stuff, so how can they implicate me in any of this? Is boffing the bad guy a federal crime?"

"It is if he's sharing the profits with you."

Anne sat back heavily in her wheelchair stunned, bewildered. "*Profits?* Sharing *what* profits? He never... Wait a minute—if I'm here in jail for this silly charge, then he must be too. Is that what he's telling them? Do they believe him just because he says it's so? Did you tell them that he's just trying to get back at me for accusing him? That's what this is all about. I just know it."

Christopher stared at her for a moment, his expression puzzled. "The records the SEC gave the U.S. Attorney show that the day before the crash of Coastal 288, Ray Thompson's flight, Warner Edelbrock gave you 5,000 shares of TransCon stock worth about $160,000. A week after the crash its market value zoomed to over $300,000. The prosecutor thinks there's a definite link, and thus the conspiracy to commit murder—the murder of Captain Ray Thompson and thirty-seven others aboard his flight. The flight that was supposed to have been yours from which, they believe, you conveniently trip-traded with an ulterior motive. They think you trip-traded that night because the weather was crappy, freezing, just what you two were waiting for. Perfect for the fake glycol setup to work. And being a pilot, they think the method was your idea."

Anne gripped the arms of her wheelchair, eyes wide. "What?" She sat forward quickly. "*What?* Earl, this is crazy! He gave me *stock* to conspire to *kill* people? Just where is this stock supposed to be? Should I look in my purse? My sugar jar?" *Up my ass? Was that what the guards were probing for?*

"It's in your account right now at the firm of Pickard, Wilmott, and DeLeury." He reached into his briefcase. "Here's a copy of it."

She took the copy and stared at it, disbelieving. Hers was the sole name on the account, and sure enough, it showed 5,000 shares of TransCon transferred into the account, transaction dated last November the ninth. It was the day before Ray's crash.

Christopher handed her another document and she saw that it was labeled *Warner E. Edelbrock, subsidiary account.* She saw by the dates that the account was opened the day before Ray's crash and closed the day after.

"What's...what's this?" Anne asked, bewildered.

"One of four accounts he had. The records show that he opened this account with the purchase of 5,000 shares of TransCon, then transferred the shares to your account and promptly closed it."

"I don't...I still don't see..."

Christopher held up his hand. "Let me finish and we can talk about it. You need to hear it all to understand how they see it. Okay?"

Anne sank her face into her hands. "Go on," she mumbled.

"Okay," he said, leaning back in his chair and locking his hands behind his neck. "Here it is: They think that as his lover you were Edelbrock's inside pipeline to Coastal flight operations while he was trying to force the airline to its knees for hostile takeover. Then, for $300,000 worth of TransCon stock, you conspired with him to help things along by concocting a method to bring a ship down by substituting a faux de-icing solution. But when the weather was right for it you happened to be flying that night, so you trip-traded at the last minute so someone else would go down with the ship." He looked up from his notes and saw that she still had her face buried. "Anne, are you listening?"

She looked up, her eyes bloodshot, misting. "Yes."

"So the ship went down, TransCon stock shot up, you made a bundle and so did he, and no one was the wiser. Neat deal, they think. Especially the faked glycol idea that probably only a pilot could think up."

Anne shook her head, regaining her composure. "It's flawed. The whole idea is flawed."

"I hoped you'd say that. How so?"

"Earl, think about it! Look at me! A useless, damn cripple! Do they think I wanted this? That's how I was nearly killed! Don't they see? Why would I engineer Ray's crash, collect a bundle, and then set up my own aircraft to crash, and come out looking like *this*? Earl, they've got it ass-backwards! He tried twice to kill *me*!"

Christopher nodded. "I believe you, but that's not the way they see it. They think he tried *once*, not twice as you see it. They think he tried to kill you on Coastal 193 to silence you, close the loop, eliminate a witness against him in the event he couldn't contain you. The drugs were an added measure to have you blamed and put away in case he failed."

Anne clenched her fists and slammed them on the armrests. "*NO!* It was *me* who proved how *both* aircraft had been iced, *me* who tipped the SEC to take a hard look at what Edelbrock was doing! Why...why would I do that if—"

"I argued that. But in the prosecutor's words, it was a clever ploy on your part to cause them to ask the same questions. It's a logic method often used by criminals, voluntarily offering apparently incriminating evidence that would make them the too-obvious choice as the guilty, thus shifting the focus elsewhere."

Anne spun her wheelchair around, her head spinning in confusion. "Oh Earl, this is double-think. I can't keep it all straight."

"You're going to have to, Anne, but now at least we've got some time to work up a strategy. They're putting the felony manslaughter trial—the drugs—on hold, in keeping with their

248

new theory that you weren't culpable in that one. That Edelbrock tried to get rid of you on Coastal 193 to protect himself."

Anne spun around again, facing him, her eyes blazing.
"Thank god for small favors, Earl. Now it's just *murder*, is that
it?"

"Anne, I'll file a motion—"

"Oh, *fuck* your motions, Earl! The only motion you know is
how to jerk off for two hundred-fifty dollars an hour. And
meanwhile I'm locked up in here to rot."

"Anne, I—"

She backhanded his briefcase, knocking it to the floor, and
began orbiting the tiny room in her wheelchair, careening off the
walls. "Don't *Anne* me! Just go out and do your job, Earl!"

"Anne, stop this! Listen to me!"

Suddenly her wheelchair slammed into a metal wastebasket,
alerting the guard outside. The door opened and he leaned in.
"What's goin' on? You okay, Mr. Christopher?"

"It's okay," he said, waving him away. "Just...an accident.
Sorry." When the door closed he turned to her. "You're not
making it any easier for me to do my job, you know. They've
got a case as well as evidence—"

She slammed her hand on the table again. "*What* evidence?
Stock I'm supposed to have received? And even if I did, what
does it prove? No jury would ever believe—"

Christopher reached into his briefcase and handed her a
document. "They will when they see this. Suppose you tell me
about it, Anne. Then maybe I can do my job more to your liking
for two hundred-fifty dollars an hour."

Anne snatched the paper from him and scanned it. Suddenly
the flush of anger drained from her face and her chest tightened.
She felt like she was suffocating. Like the document showing a
transfer of stock to an account in her name, this too was dated
the day before Ray's crash. She remembered the note well:

Anne,

Things are all set for tomorrow night at La Guardia. With the weather the way it is, the timing couldn't be better. I'll be waiting for you in a company LearJet (N64TC) at the general aviation ramp. If you decide to go ahead with this and wait until the last minute to trip-trade, then just to be on the safe side I think you'd better change out of uniform. It's less obvious that way, and less chance of your being recognized boarding the Lear right after. You DO attract attention, love, and the fewer questions asked, the better.

Other than that, quit worrying about the risk and suspicious eyes, will you? My people can be trusted—they wouldn't dare otherwise. You know how I can be.

Besides, aren't the rewards worth it?

Always,
Warner

"Oh, Jesus," Anne murmured, dropping her face in her hands.

"Yeah, he may be able to help you better than I can. And he doesn't charge two-fifty an hour. You want to tell me about it?"

She looked at him, her expression stricken. "Where...did they find this?"

"In your apartment after they booked you. It was in your desk drawer. Is it real?"

She nodded slowly, staring at the cinder wall. "Yes, it's real. But it's not...what it appears."

Christopher leaned forward on his elbows and sighed. "I guess I don't have to tell you that with the stock and all, this gives them a pretty tight case."

Anne looked away, her devastation total. "It's no longer circumstantial, is it?"

Christopher suddenly stood and began pacing the small room, tugging at his chin. "Not by much. Tell me what it means, Anne. Tell me all of it."

She tossed her hands and shrugged, staring at the floor. "It was a date. The weather had been lousy, cold, he said that because of it the timing was perfect for a trip to sunshine. So he said let's fly to Nassau for the weekend. I told him maybe, that I'd have to trip-trade in order to go. So I thought about it overnight, almost decided not to, then at the last minute I said fine. I trip-traded with Ray, changed clothes, and boarded the LearJet. You know the rest. "

"His letter is dated the day before Ray Thompson's crash."

"I know, I know. A courier from his office gave me the note the night before the crash. And the next night, just before the flight, I decided I'd go." Suddenly she looked up at him, tears streaming down her cheeks. "Ray Thompson was a friend! His wife was my friend, their ten year-old daughter, too! Do you know how many nights I've laid awake agonizing over this? That I trip-traded with him just so I could go get laid and tan my bare ass? And then he gets killed because I did? Do you? Well, *do you*?"

Christopher stood at the window, staring at the heavy wire mesh. "Yeah," he said, turning. "I think I know you well enough to know that it's been eating you alive." He reached for the letter, scanned it, then tossed it on the table. "It sounds pretty clandestine, sneaky, this business about changing out of uniform, perfect timing, risk, suspicious eyes. Was that because of Sylvia? He was afraid it would get back to her?"

Anne nodded, wiping her eyes. "Probably. He never said so, in fact he denied it, but I think that's what he was afraid of. That and what TransCon and other Coastal pilots might think if they saw me with him. With the guy who was bludgeoning our airline to its knees."

"And the `rewards'? What were they?"

She let her breath out in a rush. "What do you think?" she said wearily.

"I think Edelbrock had a monumental ego."

"Close."

"And a wankie to match." He saw her snicker as he hoped she would, lightening her mood.

"Closer. The great stud, Warner Edelbrock. Monied, macho, and meaty. His gift to womanhood. A glorious reward for spreading their thighs for His Royal Highness." She nodded, looking away. "Yeah, that was my reward as he saw it. Now look at me."

Christopher shook his head and turned away again, stretching and cracking his knuckles. "It's going to be rough-going on the witness stand, Anne. You're going to have to tell a jury and the court all of this." He turned to face her. "That damned letter can be read either way. It can be read the way the prosecutor wants it to read, or the way you say it is. But the existence of 5,000 shares of TransCon stock placed in your account by Edelbrock may convince a jury that the 'rewards' were far greater than what you're going to tell them. On the other hand, if you had no knowledge of it, weren't involved, then we have to know why he put it there so we can rebut it."

Anne wheeled quickly to his side and gripped his forearm. "Earl, you've got to convince them to break Edelbrock. Break him down, get a confession. He can explain the letter, he'll have to. It incriminates him too. If they've got him in here for trying to murder me and my passengers as well as Ray and his, surely they could press him harder. Earl, I *know* him, he's lost everything now. He's got nothing more to lose! I *know* he'll crack if they put the pressure on, and maybe we can at least find out who and where his thug Nash is. Then you can pressure Nash to plea bargain, or whatever they call it, to incriminate Edelbrock. I'd even be willing—"

Christopher frowned and leaned back in his chair, studying her desperate expression. Then it occurred to him. "You don't know, do you. About...him. About Edelbrock."

His expression was unsettling and suddenly she felt nauseous, the room tilting dizzily. She sensed what was coming and looked up at him. "What...about him? What do you mean?"

"Warner Edelbrock is dead."

John Haviland Williams

TWELVE

Warner Edelbrock is dead.

Christopher's stunning revelation still echoed in her mind as she wheeled herself around the perimeter of a cell measuring thirteen slate-gray tiles by nine, chasing and crushing bugs beneath rubber tires, anything to while away the time.

After twenty-four hours of incarceration she at last realized that Edelbrock's untimely departure now left only one person accountable for his misdeeds—she, unless Darcy's feet could be put to the fire or Nash was found. With Darcy, Christopher speculated, lay her best chance, though a slim one. Being closest to Edelbrock he might plead to the lesser charges of tax fraud and insider-trading in exchange for revealing all, including Nash's identity and whereabouts, which could help her case a great deal. On the other hand, with Edelbrock silenced, Darcy could well say as much or little as he wanted, or worse, completely disavow any knowledge of the matters involving the crashes as well as the damning bribe, and leave the existing evidence to incriminate her. Certainly with the lingering echoes of her explosive confrontation in Edelbrock's office, Darcy would be little inclined to accommodate her. And worse, he could affirm the prosecution's case as a material witness against her, saying he was well aware of the conspiracy, had tried without success to dissuade them.

Indeed, her accusing confrontation with special focus on Darcy had been a strategic error, Christopher had reminded. And she was painfully aware that of Darcy's likely choices, now that the dung had entered the revolving agitator, he was certain to be hostile.

Anne agonized and puzzled over these scenarios, but there were so many what-ifs it soon became confusing. But one thing was certain: without a living Edelbrock to deny or otherwise affirm that Darcy and Nash were significantly involved, Christopher had said that the absence of any co-conspirator in a jointly committed crime gave no relief to those remaining. Edelbrock's death now left her stranded, alone and in his place, and the legacy of his damning letter when presented to a jury would leave little question of her guilt.

There seemed no escape and Anne Ryan was terrified.

She surveyed her dismal surroundings for what seemed the squintillionth time in as many hours. It was little larger than the bathroom in her apartment, yet except for the creepy-crawlers it was surprisingly cleaner and spoke little for her own domesticity. The food was bland and starchy but edible, and most of the female guards civil enough, but those who had strip-searched her and probed deep within her body crevices were derisive and coarse, their fingers lingering too long.

She knew that the solitary quarters in which she was incarcerated were only temporary until after the trial. If convicted she would be caged with the masses, no longer would she have the "luxury" of a cell to herself, she would be just one of "the gals" fending for herself amid slashers and murderers, child molesters, drug-running biker-ladies, and...oh, Jesus, the AIDS-infested bull dykes.

She felt her resolve slipping; the seething rage that had fueled her determination had been doused with a flood of bitter truths. Despair overwhelmed her, realizing that each precious particle of progress gained in her frantic search for evidence now seemed to have turned back upon her. In her attempt to nail Edelbrock she had unwittingly steered the SEC to yet another hidden trap he had carefully laid, obviously anticipating her every move. And she sensed that somewhere at this moment he was chuckling derisively, just as he had that day on the slopes when he suckered her to *The Leap*. He may now be shoveling coal into the blast furnaces of hell, but he was chuckling nevertheless.

It was his way.

A lump welled deep in her throat and she fought back tears of bitter defeat compounded with fright of what lay ahead. Then came a rattling of keys in the lock and the creaking steel door of her cell swung open. She spun her wheelchair around.

"Come with me, Ryan," rasped the female guard.

Heart thumping wildly, she searched the woman's hooded eyes, terrified that it would be another of the so-called strip-searches, a euphemism for digital rape. "Where are we going?"

"Come *now*, Ryan, and don't give me no shit!"

Slowly she wheeled herself toward the doorway but the guard stood in her way, glaring, hands extended and palms together symbolically. Anne held out her hands and the guard cinched the cuffs tightly, then patted her cheek. "You're learning, Ryan. You'll get used to it."

As the guard wheeled her down the long hallway that smelled of a public rest room, she realized that in little more than twenty-four hours the jail system was already gaining its intended psychological effect: Demoralization of the accused and subservience to rigid authority. A sort of boot camp, initiation rites for the Sorority of the Damned. As far as the guards were concerned you were convicted and treated as such, a threat to society, shorn of your rights, and thus in need of stern correc-

257

tive measures. You felt fear deep in your bowels, a loose, churning sensation, suffering as the familiar bonds of proud confidence and dignity crumbled. You were no longer your own person. A non-entity, you belonged to *them* now. You were a ward of the state. Kenneled.

They stopped before a windowed door of lesser strength and the guard opened it and pushed her chair in.

There, hunched in her wheelchair, arthritic hands clutched in her lap, sat Edelbrock's widow. "Sylvia! Oh!"

"Ten minutes," the guard warned.

"Hello, my dear," Sylvia said, smiling pleasantly and easing her wheelchair toward Anne's. "I came as soon as I heard. I'm so sorry."

Suddenly Anne could no longer contain her tears and she buried her face in cuffed hands as Sylvia eased alongside. She felt gentle hands touch her shoulders, pulling her close, and she sagged against Sylvia's shoulder as the shuddering sobs came.

For precious minutes she let the torrent run its course as Sylvia rocked her gently against her breast. She smelled Sylvia's faint essence of rosewater, reminiscent of her grandmother of long ago and she wanted to burrow into the old woman's lap, escape the terrifying realities and once again become a child.

"There, dear. Let it all out, and in a few minutes perhaps we can talk, if you feel up to it."

At last Anne sat up, brushing the backs of her cuffed hands against tear-streaked cheeks and took the offered tissue. "Thank you. Oh, God, I'm so embarrassed—I just couldn't help it. I feel so alone, so...confused."

"I know how it feels, my dear. For so long I've been imprisoned in this contraption as well as feeling a prisoner in my own home. Now, at least I've been released from one of my prisons, however dreadful the circumstances."

"Oh, Sylvia, I'm so sorry about—I mean, I feel so sorry for you. It must have been awful."

"Yes, it was," she said without emotion. "Utterly terrifying, but in God's own way I suppose it was a trial for me; rain before shine, as they say. I have endured Warner's evil for twenty-eight years, and while the Good Lord may strike me down for saying this, his death was a blessing however ugly it was. Many more than I have suffered at his hands over the years, and I believe that my good Christian man, Romo, was an instrument of the Lord's wrath."

Anne reached for the old woman's hands. "Sylvia, I'm so glad you came to see me, and I'm grateful for your support when you visited me in the hospital, that you were at my side during the NTSB hearing, but I—I feel guilty about it. Warner and I—"

The old woman gripped Anne's hands tightly, "Shhh-shhh. Not another word. I've known about that since the beginning. Warner is—*was* so naively transparent, and you're certainly not the first female he's hoodwinked with his wretched, silver-tongued guile. I suppose that like the others he told you he had my blessing as well, didn't he?"

Anne looked away. "Yes. Yes, that's what he said."

Sylvia Edelbrock tugged at Anne's wrist. "Look at me. Look at me, child. You have succumbed to carnal flesh at the hands of an evil and unscrupulous man. He has lied to you, he has deceived you, and now he has left you with his corrupt legacy. I bear no grudge whatever against you, my dear, for the Lord asks that we forgive. That I have done."

Anne's eyes misted as the woman's hands gripped her wrists, and she bowed her head. "I'm so sorry, Sylvia."

Sylvia squeezed Anne's hands once again. "Anne Ryan, the Lord will heal your emotional wounds in time, just as he is healing your body now. But now you must put your sorrows behind you and fight, young lady, fight this terrible burden Warner has unjustly put upon you."

Anne raised her head and held Sylvia's gaze, her manacled fists clenched, emotions suddenly flooding over again. "I have nothing else to fight *with!* I'm *it*, Sylvia! He made my plane

259

crash, he drugged me to make it look worse, and then he secretly put 5,000 shares of stock into an account in my name to make it look like I took a payoff for killing all those people! And now he's *dead* and I can't prove anything!"

The door suddenly opened. "Everything all right?" asked the guard.

Sylvia waved the guard away, then turned to Anne. "Perhaps you can't prove anything—not by yourself, but you must remember that I was married to that evil man for twenty-eight years. I know more about his and Philip Darcy's corrupt ways than anyone, and I'll help you to sort this out if you'll just work with me."

"Work with you? How? Nothing I've done so far has helped anything but to get me in deeper trouble. And now I'm caged like an animal. I can't—"

"Oh, yes you can. Between what I know and what you know, I'm certain we can make some sense of this and eventually prove your innocence. But first we must get you out of this—this dungeon, so that we can go to work. There isn't much time. Tomorrow is your bail hearing and we'll begin with that."

A faint glimmer of hope was emerging, yet the offer seemed unbelievable. Could Sylvia really have evidence which, when added to what little she and Christopher possessed, would prove sufficient to overcome the charges? And if so, why hadn't she offered earlier? More, why would Sylvia even want to help? Her mind reeled as more puzzling questions arose, yet here was an unrefusable offer of assistance. What was there to lose?

"Are...are you saying that you'd help with my bail? I don't know if they're even going to allow bail. Christopher said—"

"My dear, think of how this is going to appear to the news media as you sit before the hearing judge tomorrow. There you are manacled and sitting in a wheelchair, a helpless cripple, a broken and defenseless woman with no criminal record. Do you think for one minute that the judge will deny bail because you're a threat on the streets? Nonsense. And yes, of course I'm going to help you with your bail. Oh, they'll likely set a stiff price on your freedom, but I'm willing to pay it. It's the Christian thing to do. After all, it was my husband who got you into this mess, and I have the resources to help get you out of it."

Anne eyed Sylvia warily, torn, wanting so desperately to shout for joy, to hug this marvelously compassionate and under-standing woman who, from the beginning, had shown interest in helping. But in recent weeks she had learned well of the pitfalls, the emotional dangers lurking when she placed too much hope on apparent means to her vindication. Now she was cautious; but she also was not foolish—there was little choice but to con-tinue the fight and here was the opportunity. Still, it seemed too good to be true. And someone had once said, *if anything seems too good to be true, then it usually--*

"Sylvia, I don't want to sound ungrateful, but why do you want to help me? Why would you do all of this for me?"

"I would be very disappointed in you, my dear, had you not asked that question. I suppose I'm a selfish woman, but with your freedom we can help one another. Warner, in his greed and corruption, has left me with a positively awful mess. My father, C. Gordon Preston, God rest his soul, was one of the great pio-neers of commercial aviation and he alone built Trans-Continental Airways Express to become the world-class carrier that it is today. But in a fortnight Warner Edelbrock has nearly destroyed all my father worked for."

Sylvia's eyes suddenly widened, "Just look at what he's *done!* All of his damning advertisements and other repugnant actions against Coastal Airlines over the past year, and the crashes for which I'm now absolutely certain he was responsi-ble, and then his gobbling up of Coastal Airlines which prompted these SEC investigations. Good heavens, all of this gives the appearance that the entire airline, *my* airline, is cor-rupt!" Sylvia suddenly clapped her hands and looked at the ceiling. "My *Lord!*"

Slowly she lowered her head and once again began kneading her arthritic hands. "Only by clearing you, my dear, and proving that he alone, aided only by a small circle of his henchmen scheming to profit for themselves from the capture of Coastal Airlines, can I hope to restore TransCon's great name that my father established long ago."

It made sense. Still, something troubled Anne and she reached for Sylvia's hands and took them gently in hers. "But what do you know? What evidence do you have to prove that Warner did all these things?"

"I can't tell you just yet, my dear. It's better that you not know until the authorities have Philip Darcy in custody. You may be in some danger."

Anne sat bolt upright. "Then he *was* involved! I'm not so stupid after all."

Sylvia's slender nostrils suddenly flared, her eyes narrowing, and she leaned toward Anne. "He was in the thick of it," she hissed. "As guilty as they come."

"But do you know anything about this man Nash? His fingerprints keep popping up; it seems he's the key to everything."

Sylvia leaned back in her wheelchair and waved deferentially, "Oh, a mere minion, from what I've been able to learn. A hired thug taking orders from Warner and Philip. But he's neither here nor there; with Warner dead, Philip Darcy is the key to unraveling this dreadful mess."

"So why don't they just arrest him, or have they already?"

Sylvia sighed and tossed her hands, "It seems the man has fled the country."

Anne felt the heaviness of defeat in her chest. It had happened again, the golden ring snatched from her grasp. It seemed as though someone was watching her every move, tuning in on her thoughts, her hopes, waiting for the opportune moment and then yanking the rug from beneath her once again. At last she looked up wearily and sighed. "So that leaves Nash. We have to find Nash."

"Yes, I suppose that's our only hope now, but I've never met the man. I have no idea what he looks like, but I have many loyalists at TransCon and perhaps someone who was close to Warner but not involved may be able to tell us."

Anne leaned and once again took Sylvia's hands. "I need all the help I can get, and if you put up my bail I promise that you won't regret it."

Sylvia smiled, "No, my dear, I'm certain that I won't."

The door opened and the guard entered. "Time's up."

Sylvia gathered her shawl about her and laid her hand upon Anne's knee. "I suggest that you not discuss our conversation with your attorney just yet. There is risk, you know. If he were to discuss it with the U.S. Attorney and word spreads that we've joined forces, Darcy and Nash may go into deeper hiding. Or worse, they may come for *us*!" Sylvia shook her finger at Anne. "Not a word to a soul. No one. As things stand at the moment, Darcy and Nash may well think they're home free. Let's let them keep thinking that. And in so doing we'll show them what a couple of wheelchair-ridden scheming women can do, shall we?"

The guard tapped Anne's shoulder. "Come along, Ryan."

"No, wait. Just ten seconds." She turned to Sylvia, "But what about the bail? My attorney will have to know about that."

Sylvia nodded. "Of course, but his knowing of the bail won't matter; what matters is that for the moment no one is to suspect or learn of what I know, what I have told you. Except for Pennington and Romo, I am alone in a very large house. Do you understand? These men who worked for Warner have killed to gain their profits and they will kill again and again to retain them. Look what happened to poor Milton Donnelley."

"Darcy?" Anne whispered.

"Yes," Sylvia hissed. "And Nash—he does their dirty work."

Anne nodded as the guard swung her wheelchair around, then she gripped the wheel, stopping it, and turned to Sylvia.

"I'm so grateful for all you're doing for me, I—I just don't know how I'll ever be able to repay you."

Sylvia smiled. "Please don't worry yourself about it, dear, I shall reap my own rewards. But there is a condition."

"What's that?"

"That upon arranging your bail you are to be remanded to my custody, for your protection of course. You are as valuable to me as I am to you." Sylvia inclined her head, her eyes twinkling mischievously. "You see? I told you that I'm a selfish old woman."

As the guard pushed her through the doorway she recognized Sylvia's hulking and unsmiling attendant, Pennington, looming outside. On impulse she grabbed the wheels, jerking her wheelchair to a stop. "Hello, Mr. Pennington," she said brightly, quickly offering a cuffed hand, "I guess we'll soon be seeing a lot of each other, thanks to Mrs. Edelbrock. She's a remarkable woman."

Startled, Lyle Pennington glanced at the guard then reached uncertainly for Anne's manacled hand. "Yes, she is."

Back in her cell, Anne's wariness about Sylvia's intentions had at last dissolved, and she chided herself for acting so paranoid, but Pennington's presence had suddenly tweaked her curiosity. She supposed she had a hang-up about fingerprints and that every tall, sinister-looking male was suspect as the elusive Nash, whose capture seemed the only remaining key to her freedom. But her hand-shaking ploy of moments ago with Pennington had succeeded and it had failed. He had hesitated long enough with his hand in full view for her to see that no broad, deep scar was apparent on his index finger, a scar that the experts said would be obvious, large enough to encircle the entire finger as though it had once been severed near the first knuckle.

Rain and sleet pelted Earl Christopher as he shielded his face with his briefcase and trotted up the courthouse steps. The electronic doors hissed open and a blast of blessed warm air

ɔlew in his face. He shrugged off his topcoat and laid his brief-
ɔase on the X-ray conveyor, then quickly stepped through the
metal detector.

"Morning, Earl," said William Lorenzo, the U.S. Attorney
who would try Anne's case.

Christopher snatched up his coat and briefcase and took up
stride with the prosecutor as they headed for the banks of elevators. "That's a fact, Bill, glad you're learning to recognize one."

"Earl, my friend, you disappoint me. Still testy about the
case, aren't you?"

"You could call it that. Tell me, with your myopic but
twenty-twenty prosecutorial vision that sees only what it wants
to see, is it raining and sleeting or is the sun shining and it's a
fine day?"

"If I were seeing it through your eyes, I'd say the sun was
shining. I hear your beguiling client's going to take a walk today."

"In a manner of speaking, you're right. Edelbrock's widow
is footing the bail."

Lorenzo snickered while waving to the Governor and his
entourage leaving the building. "Figures. All in the family, as I
see it."

Christopher stopped short and turned. "What? You think
it's one big, happy family? That they're all in on this?"

"Why not? Maybe you're the one who's myopic, Earl. Ever
pause to think about that? And let me tell you one other thing:
the family's getting smaller every day."

"Meaning?"

Lorenzo leaned close, "Meaning we have another body,
Earl. First was Donnelley, then Edelbrock, now Darcy. The
King and his pawns. All fall down."

Christopher was stunned. "When?"

"About six this morning in a landfill near JFK."

"Any suspects?"

"Why, counselor? Looking for another client?"

"I'm looking for anything that can help the client I have, goddammit!"

"Your defrocked client, debaucheress of the not-so-friendly skies, is beyond help, Earl, and I intend to see that she gets fifteen to twenty to reconsider her unladylike deeds. But since you're interested, you'll be among the first to know when we announce a suspect. I said *announce*, Earl, not *locate*. Drop by my office later this afternoon and we'll talk. There's something I'll let you in on if you'll keep it close, like any good officer of the court."

The ride to Sylvia Edelbrock's estate far out on Long Island was an exciting freedom spawned of two and one-half days of incarceration in a dank and smelly cell that had seemed an eternity. Although her trial for murder conspiracy now loomed, she felt re-energized and once again filled with hope and determination. With Sylvia's help and intimate knowledge of Warner's affairs and those with whom he associated, she might at last gather sufficient evidence to persuade a jury of her innocence.

Earl Christopher had been reluctant, even incredulous about her release into Sylvia's custody, had told her of the prosecutor's views of "all in the family," of Darcy's body having been found, yet what choice had she? Now, with Darcy dead, her hopes of acquittal shrank even more. Sylvia was all she had. But Christopher hadn't been the only nay-sayer. Gordy had flown into an absolute rage, but she had nailed him for it. "*You* try sitting on *your* ass in a cold concrete cell, twice daily the guards dropping your pants and bending you over a table while they poke and probe up your butt for weapons or contraband, or maybe just a feel." That had sobered him. "So I'm going, Gordy, got it?" And that had convinced him.

Anne savored the lovely rural scenery as Pennington drove, yet she now regretted her emotionally charged venting upon Gordy. When they reached Sylvia's she would call him, apologize.

266

A half-hour later Lyle Pennington swung the luxurious van between the gate pillars and onto a sweeping driveway leading to the Edelbrock Tudor-style estate known as *FieldCrest*. A late season snow had dusted the trees and grounds, yet the sun was shining and Anne was grateful for it. Such a contrast from a cell. At the top of a knoll stood the estate, and she suddenly felt as though the brief excursion from the courthouse had transcended centuries. That she had passed through some sort of time warp to Gothic times. Here before her were the mansion, grounds, and all the trappings of English nobility. It was breathtaking, awesome.

Pennington stopped the van before the grand portico and slid the side door open, lowered the hydraulic ramp, and released the clamps retaining Anne's and Sylvia's wheelchairs. The crisp air was fresh, smelling of pine and cedar, and Anne inhaled deeply as Pennington assisted them down the ramp. Clouds of steam rose from their breath as they wheeled along the freshly shoveled walk to the entryway where Pennington held the massive double doors open.

Anne had expected a butler in tails to greet them, but the doorman seemed no more than a smiling peasant from Tijuana, his wide-brimmed hat held humbly before him as he bowed and genuflected to their presence. "Buenas tardes, señora y señor."

"And good afternoon to you too, my dear Romo," Sylvia said, "I'd like you to meet Miss Anne Ryan who will be our guest for several days."

Romo bowed again, "Con mucho gusto, señorita," he said to Anne, then turned to Sylvia, "La señorita es muy linda."

Sylvia laughed, "Indeed she is. Anne, he says you're very pretty."

Anne smiled and of habit glanced at Romo's hands. His fingers were clasped around the brim of his hat and she could see them clearly. They were the gnarled hands of a laborer, thick and rough, deeply scarred. So was the right forefinger, she noticed. *Let it go, Anne,* she reminded. *Stop this nonsense before you loose your mind!*

Romo bowed again to Sylvia as he closed the doors, then made a sweeping gesture toward the cavernous foyer. "Sus almuerzo esta listo, señora."

"Thank you, Romo. Come along, Anne, lunch is ready."

They enjoyed a leisurely lunch in Pennington's absence, although Anne sensed he was hovering nearby, and at last she pushed her plate aside, sipped her coffee, then turned to Sylvia. "Did Romo cook that? It was wonderful."

"He did indeed. Not only is he a wizard in the gardens, but a fair chef as well. That is, if you can tolerate his penchant for fiery chilies and other south-of-the-border delicacies of questionable content. So long as you don't ask him what it is, I can practically guarantee you'll enjoy whatever he prepares."

"Has he been with you long?"

"Oh my, yes. He's been in the family for decades. A regular fixture, that one, and if it hadn't been for him I wouldn't be here at this moment nor would you. Nor would Pennington, for that matter."

"He's not going to be prosecuted, is he? For saving your lives?"

Sylvia waved the notion away, "Oh my, no. Justifiable homicide, they called it. The district attorney saw it for what it was, and that was that."

"Still, the funeral must have been difficult for you, even under the circumstances."

Sylvia closed her eyes and bowed her head, then took a deep breath and looked up at the chandelier over the table. "Yes, it was. He was still my husband regardless of how evil he was, and twenty-eight years of marriage is a long time. Often I find that I have to remind myself of why he's gone, so easy is it for the mind to become quickly nostalgic of better days as though shielding one from reality." She turned and grasped Anne's hand, "Do you know that I even feel guilt when enjoying release from tension and fear of that man?"

Guilt? That she couldn't understand. She despised Warner and that would never change, but she searched her mind for some comforting platitude to avoid being rude. Finding none she simply nodded.

An uncomfortable minute of silence followed until she thought of Pennington, wondering about the strange man with the frightening appearance who seemed to tend to Sylvia's every whim. "Tell me about Mr. Pennington. He seems an...interesting man."

Sylvia brightened, apparently grateful for the change of topic. "To say that Lyle Pennington is `interesting' does him little justice, my dear, but of course you, like most others, couldn't be expected to know otherwise. He's a very private person—sinister, I suppose some would say because of his un-usual appearance. Yet unless someone speaks for him he is far too modest to admit to being the courageous hero that he truly is. You see, Lyle Pennington was awarded not only the Purple Heart and the Silver Star, but the nation's highest medal of valor as well—the Congressional Medal of Honor, by President John-son, and he later served as a White House advisor on POWs and MIAs to two presidents."

"So he was in Viet Nam? Is that how...how he—"

"How he came to have that ghastly deformity of his skull? Yes. He almost single-handedly saved an entire regiment from annihilation, then a bomb of some sort exploded nearby and the shrapnel took off the top of his head. Few have ever survived that sort of grievous injury, yet his brain was miraculously left intact and surgeons were able to graft large sections of flesh from his back to cover it over. He has lost none of his mental faculties, yet he must be careful to protect the top of his head as there is no longer any bone to protect his brain."

Anne sat stunned, her stomach churning, awash in guilt for her earlier but fortunately unspoken thoughts of his frightening ugliness.

Sylvia patted her hand. "Beneath that formidable countenance with which he is now cursed, is a kind and intelligent man. He is also intensely loyal to those who care for and understand him, my dear, and you may rest assured that Lyle Pennington will protect us well in these days that you're here. Now, shall we retire to the sunroom, Anne? We have much to discuss."

They certainly did, and as afternoon became evening Sylvia filled in much of the puzzle that had daunted Anne for months. Still, there seemed little tangible proof of Warner Edelbrock's crimes and those of his associates, yet the convincing testimony Sylvia could provide would likely seem credible to a jury, considering the source, even in spite of the prosecutor's assertions of "all in the family". But there remained the question of the elusive Lt. Nash, apparently the sole surviving link in the heinous scheme that had been Edelbrock's.

"So you see," Sylvia continued, "I had long suspected Warner's shady dealings with Coastal Airlines stock, but only through my association with Milton Donnelley did I learn the truth—that Warner and Philip Darcy were scheming and profiting from the crashes they engineered as well."

"Then you don't believe that I had any involvement? That I didn't take a bribe and conspire with them to—"

"Oh my, no. Why else would I have arranged for your bail? Not for a minute do I believe such drivel."

Anne nodded, yet still she had difficulty comprehending it all. Sylvia would have to draw a clearer picture, fill in many blanks; she just wasn't getting it. "So when I gave the information to the SEC it implicated Donnelley, and Warner killed him to keep his mouth shut?"

"Yes, but it was Darcy who did the killing. Warner admitted that the night he tried to kill me. Pennington was standing outside the door to my sitting room and heard it all. He'll testify to that."

"And then he had Nash kill Darcy to close the loop?"

"Oh no. No-no-no-no. To close the loop, as you say, yes. But Warner himself murdered Philip. That too, Pennington overheard, and—"

"But why? Why didn't he just have Nash do it instead of bloodying his own hands and risk being caught? Then he could have hired someone to kill Nash and have been home free."

Sylvia laughed and waved her hand. "Oh, my dear, you should know the answer to that well enough. Warner was egocentric and filled with greed, personally vengeful if he suspected someone he trusted had turned on him. You jilted him and look what he did to you. Look what he tried to do to me with a poker while thinking that it was I who had set the SEC and IRS investigators upon him. No, I'm sure Warner took great pleasure in doing in Darcy himself after learning that the man had stolen his share of the blood-profits from Coastal Airlines and was on his way out of the country."

Anne leaned forward on her elbows, "But what proof is there that he killed Darcy?"

Sylvia's eyes twinkled. "Ah!" she said, waving a finger at Anne. "In that man's frequent and uncontrollable rages he became remarkably near-sighted, or better put, stupid. On his fiftieth birthday I gave him a 24-carat gold tie clasp with the inscription 'W.E.E.' on the back. Warner Ernest Edelbrock. It was gripped in Darcy's hand when they found him. They had obviously struggled."

Anne remembered the elegant tie clasp; he had worn it often. She sighed and leaned back in her wheelchair, digesting long-sought answers that still weren't enough. When Sylvia enlightened the jury with all of this it would present a clear and logical scenario placing Warner Edelbrock squarely at the core, responsible for the deaths of Donnelley and Darcy, the two crashes, but providing little to defuse the charge against her of conspiring with him to commit murder for profit.

And in the shadows still lurked the earlier drug and felony manslaughter charges, a convenient fallback for the prosecution. It clung like gum to a shoe.

Anne shook her head. "Forgive me, Sylvia, for seeming confused, but I don't see how much of this is going to help me. You said earlier that Warner also admitted to you while drunk that he had arranged fake de-icing for both aircraft, that Nash had done the de-icing and planted the drugs in my locker. And then he arranged the transfer of 5,000 shares of TransCon stock into an account for me to appear as a bribe, as added insurance to protect him in the event I survived and caught on to the scheme, is that right? He would have used it as blackmail to prevent me from talking, except that because of me the SEC found it first? Have I got all of that straight?"

Sylvia sat hunched over, nodding, kneading her arthritic hands. "Yes, that's correct. He admitted those things."

Anne squeezed her eyes shut, thinking. Something Sylvia had said just didn't fit... Nash! Yes, that was it!

"Sylvia, why...? Wait—let me back up a bit. Mr. Hardison told me just the other day that someone posing as Philip Darcy, and aided by another man, had de-iced my aircraft the night of the crash. Now, if as you say, it was this man Nash, then why would he set up Darcy if they were all in it together?"

For a long moment Sylvia stared at her. The silence making Anne feel as though she'd shouted a four-letter word at a church social. "Have I said something...?"

Quickly Sylvia's gaze focused. "It does seem perplexing, and I too wondered about that. But my dear, you must remember that there is no honor among killers and thieves. They feed upon one another like the carnivores they are, caring little for the value of life. It's obvious to me that the man is a dangerous and

272

demented psychotic, a crazed animal that neither Warner nor Philip could any longer control."

Sylvia leaned toward Anne and gripped her wrist tightly. "Nash is the one you must fear now, as I believe that he sees you as the only remaining threat to his anonymity and hence his survival. There is great danger, Anne, and I worry for you."

Well, that makes two of us. Anne massaged her throbbing temples, a necessity now becoming habit. Still she tried to make sense of the convoluted maze of events, of relationships, of what was and what wasn't, the whys and why nots, motive and evidence, proof. At last she shook her head and sighed. She must focus on evidence for her defense, and on that alone, avoid dwelling upon the quagmire of confusing events and assertions that were threatening her sanity.

Sylvia's hand still gripped her wrist and she gently placed hers over it. "I'm very grateful that you've gone to the expense and trouble to help me, taken me into your home, and that you're willing to testify to all of this. Everything you've told me makes sense, most of it, anyway, and I think that a jury would find it quite believable, but maybe it's because I *want* them to. I don't mean to offend you, but do you see what I mean? It may not be enough."

"Indeed I do see, my dear, and I'm not in the least offended. Suppose you tell me exactly what it is that you need."

Anne struggled for the right words. "Well...you've explained everything, but the trouble is, Sylvia, I still don't see how we *prove* any of it. Everything seems to be...well, hearsay. As my attorney would say, circumstantial." *Circumcision,* he had unwittingly said once, referring to evidence. "And if there isn't proof for my defense, and I'm convicted, it could take years for the appeal process while I'm imprisoned. Don't you see? I've got to have Nash, alive, and soon. Before the trial. He's the only one left with information that could clear me, and somehow we've got to find him."

Sylvia released Anne's wrist at last and patted her hand, a smile tugging the corners of her weathered lips. "And I believe you shall."

Anne sat forward quickly. "What do you mean? Is there—"

"My dear, you will eventually learn that I always save the best for last. As I said, I have many loyalists, not the least of whom is my very own brother, Michael. I hadn't wanted to tell you of what I just this morning learned until I knew for certain. And as yet I still don't know, but I wanted to spare you the pain of another letdown in the event that—"

Suddenly Anne's patience wore thin, wishing she'd quit treating her like a child. "I'll take that risk. What have you found out?"

Sylvia eyed her cautiously, measuring. "Very well. I spoke to my brother, Michael, this morning and he believes that he has information that may lead us directly to our mysterious Mr. Nash."

Stunned, Anne stared at her incredulously. "When will—"

Sylvia raised her hand. "Tomorrow, and not before. He will call us when he's certain, but he said to caution you not to become overconfident; he could be wrong. On the other hand he's placing himself at great risk on your behalf because I asked him to; a favor for which my brother has long been indebted."

"I—I don't understand. Why would he have this information? Why would he be in danger? He wasn't involved with Warner, was he?"

Sylvia laughed and clapped her hands, "Oh my, no. My Michael is far brighter than that." She leaned toward Anne and lowered her voice, "Michael is the black sheep of the Preston family and the youngest, yet our father doted upon the dear brat as though he could do no wrong. You see, shortly after C. Gordon Preston died, brother Michael sought his fortune elsewhere and became an electronic bookie of sorts. Land sakes, can you believe it? Poor little rich boy seeking a life of crime? Well he did, and he got himself caught."

Anne couldn't keep from laughing, "And you bailed him out, I suppose. Big sister, because father had passed away."

"Oh, law yes. Big sister to the rescue, valiantly charging in on her trusty motorized wheelchair and sweeping him to freedom, for which he has been ever grateful. We still laugh about it."

She was again caught up in Sylvia's cackling laughter. "So what's Michael doing now? What sort of work?"

A smirk tugged at the old woman's lips. "Oh, he's a consultant of sorts to the management of a very large organization." Sylvia leaned forward again and whispered, "He's called a *caporegime*. A *capo*, for short." Again she sat back and clapped her hands, laughing. "Isn't that just the limit? My baby brother—a Mafia lieutenant? Counselor to the Cosa Nostra?"

After two glasses of sherry Anne's eyelids sagged, her head nodding as she sat before the warmth of the great stone fireplace, listening to Sylvia's monologue of the history of the Preston family.

At last Sylvia realized the broken connection and wheeled herself to Anne's side. "Oh, my dear, it's been such a long day for you, let me show you your room."

Anne sighed, her eyes blinking open. "Yeah, I'm pooped. I'm sorry, I didn't mean to be rude, Sylvia."

"Quite all right, dear. Just follow me, your room's on the second floor."

The elevator was large enough to accommodate both wheelchairs, and as the cubicle whined upward Anne glanced at Sylvia's lap. Her ever-present knitting lay atop the shawl covering her legs, and with it were two of the most unusual knitting needles Anne had ever seen. The shafts appeared to be made of stainless steel, capped with ornate and finely crafted silver handles in the shape of horses necks and heads. Chess knights, that's what they were. "Those are lovely, Sylvia, may I see one?"

She examined the obviously priceless instrument closely hefting its impressive weight, admiring its exquisite detail. She touched a fingertip to the point and found it needle-sharp. How strange... "Sterling, isn't it?"

"Oh no, my dear. These were cast of solid silver in an ancient Scottish foundry. They are more than three hundred years old. Aren't they magnificent? They were a gift from my grandfather when I was a child, originally belonging to his great, great grandmother, Sarah MacRitchie, from Blackburn, Scotland."

Anne handed the unusual knitting needle to Sylvia as the elevator door hissed open. She wheeled herself into the broad hallway and paused, suddenly awestruck by its immensity. The ceiling was cathedral-like, high and coved with bowed timbers from which hung many magnificent crystal chandeliers. The polished floor was of large octagonal tiles upon which lay a continuum of fine oriental rugs for what seemed a hundred feet in each direction. More than a dozen richly carved doors as well as many ornately framed paintings gave contrasting relief to the windowless expanse of lacquered plaster walls. The effect seemed gothic, medieval. Almost sinister.

"My god," Anne murmured.

"It is rather overwhelming, isn't it, my dear. Come, follow me, your room is at the end."

Room wasn't an appropriate description. Not unless it was *The Lincoln Room, The East Room, The Red Room,* or some other quaint chamber from the White House, but she shouldn't have expected less. The carpeting was deep pile, and rich draperies adorned paned windows as well as the French doors leading to a balcony. Far across the "room" was a huge four-poster canopied bed adjacent to a sitting area in an alcove. She guessed the only other doors to be those leading to the closets and bathroom. *What in God's name must the crapper look like?*

Romo tapped at the door, leaned in and set Anne's overnight bag on the floor.

Sylvia wheeled herself to the bedside and took a small electronic console from the table. "This controls the television as
well as the heating, and the red button here at the bottom is for
Pennington. If you need him for any reason don't hesitate to use
it, dear. Are you able to care for yourself without assistance?"

Anne nodded absently, still absorbed by the lavish surroundings.

"Have a good rest, dear. There is much we must do tomorrow, especially after we speak with Michael."

"Yes, thanks. Goodnight, Sylvia."

For several minutes Anne wheeled herself about the expansive room, exploring and marveling at the less obvious yet
equally expensive furnishings and unusual objects that the Edelbrock and Preston fortunes had acquired. She had known that
Warner Edelbrock was wealthy, yet Sylvia had set that straight
earlier—all of this was Preston money of the old-line, mainstream variety. It was the fortune of empire builders no less
great than those of Rothschild, Vanderbilt, Rockefeller.

Awash with fatigue, she remembered that she hadn't called
Gordy to apologize for her harsh outburst. She looked about the
room but saw no phone, and decided she was too tired to go
looking for one. She would call him in the morning. It was time
to do her girl-things and then crash in that marvelous bed.

She brushed her teeth and relieved herself in a bathroom of
outrageous proportions. As she reached for the light switch she
considered trying out the bidet, then nixed the idea fearing that
in her unsteady and weakened condition she would slip and im-
pale herself upon it. *Or worse, receive an unwanted enema,* she
chuckled. She flicked off the light switch in the bath as well as
the bedroom and wheeled to the bedside now bathed in pale
moonlight. She locked her wheels, then peeled back the covers
and hoisted herself upon the spongy mattress and stripped off
her clothing.

As she lay naked beneath the covers she relaxed for the first
time in a week, savoring the luxurious comfort and grateful to no

longer sleep on a lumpy pad in a cold concrete cell. Still the memory of it was chilling, frightening, and much now depended upon what they would learn from Michael tomorrow.

She tried to envision what the male and younger counterpart of Sylvia might look like. She saw him as a pretty man; soft-spoken, shiny black slicked-back hair, maybe late forties, expensive double-breasted suit, and alligator shoes. And a...yes, a black fedora atop his head. Wasn't that what all exalted high priests of the Mafia looked like? Strange that a man of such means at birth and wealthy for as long as he would live, should choose the dark side of life with all its risks. But she supposed that some of the mega-rich became easily bored with their fortunes, Warner for one, and sought excitement and intrigue as an outlet...

All in the family...

Her dreams came in sporadic bursts, fragmented and kaleidoscopic, reflecting her inner fears and emotionally frustrating turmoil since that terrifying night at La Guardia that now seemed so long ago. She tossed restlessly just beneath the fuzzy surface of sleep, her legs leaden and immovable as she crawled in pursuit of a tall and heavyset man with no face, a man with a mocking, cackling laughter who stood just out of reach and hurling knitting needles at her. A muffled shriek escaped her lips when the needles struck, and suddenly she jerked awake, her eyes blinking open, heart racing. She lay still for a moment in the darkness, hearing only the thudding of her heart and blood pounding in her ears.

But was there something else? Had she also heard—

Suddenly two shattering explosions shook the room and the headboard exploded in flying splinters. Anne screamed and tumbled off the bed onto the floor. She lay naked and tangled in the covers, still shrieking when she heard a hollow shout from far down the hallway.

"Freeze!" a deep male voice called out. Then came the thundering echo of shots fired in the cavernous hallway and the

278

)ounding of heavy feet running past her door. Two more shots :ame from far down the hallway, and seconds later a shattering)f glass and shots fired outside. Quickly she rolled under the)ed and out the other side, groping for the electronic device, frantically punching the red button to summon Pennington.

"What's happening!" she heard Sylvia cry out far down the 1allway, "Pennington! Oh heavens, Pennington, hurry! Anne! Anne, I'm coming!"

"Here!" Anne shouted, "Hurry!"

Suddenly her door burst open and the room flooded with light. "Miss Ryan? Miss Ryan, where are you?" Pennington shouted.

"Here! On the floor!"

Pennington, clad only in robe and pajamas, rushed to her side and laid his .45 automatic on the bed table. "Are you hurt, Miss Ryan? Where—"

"I'm all right," Anne gasped as he gathered her up in the bedclothes and laid her gently upon the bed.

Sylvia wheeled quickly in, "What's—Anne! Anne!" she screamed.

"I think she's all right, Mrs. Edelbrock," Pennington said, covering her with a quilt and gently stroking her forehead.

"Oh, thank God! What happened? I heard shots."

"Someone shot at her from the doorway," he said, fingering the splintered holes in the headboard only inches above the pillows. "I came running when I heard the shots and got off two of my own when I saw him running from her door. Then I chased him down the stairway, fired again, and he dove through the sunroom window. There's blood on the snow outside, but he ran into the woods before I could get another shot. I'd say he's either cut from the glass or I wounded him."

Anne reached and clutched Pennington's arms. "What'd he look like?"

"The hallway was pretty dark and I never saw his face, but he was tall, a big man, about my size."

"Nash!" Sylvia hissed. "It must be! All right, quickly everyone, we're leaving. Now! Pennington, call flight operations and have the Starliner readied while Anne and I get ourselves dressed. I'll call Michael."

"Señor," Romo interrupted from the doorway. "I have found the cellar doors open. The man, he must come through there, I think."

Anne sat up, clutching the quilt about her. "Sylvia, where are we going?"

"To Michael's where you'll be safe. He has bodyguards—"

"But *where*?"

"Near Buffalo. Now hurry and dress, child, he may still be outside and try again. He's injured and desperate—we've no time to lose."

"But Sylvia, why don't we just call the police?"

"Oh good heavens, no. You're not thinking straight, child. If the police come they'll have no choice but to take you into protective custody and—"

"Never mind, I get the picture." Anne swung her legs over the bedside and began tugging her clothing on. "I've got to call Earl Christopher and let him know where we're going."

"Indeed you must. Tell him we'll be leaving from the TransCon hangar at JFK within the hour, arriving in Buffalo about an hour later. Michael's home is in the country about thirty minutes from downtown Buffalo, off the turnpike near Batavia. Now please hurry."

Anne dressed as quickly as she was able, and at five minutes to one she called and woke Christopher and told him of the shooting and their plan. When he argued she hung up.

Suddenly there came a rap on her door, and when she opened it she found Pennington dressed and ready, a .45 automatic in his shoulder holster and an Uzi submachine gun at his side. "Sorry to look like a one-man arsenal," he said, "but if he tries again I'll have him. You'll be safe."

"Thanks, but if he does try again please don't kill him. He's all I've got left and I need his testimony."

Minutes later Romo and Pennington brought the van around to the front portico and Pennington stood watch, Uzi in hand, while Romo helped Anne and Sylvia aboard. The door slammed shut and Romo stood grinning through the window, nodding vigorously; giving them a thumbs-up.

Once out of the gates Anne relaxed a little as Pennington drove at the speed limit, unwilling to attract unnecessary attention. She closed her eyes and breathed deeply for a few moments to further relax, yet the terror of only thirty minutes ago had left her legs spasming and she gripped them with her hands.

So Nash had brazenly broken in and tried to shoot her, she thought, but until now it hadn't occurred to her why—just that he had. But now as she thought about it, it was he who was the hunted, not her. And what incriminating knowledge of him could she have that Hardison, Christopher, and especially Sylvia and the others didn't? Wouldn't he have better tried to silence Sylvia? Michael? No matter. What mattered most was that someone, Nash or not, wanted her dead. Again. She thought of the Edelbrock estate deep in the woods, unprotected except for Pennington and he had nearly failed. She wondered why they had so few hired help; now Romo was all alone, the killer might—

"Sylvia, will Romo be all right? He's all alone, isn't he?"

"Romo will be fine. He's perfectly able to take care of himself."

Yes, she guessed that he could, remembering that it had been Romo who saved Sylvia's as well as Pennington's lives. Still, she found it difficult to believe that the gentle and soft-spoken man could bring himself to bury a pick ax in Warner Edelbrock's skull...

When they reached the brightly lighted TransCon hangar at JFK Anne bristled when she saw Christopher standing beside his car, waiting. She needed no more of his verbal haranguing and attempts to change her mind. But when Pennington stopped the van inside the hangar and slid the side door open, Christopher leaned in. "Anne, I need to talk to you. Alone."

"Two minutes, Earl, we're in a hurry."

He wheeled her to the side of the hangar and out of earshot. "Anne, this is foolish, insane. I can't let you do it. We've got to call the police and let them take you into protective custody. It doesn't necessarily mean that you'll be going back into a cell, they have safe-houses, places where—"

"No way, Earl, this is my life not yours. Safe-house or the White House, it's all the same to me. I'd be under their thumbs every moment, escorted and watched while I pee, shower, brush my teeth or pick my nose. Huh-uh, no way, Jose'. Two days in that stinkhole in the courthouse was enough for me, and now I've got a real chance to clear myself."

"Nash may try again, Anne."

"And I hope to God he does. I've got a war hero with an arsenal to protect me and maybe bring the son of a bitch in alive."

"You're planning on using yourself as bait?"

"*No*, I'm not planning to use myself as bait, but I'm going somewhere that he can't get to me. There are others there even better armed than Pennington. Besides, tomorrow we may know who Nash is. And guess what, Earl? It was Warner who killed Darcy. How does that strike you?"

Christopher was dumbstruck. "What?" he exclaimed, keeping his voice low. "Anne, how did you—"

"Sylvia told me. She said the police found Warner's tie clasp in Darcy's hand where he was murdered. They had struggled and Warner shot him."

Christopher leaned close to her, his voice a rasping whisper. "Anne, no one is supposed to know that yet. Lorenzo's office hasn't released the—"

They heard the dull thud of jet turbines igniting, a hollow moaning as they spooled up in a shrieking crescendo. "Never mind, Earl, now I've got to go!" Anne shouted, turning and wheeling toward the twin-engine Starliner.

"Call me when you get there!" Christopher shouted back.

Pennington stood at the boarding steps and helped her out of the wheelchair, then scooped her in his arms and carried her up the steps. As he turned and ducked to enter the aircraft, Anne saw Christopher standing to the side, his hands planted on his hips. She blew him a kiss and waved.

Earl Christopher stood watching as the sleek corporate jet taxied across the ramp and turned, a gust of hot, stinking burned kerosene suddenly blowing in his face. Deep in his gut he sensed he might never see her again. Not alive, anyway.

All in the family, Earl.

Lorenzo's words may not have been so far off the mark after all. He shook his head and walked quickly to his car where he reached for his cellular phone.

John Haviland Williams

THIRTEEN

Mitchell Hardison stood amid an electronic maze in the near darkness of the New York Terminal Radar Approach Control (TRACON) operations room, munching a Snickers bar and watching the eyeball-numbing luminescence of a radarscope, waiting. At last came the call.

"Hardison," he answered.

"Christopher. You ready?"

"All set. The boys here show them filed on an IFR flight plan direct to Buffalo. We can watch them on the screen here until they descend into Buffalo, then we'll switch to Buffalo Approach Control who'll track them right down to the runway. You got someone watching at the other end when they land?"

"Yeah, a couple of U.S. Marshals. As an attorney, I'm also an officer of the court and I had to let the U.S. Attorney in on it. God help me if Anne finds out."

Tough shit, counselor. "Okay, I'll stay here until these guys hand off the flight to Buffalo Approach Control, which'll be in about, oh--forty minutes, it looks like. Call me if anything happens at your end."

"Yeah. Wait—okay, there they go," Christopher said, watching the blinking lights of the Starliner as it accelerated and thundered down the runway.

A muffled roar like rolling thunder came through Hardison's receiver and he glanced at the radarscope but it was too soon "We'll have them in a minute," he said. "Stay there until we do, okay?" He counted the seconds. Climbing at three thousand feet a minute he calculated that the Starliner would pop onto the screen in a few more seconds.

He watched patiently as Frank Serra, one of roughly a dozen air traffic control specialists populating the TRACON, adjusted the gain on the glowing screen, the sweepline pegged in the center and making a sweep of the screen's circumference every five seconds. It was just past two a.m. and there was little air traffic, mostly military stuff, and the sweepline illuminated them as glowing "targets" quickly dimming as the sweep passed, then glowing again on the next sweep. He watched two military aircraft inch their way slowly from right to left, then a third aircraft came from the top of the screen on an apparent collision course.

"They gonna hit, Frank?" Hardison asked the controller.

"No sir. That Canadian flight from the north'll pass a thousand feet under, heading southward. Watch."

Hardison peered at the screen, the northern target converging at right angles to one of the westbound targets. The sweep came around again and the converging targets merged as one and Hardison stiffened. On the next sweep the targets separated and continued on their respective headings. Hardison let out his breath in a rush. He'd seen the detritus of too many accidents over the years and he thought he'd just witnessed another.

The air traffic controller grinned, "You get used to it."

"Not in my business you don't, son." He watched the radar sweep again and looked at his stopwatch. Any second now.

"Radar contact," said the controller, pointing to the screen where an electronic data tag appeared adjacent to a target west-bound for Buffalo. "November three-four Tango Charlie. That he one you're looking for, sir?"

"Yeah, that's it. N34TC."

Anne loosened her seatbelt as the Starliner climbed high above New York City, wishing that she were forward in the cockpit in spite of the ultra-luxurious interior of the passenger cabin. She had never been in a Starliner before, or any of the so-called 'bizjets" used by the high cockalorum of corporate inner circles, and she marveled at how quiet the twin fanjets were in the rear. She reached down and unlatched the comfortable seat and swiv-eled to face Sylvia across the narrow aisle. "Thank you," she said, more with her eyes and lips.

Sylvia smiled faintly, avoiding Anne's gaze, and returned to her knitting. Knit and purl, knit and purl, the sharp needlepoints rapidly stitching as though a machine, her concentration total as though the horror of an hour ago had never happened.

Anne shrugged and glanced at Pennington sitting in the rear in a forward-facing seat beside the lavatory door, his Uzi no-where in sight, but beneath his jacket she knew the heavy .45 was at ready. She abhorred guns but now she was grateful that Pennington had his. Only an hour ago he had saved her life, risking his. Just as Sylvia said he would. A war hero several times over. She smiled and nodded to him; he nodded back but didn't smile.

Anne leaned back in her seat, puzzled and just a little miffed that Sylvia and Pennington now seemed so aloof. Suddenly she felt foolish, realizing that her emotions were again gaining the upper hand, that she was reacting like a selfish child starved for affection, attention. She sighed heavily, realizing that she had been alone for so long, her body brutally injured, her mind and soul persecuted by the hurled stones of her many detractors, that she had grabbed and clung frantically to a kind and understanding hand offered in her darkest moments. In little over twenty-four hours she had become dependent, addicted to Sylvia's warmth and confidence, and now that it should ebb even in the slightest seemed a threatening tug at her newfound security.

For twenty minutes Mitchell Hardison watched the radar target that was November three-four Tango Charlie move unerringly westward, on course for Buffalo, speed three hundred knots, altitude sixteen thousand. He had waited and watched impatiently, primed by Earl Christopher's suspicions, expecting at any moment that the target would change course for parts unknown, Anne Ryan with it. But it hadn't. And it probably wouldn't. Christopher was probably just overagitated, understandable in light of his client's desperate state.

He sat back in the chair beside the air traffic controller and scanned the near darkened room, only now realizing that he and Frank were not alone. He knew better of course, but only now had he become aware of the muted voices of the other controllers speaking into their microphones, their shadowy figures seated before glowing screens arranged in horseshoe fashion about the TRACON radar room. Spooky way to make a living, he thought. The environment seemed unreal, almost funereal and severed from the real world, a place where you sat in relative quiet for eight hours daily and cloaked in near darkness, seemingly alone, gazing at radar blips that were the lives of thousands encapsulated in aluminum chambers aloft inching their way across the glowing screen. The boredom from time to time would be interrupted only by an occasionally disoriented pilot seeking direction, an errant pilot unwittingly flying in harm's way, and infrequently a pilot whose radar blip is suddenly no more. He wondered if controllers felt detachment from the scenes played out before them, electronic scenes that seemed no more real than computer games.

Hardison shook away the thoughts and peeled the wrapping from a fresh cigar, snipped the tip, and reached for his lighter.

"There's no smoking in here, sir," said Frank, the controller sitting at his elbow.

Swell. He pocketed the cigar and rubbed the stubble on his cheeks, blinking his grainy eyes in the near darkness of the radar room, wishing he hadn't answered his bedside telephone and taken Christopher's urgent call. And he was on his own time, not the NTSB's. At this moment Dog probably lay comfortably curled on the bed, more likely the pillow, snoring contentedly and drooling as he lay claim to the bed in which he allowed his master to sleep. Tomorrow the sheets and pillowcases would need changing after only three weeks, a full seven days before his much-dreaded monthly event, Laundry Day. Damn.

He glared at the radar screen, seeing the target move inexorably toward Buffalo. And what if it *did* turn? What if it suddenly did a right-face and shot north to Canada, as Christopher feared, what could he do about it? Send up the air force to shoot it down? Press his thumb to the screen and hold the aircraft in place? There wasn't a damn thing he could do but watch if it turned.

And give Christopher the bad news. Sayonara, Ryan.

He rose slowly from his chair, stretched, and fished in his pocket for the cigar he craved. "I'll be out in the hall, call me if it changes course, Frank." He turned and stumbled over his chair in the darkness, cursing it as he parted the doorway curtain and reached for the knob.

"Radar contact," Frank droned.

Hardison fumbled his way back through the curtain and came up behind the controller and peered at the screen. "Whatcha got?"

"Nothing remarkable. Just a Starliner inbound from Canada."

Another--*two* Starliners at *two* in the morning? What had roused the fat asses of corporate America at this hour? Hardison watched the southbound target that was the second Starliner, saw that it was converging at right angles to N34TC, the one westbound and carrying Anne Ryan. "They're not going to hit either, right?"

Frank grinned and shook his head. "Like I said, you get used to it." He pointed to the screen, "This one southbound is November three-two-one X-ray. He's on a VFR flight plan en-route to Harrisburg, Pee-A. Looks like they'll cross just about over Binghamton."

"Isn't that kinda unusual—twenty million bucks worth of corporate jet flying under visual flight rules at night?"

"It happens. Long as they're below eighteen thousand feet they can pretty much fly any way they like. Easier for them to divert if they want to. The corporates sometimes do that; some exec changes his mind, wants to go somewhere else, that sort of thing."

"Like stopping to pick up a broad if he gets horny, or something."

"Or something."

Anne stared out the window of the Starliner at the thousands of pinpoints of light that were stars and constellations, thinking of what lay ahead. Since they were going to Michael's tonight he may already have answers. No matter that Nash was somewhere back on Long Island, maybe injured and wandering through the woods; if his identity and description were known the police could surely catch him. Then, with a confession, things could begin to wind down and the nightmare would be over.

Amid the blinking stars she saw two that flashed in sync and she focused on them, suspecting and at last seeing a flashing red one above and between them. They were the lights of another airplane heading straight for them, converging on their course at an altitude approximating theirs. It was a common sight at night for airline pilots and it troubled her little, knowing that at a distance the required separation in altitude often appeared minimal, if not nonexistent. She watched as it came closer, probably at a closure rate of nearly 400 miles per hour.

It had to be another jet.

Suddenly the cabin tilted steeply to the left and she instinc-ively gripped the armrests as they swung away from the other aircraft. Obviously an evasive maneuver, she thought, the pilots up forward uncomfortable with the proximity of the other air-craft. She looked first to Sylvia then to Pennington and saw not a hint of alarm, she knitting, and he scanning a magazine. Their relaxed attitude after an abrupt turn seemed far different from that of the typical airline passenger to whom she was accus-tomed, yet considering that Sylvia owned a major airline, she allowed that these were not typical passengers.

Hardison watched the radar targets that were the two Starliners converging at right angles, as had the military flights earlier, but still he couldn't get used to it. He held his breath again until the revolving line on the radar screen completed its next sweep and the targets separated and continued on their respective courses. He heaved a sigh, "You keep your job, Frank, and I'll keep mine," he said. "I couldn't sit here on an eight-hour shift every day and watch those blips come together like that. Like, smacko!" He shook his head. "Those are real airplanes; this is nuts."

"This is nothing. You should see it in the daytime when there's a lot of traffic. The target data tags overlap all over one another. Pure hell to track aircraft and keep them apart."

Hardison nodded grimly. "I know. And when you can't, that's when I have to pick up the pieces, Frank."

Twenty minutes later in a similar radar room near Buffalo an air traffic controller vectored November three-four Tango Charlie to the outer marker inbound to the Buffalo airport. The aircraft was five miles from touchdown when the controller called the Buffalo control tower on the direct line. "Yeah, Lou, this is Max at Buffalo TRACON. You got three-four Tango Charlie in sight?"

The tower controller squinted at the darkness outside the tower windows. "Hold on...yeah, I see his landing lights about a mile out. I cleared him to land a couple minutes ago. You want to hold until he touches down and I verify?"

"Roger that. I'll hold."

The Buffalo tower controller watched as the distant lights grew larger, and then he saw the Starliner flare over the end of the runway and touch down. "Looks like him," he said into the telephone. "Wait-one while I get the glasses on him." A minute later the Starliner taxied past the tower and the controller saw clearly the large numbers on the engines, N34TC. November three-four Tango Charlie it was. "Yeah, it's him. You want to talk to him?"

"Negative. Thanks, Lou. Just checking." The Buffalo TRACON controller broke the connection and called Hardison. "They're down, okay... Yeah, I'm sure. It's them."

Deputy U.S. Marshals Tolliver and Marchetti sat in darkness in their unmarked sedan at Buffalo airport, watching through night-vision binoculars as the howling Starliner taxied to the itinerant aircraft ramp and shut down. Large numerals on the engines read N34TC, just as they had been told to watch for. Far to their right they saw a black Oldsmobile emerge from the darkness behind a hangar, proceed across the ramp and stop near the plane's left wingtip. The car appeared empty except for the driver and they watched him get out and open the passenger door, waiting while the aircraft's cabin-stair door opened.

"There's supposed to be three of them, right?" asked Tolliver.

"Plus the two pilots."

They watched as a young man in uniform walked quickly down the aircraft's steps with a folded wheelchair hooked under each arm, then stood on the ramp, waiting. "That one of the pilots?" Tolliver asked.

Marchetti nodded as he peered through his binoculars. "You can tell by his sleeves—three stripes; he's the first officer."

Moments later a tall, heavyset man emerged from the aircraft with a blanketed woman in his arms and walked carefully down the steps. He set her in one of the wheelchairs and trotted quickly back up the steps and into the aircraft. A minute later he emerged carrying another woman, much older, and set her in a wheelchair also. The driver of the Olds seemed to be introducing himself to the small group.

"The woman on the left is Ryan," said Marchetti. "Fits the description."

"You get a make on the driver?"

Marchetti held the binoculars to his eyes, studying the shadowy face. "Nope." He watched as the driver assisted the woman identified as Ryan into the front seat, then collapsed the wheelchair and opened the rear door, quickly stuffing it inside. "Looks like she's the only one going for a ride."

"I thought Lorenzo said they all were."

"That's what he said, but no matter what happens we're supposed to tail Ryan. Let's get back to the car; they're leaving."

"Hold on a sec, I want to watch this." Tolliver trained his binoculars again on the aircraft, saw the tall, heavyset man carry the older woman back up the steps and the plane's first officer quickly followed with the wheelchair. Then the door thunked shut and the jet engines began spooling up. Tolliver watched the Oldsmobile drive slowly toward the road leading to the airport exit. He quickly stuffed his binoculars into the case and tagged Marchetti's elbow. "Okay, let's go. We'll pick up the tail on Ryan as they pass through the front gate."

Four minutes later the marshals positioned their gray sedan between two parked cars near the front gate to the airport and waited. Moments later the departing Starliner thundered overhead then swung eastward and disappeared into the night. Tolliver looked at his watch nervously. "There any other gate out of here?"

"Not any more. Airport security."

"Think we ought to go back for a look? They should have come by us by now."

"Yeah." Marchetti dropped the sedan into gear and crept back toward the itinerant aircraft ramp. He stopped in the shadows beside a hangar and scanned the deserted expanse of runways and taxiways. The Olds had vanished and so had Ryan.

"There! Over there!" Tolliver shouted, pointing toward a row of aircraft hangars a half-mile distant. Marchetti saw the brake lights of a car stopping before one of the hangars and quickly reached for his night-vision binoculars. "It's the Olds, all right, and Ryan too." He saw the hangar doors rise and a sleek LearJet roll out as the car's driver hurriedly pushed the woman in the wheelchair toward it. "Christ, they're going to beat it out of here!"

Marchetti slammed the car into gear and the tires shrieked as he sped down the taxiway, knowing they were too late. They had bumbled it. His speedometer edged toward seventy as the LearJet carrying Ryan turned onto the taxiway ahead of them and accelerated.

"He's not going to wait for clearance!" Tolliver shouted, his hands gripping the dashboard.

"Or a runway, for that matter." Ahead, Marchetti saw twin gouts of blue flame burst from the aircraft's jetpipes and it quickly shot ahead of them, widening the gap as it accelerated then lifted off the taxiway and climbed into the night. He slammed his hand against the steering wheel and stood on the brakes. "Skipped! She goddamn fucking skipped!"

Tolliver was already on the radio to dispatch. Lorenzo would be pissed as hell.

Several minutes had passed since they banked abruptly away from the converging aircraft, and Anne became uneasy. When

294

pilots make an evasive maneuver to avoid another aircraft they got back on course as quickly as possible, she knew. But the pilots up forward hadn't. Now the Starliner in which she rode was clearly heading southward, no longer west toward Buffalo. She glanced again at Sylvia, then to Pennington. Still they seemed unconcerned, ignoring her.

What was going on?

Anne reached across the narrow aisle and touched Sylvia's wrist. "Why did we change course?"

Still the old woman knitted intently, knit and purl, knit and purl, at last looking up and meeting Anne's questioning gaze. "Because, dear, we're following our flight plan. Isn't that the way you pilots say it?"

Anne stiffened, her heart thudding as she slowly withdrew her hand. "We're...not going to Buffalo, are we."

Sylvia shook her head slowly as she again concentrated on her knitting, her weathered lips forming *no*.

Anne glanced quickly at Pennington sitting in the rear by the lavatory door. Then she screamed. His .45 automatic was pointed squarely at her midsection.

"You! It was *YOU! You're* Nash!"

His now cruel eyes bored into hers and he slowly raised his left hand, fingers spread, palm forward. The broad, ugly scar on his index finger was now unmistakable as he rotated it for her to see. It was his *left*, not his right. No wonder she had missed it earlier.

The awful realization struck like a bludgeon and suddenly she felt light-headed, dizzy and nauseous, her fingertips tingling as though she were standing at the edge of a yawning precipice and losing her balance. Her legs began spasming uncontrollably as she looked incredulously at Sylvia. "Why?" she asked, her voice suddenly cracking, "Why have you...why have you done all this just to get at *me*? What have I ever—"

Sylvia's eyes narrowed and she leaned toward Anne, waving a knitting needle for emphasis as she spoke. "Because you are the last of them, you wretched, perverted, filthy adulteress. You are the first and last links in the encircling chain of conniving evil that have putrefied my life! You, Warner, Milton, Philip, all of you! And soon you shall join them to rot in hell where you justly belong! Do you *hear* me? ROT! ROT! ROT!"

Insane. The woman's demented... Anne felt her throat and chest tighten as though she was suffocating, claustrophobic, sealed in an airless chamber. Suddenly the old woman's eyes widened demonically, her voice becoming a shrill screech, ranting as though preaching fire and brimstone from some bully-pulpit.

"Scripture!" Sylvia shrieked. "You have defied scripture! Such is *your* crime! For out of the heart proceed evil thoughts, adulteries, fornications... Know ye not that the unrighteous shall not inherit the Kingdom of God? Neither fornicators nor adulterers nor abusers of themselves with mankind shall inherit the kingdom of GOD!" As though punctuating her venomous diatribe she suddenly thrust a knitting needle at Anne's face, its needle-sharp point wavering only inches from her left eye. Anne recoiled instantly, cringing and grimacing as she pressed her head back hard against the headrest, her eyes crossed and staring at the murderous needle.

For a long moment Sylvia was silent, her demonic expression frozen in a rictus of boiling hate as she inched the needle closer to Anne's eye. "Now do you understand?" she wheedled, giggling like a child. "Do you now understand the writings of St. Matthew? Of Corinthians? You have committed evil acts of carnal filth with the man who was my *husband*! You have romped and fornicated upon my very bed with your wretched and filthy body! You have stolen his soul from me, and it was mine! Mine alone!"

Anne clenched her teeth tightly and swallowed hard to control the churning of her stomach and the bitterness of burning bile quickly rising in her throat. If she threw up now the knitting needle would puncture her eye. She didn't dare move or even

296

breathe, and she prayed that the aircraft wouldn't lurch or again turn abruptly.

Slowly Sylvia pressed the knitting needle into the tender flesh beneath Anne's left eye, just pricking the surface, then quickly withdrew it, satisfied with the resulting yelp of pain and the terrorizing effect. Her expression softened as she settled back in her seat. "Now I believe we understand each other, don't we, my dear?"

Anne let her breath out in a rush, cautiously touching a trembling fingertip to the flesh beneath her eye and finding a droplet of blood. "Can...can we...talk?"

"Of course, my dear. Perhaps you'd care to purge your soul? It's ever so much easier that way."

Anne closed her eyes for a moment trying to calm her wildly beating heart and keep from vomiting. When she opened them Sylvia was smiling pleasantly, patiently. "What are you...what are you going to do? Are you going to...kill me?"

"Oh, I must. Oh yes, there is no other way, don't you see?"

"Then it was you who had all of the others killed? That broker, Donnelley? Darcy? And your husband too? You did have him killed, didn't you. You set it up that way. He had nothing to do with any of this—the two crashes, the drugs in my locker, the stock that appeared to be a bribe, it was all lies, a set-up, wasn't it?"

"Of course!" Sylvia exclaimed gleefully, clapping her hands together. "And it worked beautifully. You and Warner and the others did exactly as I had planned. I had little more to do than arrange the stage and nudge the lot of you, and like the corrupt little puppets you are, you acted out the script as I called the cues. Oh, you were all so terribly predictable, it almost robbed me of amusement."

"...you acted out the script as I called the cues...so terribly predictable..." Realization suddenly dawned. Released into Sylvia's custody, the shots in the house, the rush to seek protec-

tion at Michael's, how cleverly they had arranged the ruse to get her aboard the aircraft.

Another wave of nausea swept over Anne and her mind spun dizzily as she absorbed it all. How foolish she had been, how incredibly blind not to have seen through it. And it was Gordy who had long ago warned that Sylvia might be a Trojan Horse, and she hadn't listened. The demonic woman's grandmotherly visits to the hospital, the NTSB hearing, the courthouse jail, all had been a carefully calculated ploy rigged behind a cruel veil of compassion for which she had fallen victim. And all the while Nash had been watching her every move and those of Warner, Donnelley, Darcy, feeding Sylvia the information from which she plotted and he killed. And Warner...he had been innocent all along... Profiting from the crashes, yes, yet innocent of causing them. And his suspicious words of that afternoon months ago now had a haunting echo: *"It looks pretty bad out there, Anne, maybe you ought to trip-trade tonight—let someone else fly the trip to Detroit..."*

He cared, the bastard really cared after all...

The aircraft banked slightly to the right, reminding her of where she was and why, and suddenly she felt the familiar rage building again, nudging fear and caution aside. "You're insane, Sylvia. You're sick, evil."

Sylvia cackled with amusement and clapped her hands appreciatively. "Insane? Sick? Evil? No. No, insanity, my dear, is when someone does the same thing over and over, each time expecting a different outcome that somehow never materializes. *That* is insanity by definition; hardly comparable when you consider that the outcome I seek is in fact about to become reality in my little play. It can end no other way, because I choose it to be so.

"And *evil*? *Sick*? How foolish and naive you are that you and the others could not see of yourselves, that all of you are the very manifestation of that which infects our society. You, the adulteress and deceitful vixen, lusting for the flesh of those who

298

belong to another. Warner, Philip, Milton—the power mongers, insatiable in their treachery, their cunning greed and thievery, willing to slice any throat to gorge themselves upon the blood of others.

"No, my dear. Your perception of sickness, of evil, is but a distorted simile of your own faults, which you and those like you project upon others, but failing utterly. Yes, you and the others would like very much to believe that I am the sick and evil one, because those of your ilk are fearful if not incapable of looking upon yourselves.

"No, my dear, your desperate yet futile invective is lost upon me, your words are but a mirror of what you fear may be yourself. Words reflect the mind, the mind the soul."

Time. Buy time, keep her talking. Think of something. "You don't consider murder and deceit sick? Evil? If you believe we're all as you say, what sets you apart from us, Sylvia?" Anne stiffened when the old woman began toying with a knitting needle, her expression one of weary tolerance. Then with a faint smile she looked again at Anne.

"What sets us apart? Why, the end result, my dear. Of good and evil, that's what sets us apart. In choreographing our little play I merely arranged all of you, the forces of evil and greed, in a circle to feed upon one another like toppling dominoes. In so doing I have rid society of yet another element of that which has welled up from the sewers of hell. *That*, is what sets us apart. It's what I believe the authorities would call a `sting' operation. You have all followed your corrupt instincts and now..you..have..been..*stung*."

Anne glanced quickly at Pennington, or Nash, or whoever he really was, and saw that he now sat relaxed, confident, yet still he held his .45 unwaveringly aimed at her midsection. He couldn't miss if she moved toward Sylvia. *So draw her out, buy time, keep her talking and watch for an opportunity...*

"So it was Pennington who was on the de-icing tanker the night of my crash? He doctored the de-icing fluid for both crashes, left out the glycol?"

Sylvia nodded, a hint of a smile tugging the corners of her mouth. "With a little help from his associate, Esposito. He even watched you crash, my dear, then called and told me of your terrible fate."

"And the drugs in my locker? How did he get them in there?"

Sylvia looked at Pennington fondly, "Why, he was a janitor, of course. Lyle is capable of acting many roles convincingly as well as acquiring the necessary identification."

"Then it was you, not Warner, who put the TransCon stock in an account in my name to make it look like I took a payoff for the first crash?"

Sylvia clapped her hands in her now familiar gesture of light-heartedness. "A mere pittance of a price considering the benefits I have accrued, wouldn't you agree? Oh, dear Milton was always such a malleable wimp, a weathervane if ever there was the scent of a dollar in the wind. Such a miserable soul whose treachery took him to the grave."

Anne nodded toward Pennington, "Courtesy of the much-honored war hero? The White House advisor to two presidents? Mr. Frankenstein incarnate? What a bunch of crap!" Too late she realized the error of her unguarded words.

Sylvia sat forward, her eyes narrowing. "A sarcastic tongue, my dear, will only serve to enhance his wrath when *your* moment arrives." She tapped her finger meaningfully on the tip of a knitting needle. "It may well be his choice in which of your bodily orifices he may wish to insert my little Scottish antique. So? Ah, I see that I have your complete attention again. He knows well the female anatomy, such that your death could be a most agonizing one if you tempt him."

Anne's stomach churned as she again stared at the murderous knitting needle, certain of Pennington's perverted choices undoubtedly to be guided by Sylvia. Her knees trembled as she unconsciously squeezed her thighs together. "But why kill me now? Why not back at the house when you had every opportunity? Why didn't he just aim lower when he shot at my bed?"

Sylvia chuckled and shook her head condescendingly. "That would have been an utterly stupid thing to do. Can you imagine the questions the authorities would ask of us, your bail custodians? Anne Ryan, last seen in our custody, in our home, and suddenly she is missing? Never again to be found? No, child, as far as the authorities at this minute know, you have skipped bail right before their very eyes and left me forfeiting the $1.3 million I put up on your behalf. You are a fugitive never to be found, and soon when Pennington and I are seen arriving back in New York we will learn of your treachery. We will be absolutely astonished and crestfallen that you had broken our trust and substituted one of Michael's drivers with one of your own in a stolen car, and then fled the country in a chartered aircraft."

Anne shook her head in disbelief, "But my attorney saw me get on this plane. How will you explain it when I don't get off alive in Buffalo, or back in New York?"

Sylvia looked at her watch and smiled. "Oh, but my dear, you have already gotten off in Buffalo. About ten minutes ago. At least someone who looks very much like you. And then you quickly fled the country right before their very eyes."

Shadowed in the near darkness of the Buffalo TRACON radar room, air traffic controller Max Kastan watched the target that was Starliner November three-four Tango Charlie now heading eastbound on its IFR flight plan from Buffalo back to New York. Quick turnaround, he thought. It hadn't been on the ground in Buffalo for more than a few minutes, at best. Near the bottom of his screen the earlier target that was Starliner November three-two-one X-ray continued routinely on its route southward. But he frowned and shook his head as he looked again at the target that was the unidentified and illegal LearJet speeding northward over Lake Ontario without clearance. A scant fifty miles ahead of the aircraft lay the Canadian border, and not far beyond was wilderness.

He watched for several minutes as the LearJet flew across the lake, then another five as it busted into Canadian airspace and continued northward. Then it disappeared from the screen. It looked like a crash, but after the call from the U.S. Marshal he suspected that it wasn't. The brazen pilot with the fugitive on board had probably dropped below the radar scan and was stealthily tree-topping his way northward or to wherever. There was little he could do but watch and alert Search and Rescue, but he sensed it was useless. He flicked the switch for the direct line and called Mitchell Hardison.

FOURTEEN

Gagged with duct tape and her hands bound before her with Sylvia's yarn, Anne realized how they had done it. She had once heard military pilots talk of it; how one aircraft aloft could be switched with another at nearly the same altitude by intercepting at right angles. Then, at the point of crossover, when the radar targets merged, one would turn away just as the other turned into its course. Executed carefully, the radar targets would separate and appear as though neither had altered course when in fact they had exchanged courses. Anne nodded absently, staring out the window at pinpoints of light far below. Yes, that was how they had done it, the other jet she had seen converging upon them had assumed their original course for Buffalo. As far as anyone knew, she was on that other plane.

She thought of Christopher, that it would be like him to have someone watching in Buffalo when they landed, but he would be fooled. The switched aircraft, arriving in Buffalo in darkness and probably bearing the same identification numbers as the one in which she now rode, had already offloaded stand-ins as Sylvia said. Unless Christopher's man in Buffalo suspected otherwise he has probably already called and advised that they had arrived safely.

She was trapped without hope of assistance. And it was her fault. Only thirty minutes ago she had rebuffed Christopher's pleas. And in her haste she had ignored what he was trying to tell her about the evidence linking Warner to Darcy's murder, the gold tie clasp. Now it was clear that Pennington had planted the evidence after murdering Darcy.

She glared at the man that was Pennington, also known as Nash, realizing how cleverly she had been duped, how they had skillfully carried out the entire confusing scenario of death and deception beginning with Ray Thompson's crash that should have been hers. But she also realized that for their plan to work they would soon, probably in minutes, have to dispose of her and rendezvous with the switched aircraft and reverse the sequence, arriving back in New York without her aboard because she was seen getting off in Buffalo.

She took slow, deep breaths to calm herself, to force herself to think clearly with maybe only minutes remaining before they did whatever they had in mind. There were two pilots up forward—were they in on it? She had to assume that they were, yet for Nash to dispose of her body they would either have to land or else...*he would throw her from the plane!*

Suddenly the aircraft decelerated and the nose dipped steeply, her stomach surging against her ribcage as they dropped like a fast elevator. She looked out the window, saw the flaps and speed brakes deploying on the wings as the aircraft began a high-speed descent. Nash was still buckled into his seat in the rear only a dozen feet away, now aiming the murderous Uzi squarely at her midsection. Across the aisle Sylvia was kneading her gnarled hands and staring out her window, waiting as they descended.

So they had chosen landing, and a quick one, probably at an abandoned airfield. There they could easily rid themselves of er body and leave in time to rendezvous with the other Starliner aircraft and reverse the mid-air switch.

Hurry! Think! Think of something, anything!

Gagged and her hands bound before her, Anne sat in the rear-facing seat outside the closed cockpit door and moved only her eyes, searching for something, anything she could use as a weapon.   Except for the knitting needles Sylvia seemed unarmed, but Pennington with the menacing Uzi could easily get off a burst if she made even the slightest move toward her.

She yawned to clear her ears as they descended rapidly, the slipstream outside a buffeting roar.   They would land in minutes.

Think! Think, goddammit!

She stared at the cabin wall by her left knee, her mind racing, when suddenly she saw it. It had been there all along, innocent, innocuous, standard equipment in aircraft.   There, clamped to the wall, was a small red fire extinguisher hidden from Nash's view by the side-facing sofa ahead of her. A wild idea began to form but it would involve terrible risk and possibly her death, yet she had nothing to lose by trying; she would soon die anyway.   The aircraft shook and buffeted as it descended steeply, and that in itself would help.   Her heart beat furiously as she thought about what she would do. She moved her eyes slowly and glanced at Sylvia.   She was still looking away, staring out the window.

All right, do it. Just do it!

Slowly she leaned forward and closed her eyes, knowing that Nash was watching her every move. Feigning hiccups, she puffed her cheeks, grimacing as though about to vomit as she carefully released her seat belt and groped by her knee for the latch releasing the fire extinguisher. When it came free she gripped the heavy metal canister between her bound hands and blinked her eyes open, measuring Nash's distance. He frowned and leaned forward, suspicious, alert.

Now!

Anne rolled her eyes back in her head and slumped forward falling to her knees on the floor by the sofa and counting.

One...two...now!

She looked up and saw him coming fast, startled, then she thrust the fire extinguisher at him and jerked the trigger as she dove for the floor. A foamy blast of pressurized chemical instantly engulfed Pennington as though an avalanche had buried him. He bellowed a gargling howl as the chemical seared his eyes, and she felt the jolt when he stumbled and fell forward against the sofa and then upon her, blindly unleashing a chattering burst of machinegun fire inches over her head. The passenger cabin suddenly exploded in a screeching hurricane of rushing air as the hail of bullets stitched through the cockpit partition and pierced the aircraft's pressurized skin beyond. A whirlwind of foam, litter, dust, and small objects pelted them as the diving aircraft explosively decompressed, and Anne rolled from beneath his now slippery and struggling weight while clutching the fire extinguisher to her breast.

"...he has no bone there, he must protect the top of his head..." she remembered Sylvia saying.

She gripped the heavy steel canister with her bound hands and slammed it against the side of his head instead of the top, to avoid killing him. Grunting and screaming with uncontrollable rage, she battered him again and again until at last he lay motionless.

The aircraft shuddered and heaved as it dove for the earth, and above the roar of the decompressing cabin Anne heard Sylvia's maniacal shrieking. Her rage now unleashed and adrenaline pumping, she swung the extinguisher and shot the old woman full in the face. In an instant of insane fury she wanted to smash it upon the flailing, shrieking bitch's skull, but instead she dropped the extinguisher, tore the duct tape from her mouth and grabbed for Nash's weapons, carefully avoiding the Uzi's trigger. Inside his coat she found the .45 and yanked it from its olster. She had no idea how to use it but she could quickly earn.

Gasping and trembling, she bit through the yarn binding her hands, suddenly aware that the decompression whirlwind had ceased as the pressure equalized. Only the increasing roar of the slipstream outside remained.

The pilots! What would she do about the pilots?

She glanced at Sylvia, now a flailing, macabre mask of foam, then at Nash. He seemed unconscious. Quickly she dragged herself to the cockpit door and lay there with her hand on the knob, frightened of what awaited inside.

Head low, she took a deep breath and clenched her teeth, gripping the heavy and unfamiliar .45 in her right hand. She yanked the door open. "Freeze!" she yelled, her voice cracking as she thrust the heavy automatic into the cockpit.

Anne recoiled at the gruesome sight. The two pilots sat slumped in their seats in the darkened cockpit, only the glowing of the instruments revealed the bloody havoc that Nash's wild bullets had wrought. Their bodies were restrained partially upright by their shoulder harnesses, but she saw two dark, blood-splattered holes in the center of the captain's back. He was obviously dead. The first officer had taken one through the neck but seemed still alive, his head lolling to one side as he mumbled incoherently, blood dripping from his mouth and pumping in gouts from the terrible wound in his throat. He would die in seconds.

She was stunned by the grisly scene, still gripping the .45, at last realizing that the aircraft was diving out of control. She clambered onto the control pedestal between the pilots, dropped the heavy .45 in the captain's lap and grabbed for his control wheel, pulling hard against the pressure building up from excessive speed.

Slow down! She had to slow it down! Get the nose up!

She slapped the throttles to idle and shoved the landing gear lever down, praying the wheels wouldn't tear away from the excessive speed. Suddenly the aircraft shuddered and bucked as though harpooned, the instrument panel now a chattering blur as three sets of wheels reluctantly pushed their way into the howling slipstream and locked into place. Still the control wheel seemed anchored in concrete, her shoulders aching as she strained and pulled frantically to bring the nose up, the altimeter unwinding like a clock gone berserk.

9,000, 8,000, 7,000 feet...

Gradually the control wheel began to ease back in her hand as the hurtling aircraft slowed, its nose reluctantly rising and her face sagging grotesquely as gravity forces quickly compounded.

4,000, 3,000...

At last the altimeter steadied at two thousand feet and she had the aircraft level again, under control, and now a wallowing, docile giant humming along at a stodgy hundred and fifty knots. Anne let out her breath in a rush, safe for the moment, but she was trembling from an adrenaline overload and now acutely aware of the bloody bodies on either side of her. She steeled herself to lean over the captain's body and peer out his side window. Mountains loomed in the darkness not far below, an area with which she was completely unfamiliar and in fact now lost. That, she would worry about in a minute or two, but first she'd better climb to a safe altitude fast before she bored a new tunnel in the mountains of Pennsylvania.

Anne pushed herself away from the side window and her cheek brushed the dead captain's chin, knocking his lolling head to one side and causing a noisy release of trapped gases from his throat. The foul odor of his last meal quickly permeated her nostrils, setting off a gag reflex she couldn't control. Hot, acidic vomit rose quickly in her throat before she could swallow it back, and it spewed from her lips and onto his lap. Coughing and gagging and nearly apologizing, she resumed her painful and awkward side-saddle position on the knobs and switches of the control pedestal. Then she groped for the landing gear lever, raised it, and shoved the throttles to climb power. The ship was

308

powerful, far more responsive than the aging DC-9s to which she was long accustomed, and it surged forward eagerly.

Anne wiped the vomitus from her chin as she gripped the captain's control wheel with her left hand and held it back for the climb to higher altitude. Once again she was in command of an aircraft, yet the irony that she was a defrocked pilot and no longer legal brought an involuntary snicker to her lips. *So sue me,* she thought, *everyone else is.* Maybe she would chart her own course and fly the damn thing to Havana, take advantage of the disappearance setup that Sylvia had so carefully orchestrated. Give the world the finger.

Yeah, and then what?

She leveled off at five thousand feet on a southbound heading, grimacing and gagging again as she reached past the blooded body of the young first officer and set the autopilot. The cockpit reeked of her vomitus and the sicky-sweet smell of spilled blood, and she breathed through her mouth, avoiding also the stench of feces released when the bullets struck the pilots. She monitored the autopilot for a few moments, wary of its condition, fearing it might be damaged and release suddenly when she wasn't expecting it and could lose control. But it seemed functional, feeding in corrective control inputs as it should.

In the dim glow of the cockpit lights she glanced quickly about, looking for the pilots' weapons and saw none. It was then that she realized that these had been professional pilots in freshly pressed uniforms, not rag-tag armed renegades. The poor guys had probably been pulled from TransCon line duty without the slightest notion what their deceptive and ill-fated trip was about. Two more airmen, her brothers of the cloth, dead because of Sylvia. She hoped they had no families, but a gold ring on the young first officer's finger told her otherwise. There were probably young children as well.

Tears suddenly welled in her eyes and her hands trembled as she punched in code 7700 on the radar transponder, an international distress signal that would highlight and blink their target

309

image on FAA radar receivers within range. She scanned the instruments from her awkward and uncomfortable perch, saw that several were blood-spattered and smashed by stray bullets and those that had torn through the captain's chest, but the instruments that she needed most seemed still operable. The global positioning system, a device that could pinpoint her location, was hopelessly shattered, but the radios appeared to be intact and operable and the fuel supply was in good shape. Now she had to find out where she was and locate a place to try to land.

Land. But how?

Her legs were strong enough to work the rudder pedals, but there was no way she could drag either of the pilots from their cramped seats and take their place. She could do without the rudder and brakes while in the air by manipulating the autopilot controls for turns, descent, and final approach. But landing and bringing the aircraft to a stop was another matter. She would somehow have to land the aircraft from her awkward position on the control pedestal and without use of the pedals that controlled the rudder and brakes. It would be like trying to drive a speeding automobile from the back seat. And then park it.

Pennington! Sylvia! In her panic to gain control of the aircraft she had nearly forgotten! Fear gripped her once again as she grabbed the slippery vomit-spattered .45 from the captain's lap and spun around...

"Son of a bitch," Hardison swore quietly as he cradled the telephone. It was the Buffalo TRACON controller relaying the U.S. Marshal's urgent message. Ryan had skipped in a LearJet and disappeared from the radar screen. For a long moment he stood with hands jammed in his pockets, rocking on his heels and lateraling a cigar butt about his mouth, cursing the woman he had come to know and eventually respect.

Yes, he'd been her nemesis at first, and with good reason. But the revealing DC-9 simulator runs she had made and the

ood coloring he found corroborating her notion of criminally-
nduced wing icing had changed all that. He'd even scoffed at
he murder conspiracy theory and had developed a grudging
sense of admiration for the gutsy female airline captain who
eemed willing to go to any lengths to prove her innocence.
Hell, he'd even gotten to like her.

But now she had skipped bail and fled the country, dumping
all she had worked toward and sealing her guilt. Now there was
no way anyone would believe her story.

But it didn't fit. Why, when the evidence was mounting on
her side, would she up and make like a jackrabbit? He wondered if others would see it that way as well, but he doubted that
prosecutors could be such Pollyannas. No, it wasn't their ilk any
more than his. You drew your conclusions based upon evidence
and probabilities, not wishful thinking. Now she had given them
just what they wanted. A done deal.

He shrugged and walked into the radar center's snack canteen, poured the last of the rancid coffee from a clouded pot,
sipped it and grimaced. Chewable. No wonder air traffic controllers were sometimes a bitchy lot. He tossed the dregs into
the sink and sighed, rubbing his weary eyes and looking at his
watch. What to do now. It was nearly three a.m. and he should
go home and forget about Ryan. His job was done. Besides,
Dog probably needed to poop.

But he couldn't forget about Ryan. The whole damned
business niggled at his senses, there had to be something--

"Mr. Hardison?"

He turned and saw the TRACON supervisor standing in the
canteen doorway. "Don't tell me—the LearJet's back."

"No sir, but we've got a distress signal from another aircraft
and I think you might want to come have a look."

He peered over the air traffic controller's shoulder at the
glowing radar screen. The sweep resolution showed targets of
several aircraft, one of which was blinking. "That the one?"

"That's it. He's squawking 7700, the ident for Mayday."

"What is it? What's his number?"

"It's one of the Starliners you saw earlier. November three-two-one X-ray, the one that was southbound out of Canada."

"The one I thought was gonna hit the other that was west-bound for Buffalo?"

"That's it. We've tried repeatedly to raise him since he idented but he doesn't answer. The weird thing about it is he disappeared from the screen for about thirty seconds then popped up again and began identing 7700. His course is erratic, all over the sky."

Hardison sensed something more than just an aircraft in distress. "What's his altitude and location?"

"He's encoding 4,900 feet about four miles southwest of Tunkhannock, Pennsylvania. There's an abandoned military airfield near there, and a few minutes ago it looked like he was heading for it." The controller pointed at the screen. "Now you can see he's kind of wandering south, like he's lost."

A twenty million-dollar corporate aircraft lost? Hardison shook his head. No way. "Call 'em again."

"Starliner three-two-one X-ray, New York approach control, do you read?" The air traffic controller repeated the call then turned to Hardison and shook his head.

Hardison turned away and reached for the telephone to call the duty officer at his office. For the moment he'd have to forget about Ryan. The errant Starliner displayed all the signs of an aircraft soon to crash, and he'd better alert the Go-Team. Ethel would have to let Dog out.

Then a thought struck him and he turned to the TRACON supervisor. "Can you raise the FAA records branch in Oklahoma City and find out who owns that wandering Starliner?"

"No problem."

He waited all of three minutes. When the TRACON supervisor handed him the fax he wasn't surprised. At least not now. The aircraft belonged to TransCon. Now there were *two* TransCon Starliners cavorting about the skies tonight, one southbound from Canada and apparently in trouble, and the other, N34TC, that had carried Ryan earlier and which was now eastbound out of Buffalo on its return to New York. But it was strange that the two related aircraft weren't communicating with one another, especially with one of them apparently in trouble. Hardison crumpled the fax. "Try calling that southbound Star-iner again. The one identing Mayday."

Anne spun around with the .45 and saw the blur of motion in the cockpit doorway too late. "NO—Jesus! Oh God!" she shrieked. A hand flashed downward, driving the shaft of a steel knitting needle deep into her left breast, her senses exploding with sear-ing white-hot pain. Sylvia lay braced in the doorway and shrieking obscenities, jabbing blindly, her face a swollen, con-torted mask of venomous hatred. Screaming in pain, Anne thrust the barrel of the .45 in the old woman's face and jerked the trigger but nothing happened. Sylvia jabbed again and again, driving the needle shaft deep into Anne's forearm and thigh. Scalding pain shot up her arm and leg as she grunted and slammed the heavy .45 into the side of Sylvia's face with all of her might. Blood gouted from the old woman's nose as she crumpled to the floor unconscious, the deadly knitting needle still clutched in her gnarled hand.

Gasping, blood streaming from painful wounds in her breast, arm, and thigh, Anne looked at Nash and saw that he still lay unmoving near the cockpit doorway. Was he unconscious? Faking? Was he waiting until she turned her back again? Sud-denly she felt her churning stomach surge against her rib cage as though she were descending in a fast elevator. She glanced quickly at the night horizon, saw that the aircraft was diving again for the mountains below. The autopilot had released! Cursing, she whirled and grabbed the captain's control yoke again, leveled out and reset the autopilot. Again she waited, not trusting it, and again it seemed to be holding.

Waves of nausea and blinding pain flooded her senses as she slid off the control pedestal and grabbed the blood-streaked knitting needle from Sylvia's hand. Wary, she crawled toward Nash who lay sprawled face up on the cabin floor, mouth open and eyes closed, his breathing slow, shallow. She nudged his ribs with the .45 but he didn't move. Blood pounded in her ears as she lay near him for seconds, unconvinced, yet wondering what to do, certain that at any moment he would spring to life and it would all be over. She could lock herself in the cockpit but the door was too flimsy. He could kick through it in seconds. Tie him up? With what? Yarn? Not for a behemoth like him. She lay there paralyzed with indecision yet desperate to do something to contain him, and quickly. She had to be certain he was no longer a threat before she went back to the cockpit!

What if she held the gun to his temple and prodded him in a painful spot? But suppose he sprang to life, then what? The .45 wouldn't fire, that she had found out, and there wasn't time to figure out why. She grimaced, steeling herself as she raised the steel knitting needle above his face and slowly eased it between his teeth. *Stop! Far enough!* Her hand trembled as she held the knitting needle poised, ready to jam it deep into his throat if he moved. She reached for his crotch and fumbled with his zipper, her stomach churning as she felt for his flaccid warmth, found his testicles and curled her fingers around them. With a quick jerk she twisted and squeezed hard.

Nothing.

She quickly drew away, suddenly wanting to vomit again, wiping her hand of the sweaty filth she had touched and realizing she had hit him too hard with the fire extinguisher near the unprotected area of his skull. He was probably brain-dead or in a coma, no longer capable of a confession, and once again she had screwed herself into a corner. That left only Sylvia; she would have to keep her alive at all costs.

Dizzy with pain and trembling, blood seeping from her wounds, she crawled to Sylvia and turned her over. The old

314

woman's face was a ruined mask of blood and she mumbled incoherently, making obscene gawing sounds through shattered teeth as Anne quickly bound her wrists with yarn. Then she crawled back into the cockpit and once again dragged herself onto the control pedestal between the dead pilots. It was time to somehow get the aircraft onto the ground.

Suddenly the cockpit pitched down steeply again and Anne catapulted upward, cracking her head on the overhead switch panel. The autopilot had released its electronic grip on the controls again! Tears of pain stung her eyes as she again reset the errant device, and instantly the aircraft yawed sharply to the right, then pitched wildly down again, then up! The autopilot was going berserk! Its electronic brain had gone schizo, likely from a bullet lodged somewhere in the circuitry. Quickly she snapped the switch to off and grabbed for the captain's controls again.

All right, then, I'll have to fly it myself as best I can!

"November three-two-one X-ray, do you read?" came a voice through the cockpit speaker. Anne ignored the call to what she thought was another aircraft. She glanced at the ID placard on the instrument panel assuring herself that the aircraft she was flying was N34TC, November three-four Tango Charlie. Yet she was puzzled. By now radar should have picked up her distress signal. So why weren't they calling? She checked the transponder, saw that it was still squawking code 7700, and then grabbed the copilot's mike. "Any radio, any radio, this is Starliner three-four Tango Charlie, do you read?"

"Three-four Tango Charlie, New York approach control, go ahead."

"Three-four Tango Charlie, mayday, mayday, mayday," Anne said quickly.

"Three-four Tango Charlie, New York approach control, do I understand that you're declaring an emergency?"

Fueled by pain and fright, her frustration suddenly boiled over. "Goddammit, what do you think I'm declaring, a national holiday? Christ, you guys, get your frigging act together! I've been squawking 7700 for the past several minutes, don't you guys look at your radar scopes?"

"Easy now. Three-four Tango Charlie we show you as eastbound over Elmira at flight level two-three-zero enroute to JFK. We're not showing a 7700 squawk on you."

Eastbound? At 23,000 feet? Anne glanced at the directional gyro, then to the compass: her heading was 170 degrees. South. The altimeter read 4,900 feet. She scanned the night horizon and saw few lights, nothing like the vicinity of Elmira. Suddenly it dawned on her. The other Starliner had assumed her call sign, N34TC, when the switch had taken place. No wonder air traffic control thought she was three-two-one X-ray. She was out of step with what was going on. She keyed the mike: "New York approach, this is three-four Tango Charlie level at 4900 feet, heading one-seven-zero degrees and way south of Elmira. Look again at your scope. That's me squawking the mayday."

A different voice came back: "Ryan, is that you?"

She recognized the coarse, gravelly voice instantly. "Yeah, shall I wave? Is this Mitchell Hardison? Halo, estatue?"

He chuckled. The woman had grit. "The same. You've got us—"

"I thought I smelled a cigar."

"Yeah, well you've got us a little confused here. We've got two Starliners on the scope and three-four Tango Charlie is tagged as an eastbound Starliner near Elmira. From what I hear you're supposed to be northbound in a LearJet skipping the country. So, Ryan, if you're what and where you say you are, let's see you cancel the 7700 mayday and squawk 3482 on the transponder."

Anne dialed the numbers in and punched the transponder ident button. "How's that?"

Hardison watched the radar screen, saw the blinking target for the southbound Starliner that was known as three-two-one X-ray quickly fade and code 3482 appeared. "On the money," he aid, "What's going on up there, Ryan? You've been wandering all over the sky like some kind of carnival ride, like you're lost. 've seen you fly better than that."

"I'm not on drugs, I can tell you that."

Anne explained her desperate situation briefly while glancng back at the motionless figures of Nash and Sylvia. Then Hardison signed off and the controller's voice came back: "Miss Ryan, I understand that your global positioning system is inoperable, so we're going to hand you over to Scranton Approach Control for radar vectors and get you on the ground there. Advise you use three-two-one X-ray as your call sign to avoid confusion since the eastbound Starliner also using three-four Tango Charlie is now turning north for Canada and following the route of the LearJet."

Anne shifted uncomfortably on the control pedestal. "Roger that, but you'd better track him because it's my guess he's heard us on the radio and he's running. It was a switch, got it? A switch as we flew toward Buffalo, and then he was probably supposed to rendezvous with us on the flip-flop and switch again. He is me. Sleight of hand, mirrors and all that." She looked over her shoulder at Sylvia again. "And now I've got their boss and her flat-topped Neanderthal by the...scrotum."

Hardison came back: "Can you handle it, Ryan?"

"I already did."

"What?"

"Never mind, just—"

"How about the aircraft? Think you can get it down okay without the autopilot?"

"And if I can't? Then what, another hearing? Pilot error again?"

Hardison's voice became impatient. "Look, Ryan, we're on your side down here, okay? I'd just as soon go home and go to bed than have to roust the Go-Team and scrape your butt off the landscape. Now how about Scranton? Can you fly the aircraft well enough to handle the vectors?"

Anne closed her eyes and breathed deeply. The terror she had endured and the massive doses of adrenaline had left her giddy and flippant, an unnatural high that was dangerous and she was wasting time sparring with them. And the worst was yet ahead. "It'll be difficult and I'm injured, but I think I can do it. But negative on landing Scranton, it's too risky trying to land in a populated area. I've got to try to fly this thing sidesaddle between two dead pilots, so I won't have use of the rudder or the brakes. I don't know if I'll even be able to land without busting it, let alone bring it to a stop."

"You'll do okay, Ryan. Make like it's a simulator and impress me again. Now here's the controller; he's got another idea."

"Ah, three-two-one X-ray, understand negative on Scranton. There's an abandoned military field about eight to ten miles northeast of you. Scranton Approach can vector you in and it has a long runway, but it's probably in poor condition. There are no lights and no instrument landing system. Do you want to try for it?"

She would have to; there was little other choice. If she chose Scranton or any other populated area and lost it on landing, the three thousand pounds of jet fuel now sloshing about in the tanks would light off a spectacular fireball and probably torch surrounding buildings, aircraft, and people as well. Coastal 193 revisited. No, it would have to be the abandoned military airfield.

"All right, let's do it," she said at last.

Her back ached miserably and pain throbbed in her bloodied wounds as she sat sideways on the center pedestal, her upper body twisted forward while she gripped the dead captain's control wheel with her left hand and worked the radios, instruments, and throttles with her right. Worse, she couldn't see out the windshield without leaning down and forward, an impossible position for controlling the aircraft, especially during landing.

She eased herself painfully from the center control pedestal, then turned and straddled it, leaning forward like a jockey. Knobs and switches poked painfully in her groin as she resumed what awkward control she could, but at least now she could see forward. She experimented with turning the aircraft at reduced speed without the rudder, but it slipped and wallowed dangerously each time she banked left or right.

No good.

All right, she would use the throttles instead; try steering by using asymmetrical thrust from the twin engines far to the rear. That was how Captain Al Haynes had done it in a disabled United DC-10 at Sioux City years ago. He'd busted it on landing, but still a lot of lives were saved owing to his remarkable skill. She pulled back the throttle to the left engine as she banked left and simultaneously advanced the right throttle. The aircraft was sloppy and dangerously unstable at low speeds without the rudder, porpoising and wanting to slip away from her and fall off into a fatal spin as it reluctantly swung around in a shallow turn, but at last she managed to reverse course and head northeast for the darkened airfield that lay somewhere ahead.

"Now start your descent and turn right to a heading of zero-four-five degrees," the air traffic controller instructed.

Anne eased the throttles back and let the ship slow and begin to settle in the darkness, her heart thumping in her throat as the altimeter began unwinding. She began a shallow turn to the right when suddenly the control wheel shook in her hands and she felt the familiar sinking in the pit of her stomach.

Stall!

Instinctively she shoved the wheel forward to get the nose down and pushed the throttles forward, cracking her head painfully again on the overhead panel as she dove the aircraft to regain precious airspeed.

Too fast! Get the nose up! No--too much—down!

For seconds that seemed minutes she porpoised and careened about the sky, seeking the delicate balance of control that

319

would otherwise have been easy had she been able to sit in a pilot's seat and use the controls properly. Her hands darted about the cockpit, manipulating the control wheel, throttles, flaps, radios, and landing gear, at last gaining control and dreading the landing only minutes away that now seemed impossible. Worse she would have no brakes. They were an extension of the rudder pedals she couldn't reach.

"Turn right to one-zero-five degrees," came another vector.

Straining to see ahead and searching for the field with no lights, she managed another turn, her legs and back aching miserably as she sat hunched forward and worked the throttles, unmindful of the blood still dripping from her wounds. Then again came the controller's voice: "Turn right to one-nine-zero degrees and tune in Tunkhannock VOR on one-one-nine point-five for the zero-one-zero radial. It will lead you directly to the runway now four miles ahead. We're losing you from the radar screen, so good luck. Search and rescue have been dispatched."

"Ryan!" Hardison broke in, "You...you can do this one. I know you can."

Now below the protective guidance of the radar net and on her own, she hunched down on the control pedestal, unhearing of his words and straining to see ahead, concentrating on the difficult approach over mountainous terrain in the darkness. Her left arm ached miserably, a compounding of the searing pain from the deep puncture wounds in her forearm and breast, and the strain from reaching far to her left and gripping the captain's control wheel. Slowly she eased the throttles back, descending, praying that she was on course for the runway and not a mountain.

The altimeter slowly unwound...2,000 feet, 1,900, 1,800... Time to make ready. She chanted a brief landing checklist from memory and set the flaps, trim, power levers and boost. Then she eased the landing gear lever down. Now: Landing lights...*on!*

The powerful beams stabbed ahead in the darkness but still she saw nothing, only the tops of dense trees whipping past not far below. Her heart raced and her breath came in labored gasps as she strained to hold herself upright in an awkward squatting position. Suddenly a road flashed past close beneath and she instinctively jerked the wheel back and the nose shot up dangerously. The stall warning device blared its raucous honking and she quickly shoved the nose down and pushed on more power, leveling out only scores of feet above the treetops.

Close! So damn close! Then she saw it.

Less than a half-mile ahead stretched a broad ribbon of concrete bordered by rows of abandoned aircraft hangars. This was it; she was committed. There could be no second try. The runway threshold grew in the powerful beams as the Starliner raced over the treetops at a hundred-thirty miles an hour.

Do it right...don't screw it up...

She eased the throttles back, judging her altitude and tensing as the aircraft sank lower and the runway neared, the landing gear an extension of her own legs, reaching, feeling...

Forty feet...thirty...twenty...power back a bit, slide right— easy, easy, not too much, left throttle ahead—now back...nose up. Nose up! Too much—down!

Suddenly the wheels slammed onto the runway and the hurtling aircraft swerved dangerously to the right, its wheels chattering and skidding over the pavement, torturing the landing gear and quickly stripping away the tires. *She was losing it!* Desperately she worked the throttles, yanking the left to reverse thrust, shoving the right full forward. The jet engines shrieked and thundered in opposite thrust, tugging the tail around an instant before the speeding aircraft skidded off the runway. Quickly she yanked the right throttle to reverse thrust also and both engines screamed their hurricane thrust forward.

It was too little too late.

Ghostly hangars raced past in the darkness at a hundred miles an hour as she feverishly worked the throttles to keep the careening aircraft straight in what she knew was a losing battle. Now less than half a mile ahead loomed the end of the runway, and a solid stand of trees awaited beyond. There was no way she could stop in time.

The boonies—her only chance! Take a ride on the wild side! She had done it for Hardison in the simulator and now she would do it for real. It was a frightening and deadly risk but there was no choice. *I love you, Gordy. I love you, Titus. God help me...*

Now! With both engines screaming in reverse thrust, she jerked the left throttle to idle and the aircraft went berserk, suddenly lurching sideways and skidding down the runway on bare wheels. Anne gritted her teeth and held on as the landing gear tore away, felt the tremendous jolt as the aircraft pancaked onto its belly and the wild ride began. She slapped the fuel and electrical switches to off and blew the fire bottles into the engines as the ship spun dizzily in a shower of sparks and shrieking metal and slammed into a low berm adjacent to the runway, skidding minus a wing across a frozen field where at last the wild ride ended.

Suddenly it was still, the quiet almost overwhelming in the wake of thundering engines and shrieking metal, and Anne crawled from the floor and peered out the side window, the stench of raw kerosene filling her nostrils. A concussive *whumph* suddenly shook the shattered aircraft and a gout of brilliant flame shot skyward from where the right wing had been and she ducked, already feeling the searing heat baking the fuselage. In seconds she would be fried meat.

Ignoring the burning pain in her breast, arm, and thigh, she crawled out of the cockpit and into the passenger cabin where Sylvia lay bound and struggling, screaming demonically amid clouds of choking black smoke. She had to save them for confessions, one of them at least, but Nash was impossible; there was no way she could move his bulk.

Another explosion rocked the aircraft and she saw the cabin windows melting away. Clouds of acrid smoke billowed into the cabin and filled her lungs as she struggled choking and gagging to drag Sylvia's flailing body toward the cabin door on the opposite side. She grabbed the latch, levered it aside and pushed the door out. Instantly the vacuum created sucked the flames through the melted cabin windows and Anne screamed as the terrible heat seared her back and set her hair afire. She let go of Sylvia and grabbed for the old woman's shawl, quickly wrapping it about her head, then dove headfirst for the doorway only to be jerked up short, cracking her chin on the threshold. Nash's powerful hands clasped her ankle in an unyielding vise-like grip, tugging her back into the flaming cabin. Grunting and screaming, Anne kicked wildly at the face that was a tormented rictus of demonic eyes and bared teeth. Then with a wail of pain and frustration she brought her heel down squarely upon the sponginess that was the top of his mutilated head. Her release was instant and she dove through the open door as another gout of flame shot after her.

Dazed and gasping in agony, Anne dragged herself forward on her elbows, struggling to distance herself from the flames engulfing the aircraft. A piercing wail came from within the inferno and she closed her eyes tightly and clenched her teeth trying to shut out Sylvia's unearthly screams. Any second would come the big one, the thundering holocaust when the remaining fuel tank ignited and exploded, and she wrenched herself forward frantically. Behind she heard the popping sounds of the ammunition in Nash's weapons going up and she ducked as bullets buzzed over her head.

Run! For God's sake, RUN!

She couldn't, her legs just wouldn't work. Whimpering and panting, she pulled herself ahead faster with her elbows but still she was only fifty feet from the flaming aircraft.

On your KNEES! Get on your KNEES!

Crying out in pain and frustration, she forced herself onto her knees and tried to scuttle forward but fell instead on her face, bloodying her nose. Again she got upon her knees, remembering the elderly man at the hospital with odd prosthetics for legs, how he had strained in dogged determination as he worked his way purposefully along the parallel bars.

Purpose! Purpose!

She wailed frantically as she spurred herself forward, scuttling painfully on hands and knees when suddenly a concussive explosion blew her to the ground and great shards of flaming metal scythed over her head, slashing into the forest beyond and igniting the trees. She rose to her knees slowly, swaying drunkenly when darkness overcame her.

FIFTEEN

'Good afternoon. We meet again."

Anne's eyes fluttered open and she stared through a gauzy haze at the figure standing near. She blinked her eyes several times and still the cloud wouldn't dissolve. She tried moving her hands and fingers but they were bound, and her face felt encased in a mask. Her entire body seemed aflame as though she'd been parboiled. She tried to sit up but firm hands pressed her back. Then she remembered.

"Don't try to sit up, you've had a rough time. Again."

"Who...?" she said through puffy lips. The figure hovered nearer, only inches away, and she strained to make out the face.

"I'm sorry, I won't play any more games with you. It's me, David Levinson. Welcome back to Queens Memorial, we've missed you."

"Oh, Jesus," she rasped through seared membranes, "This is where I came in."

"It is, and it's where you're going to stay this time until I'm finished with you. No jumping ship to play detective this time."

"My eyes...why can't I—"

"The lenses were scorched somewhat, but you'll regain you sight in a few days."

"And the rest of me?"

"Puncture wounds in the left breast, forearm, and thigh some infection, but we've got that under control and they'll hea well enough. You've got second-degree burns on a good part o your body, including your scalp, but I don't think any grafting is necessary. You're just going to be pretty uncomfortable for a few weeks."

Anne sighed and closed her eyes. "So what else is new."

"Oh, a good deal. Would you like to entertain some people who've been waiting to see you?"

"Who are they—U.S. Marshals?"

Levinson chuckled, "I think we can do better than that."

"Wait...how long have I been here?"

"Two days and two nights, all the while rambling on about a ride on the wild side, or something like that. From the looks o you, I guess you did."

In the hallway outside her room they drew lots to see who would go in first since Levinson would allow only one at a time. Gordy lost the first three rounds, only because Titus had arranged the lots. He knew best the order of appearance for Miz Annie.

Titus settled himself gently into the chair at her bedside, testing its strength before allowing the full weight of his enormous bulk upon it. "Miz Annie, it be me," he rasped quietly. "I...I'm jes' so glad you is goin' be okay. Lord knows, missy, we's all been prayin' for you. You been done wrong, okay, but it all be fixed soon enough. You'll see. Titus knows."

She reached toward the sound of his voice with a bound hand, wanting so badly to touch the gentle giant she adored. "Thank you, Titus. I hope you're right."

326

"Oh, I be right, okay." He leaned toward her and gently patted her shoulder. "Others waitin' to see you now, Miz Annie. Take care now, you hear? Everthin' be okay soon. Hold on to that, hear?"

A lump welled in her throat as she heard him leave. "Goodbye, Titus," she said softly. "I love you too."

She saw another hazy figure approach her bedside and pull up a chair. Before he spoke she knew who it was; the gagging scent of rancid cigars preceded him.

"Hello, Anne," said the gravelly voice. "I just want to say that you're a hell of a pilot, tops in my books. What you did at that abandoned airfield was even better than what you did in the simulator. If you're still trying to impress me, you've damn well succeeded."

Anne tried to smile but her lips stung like fire. "I'll bet you wouldn't fly with me, though. I have a knack for busting airplanes."

"You'll improve with practice. I'll let someone else tell you why that's going to be so. Take care, kiddo, talk to you later."

Another figure settled in the chair and sat quietly then cleared his throat. "Miss Ryan, I'm William Lorenzo, Assistant U.S. Attorney, and—"

"I know who you are. I suppose you can't wait until I get out of here."

"We'll need a pretty lengthy statement from you, and there'll be a hearing, but it can wait. It's seldom that I lose a case, but I can honestly say that I'm glad I've lost this one. Forfeited, better describes it."

Anne sat up quickly but searing pain shot through her body and she laid back. "I—I don't understand. They're all dead, there's nobody to testify—"

"Oh yes there is. We have Nash's accomplice, a fellow named Esposito, also known as Luis Alvarado, who helped him spray that stuff on your aircraft the night you crashed."

Anne tried to sit up. "What? How did—"

"The local police responded to a silent alarm at the Edel-brock estate shortly after Sylvia died, and when they arrived your friend Romo had him collared. They thought he was just a burglar, but when they took him in for questioning they found that he was an illegal alien and called Immigration."

"What was he doing at the estate? How did you link him with Nash?"

"He was looking for Nash. And money. Nash apparently had stiffed him or else Alvarado was coming back for more, trying to squeeze him because of all the media coverage. So in exchange for deportation he talked. Said he drove the tanker, saw Nash put the stuff in the water but didn't know what it was, etcetera, etcetera. When we told Hardison about it, he put us in touch with his assistant, Westphal, who identified Alvarado, a.k.a. Esposito, as being one of the two guys on the tanker that night."

Anne stared at him uncertainly. "But is his testimony enough?"

"Not by itself, but collectively we have enough. Penning-ton's prints, Nash's, I should say, were all over objects at the Edelbrock estate and they match those on the aspirin bottle and the food coloring can that Mitchell Hardison found."

"Circumstantial," she mocked.

"Maybe, but convincing nonetheless. And thanks to your alerting the flight controllers, we have the pilots of the other Starliner aircraft. They confessed to the in-flight switch that fooled everybody watching on radar. Sylvia Edelbrock had ar-ranged it, and Nash, as you know, was a former navy pilot. It was his scheme. Add to that the documents we found locked in a file at her estate and we go well beyond circumstantial."

"What documents?"

"Typed instructions, for one. Instructions she apparently gave to Milton Donnelley, directing him to transfer 5,000 shares of her TransCon stock to an account she had set up in your name. Also included was how to do it so that it appeared as

hough the stock had come from Warner Edelbrock. We com-
ared the method to the firm's client records and they matched.
With that information we concluded that Warner Edelbrock's
ransfer to you was bogus, a smokescreen engineered by Sylvia
Edelbrock."

One of many. "So you're dropping the charges against me?"

"That's up to the judge, but with the testimony and the evi-
lence we now have, and my recommendations, I think that he
will. Especially convincing will be the evidence of how Sylvia
Edelbrock arranged the crashes, implicated you with drugs, and
hen with a mid-air aircraft switch attempted again to kill you to
close the loop."

Anger suddenly stirred her. If she hadn't played detective,
stubbornly set out to clear herself and nearly gotten herself
killed, she'd be going to prison. As it had been all her life, only
Anne Ryan could help Anne Ryan.

As though he knew what she was thinking, Lorenzo added,
'We were wrong, and I'm sorry. Perception is reality, and what
evidence we had going in strengthened our perceptions. Unfor-
tunately, this human failing extends to law enforcement as well.
We're not immune."

It was over at last. Anne closed her eyes and shook her
head. *Close. It had been so damned close.*

"It took a lot of courage to do what you did, Miss Ryan, and
you almost didn't live to tell about it. If you hadn't comman-
deered that airplane we might still be believing—"

Her eyes suddenly blinked open painfully. "Courage? Are
you kidding? I was scared to death! I didn't have any choice! If
I hadn't done something you'd still be looking for me, dead meat
somewhere, but as far as you knew a fugitive who'd skipped
bail. But when I found out we weren't going to her brother's
place it all came together, how I'd let myself get tricked into all
that, the faked shooting in my room—"

"Sylvia Edelbrock does have a brother. Or did."

329

"Yeah, she said he's some Mafia lieutenant, or something. A *capo*, that was it. He's probably in on it too. Did you check that out?"

Lorenzo chuckled and shook his head, "He might have been in on it if he'd lived beyond the age of seven. There's a lot more about Sylvia Preston Edelbrock that we've learned and you don't know, although it's inadmissible as evidence—"

"What—she killed him and had Romo roast him for dinner?"

"Close. Sylvia Preston, long before she became Warner Edelbrock's wife, spent twelve years in a mental institution. When she was fourteen, crippled, she gouged out her younger brother's eyes with a knitting needle and then drove it into his brain. The psychiatric records show that she did it because he took something of hers. Sound familiar?"

Anne thought a moment and then it dawned. "Loud and clear, I think. She saw that my affair with her husband was like stealing something from her, that I had stolen his soul from her, that it belonged to her. Is that what you mean?"

Lorenzo shrugged, smiling. "Suits me. He was also trying to wrest the airline away from her as well. That may have something to do with it. Who knows what goes on in the complexities of the psychotic mind. By the way, do you realize that because of that psychotic mind you're now a wealthy woman?"

"Mr. Lorenzo, I'm not up to mind games. What do you mean?"

"Under New York law, a gift is a gift, irrevocable if the donor predeceases the donee unless a will provides otherwise. The stock she transferred into your name to incriminate you remains yours, and so it seems the only mistake Sylvia Edelbrock made."

Anne looked at him and slowly shook her head. "No, she made two. She took me for an airplane ride. That's my territory. If it'd been a car or anything else, she probably would have succeeded in killing me."

SIXTEEN

Mitchell Hardison stood on the front steps of Queens Memorial Hospital, pondering his brief visit with Anne Ryan. Below on the street a honking melee of homebound traffic sped past. Already it was late afternoon, too late to fight the traffic back to the NTSB offices across the river in Parsippany. He supposed he should just go home and feed and walk Dog before going to his weekly dinner at Ethel's.

Boiled chicken and Brussels sprouts—no butter. Christ!

No longer was there chicken-fried steak, taters and thick gravy, homemade bread with mounds of butter, coconut cream pie...

"You are entirely too portly, Mitchell dear."

He sighed at the depressing thought of Ethel's Spartan menu designed to produce the Incredible Shrinking Man, but already he had a plan. It was deceitful, but then a guy had to take care of himself during hard times.

He reached into a pocket and drew out a fresh cigar, lighted it, and exhaled a suffocating cloud rivaling that of a passing bus.

331

He thought again of Ryan. He'd thought of her often since he revealing demonstrations in the DC-9 simulator weeks ago, and he'd probably think of her for a long time to come. She could fly again, maybe soon, no question about it. And well she should, the FAA was going to reinstate her license. But *would* she? The woman still harbored a great deal of guilt about matters that weren't her fault. She may never again want to haul passengers.

As for himself, his handling of her pilot error case troubled him. What could he have done differently? He had followed what evidence there was, had even gone the extra mile looking for more before putting the cap on the case and handing the Board its probable cause. And he had been wrong.

Probable Cause. *Probable...* The very language of the law seemed flawed, it seemed to allow a convenient off-ramp from the route in pursuit of a problem. An opportunity to be snookered by what *appeared* to be.

Perception is reality... Hardison shook his head. Lorenzo had said that. For some, maybe he was right. Certainly the public reacted as such. Laymen. But there was no place for it in law enforcement or at the NTSB, as far as he was concerned.

Not that the NTSB lived by perceptions. They didn't. They scrupulously adhered to fact, evidence. But as far as he was concerned the qualified language of the NTSB's congressionally-mandated goal to seek *probable* causes left a good deal to be desired.

He stared at the sky as rush-hour traffic sped past, deep in thought. Cogitating, he called it, while lateraling the cigar from one corner of his mouth to the other. Okay, so after much searching for and sifting of information, you state the probable cause of an accident for the record and for the learning benefit of other pilots, air traffic controllers, and the aircraft manufacturers. But too often what you're really saying is that you don't *know* the cause. What you have is an educated and deductive guess when things turned gray. A conclusion based upon the best objective information available. Nothing wrong with that. But is it enough? Just where do you, where *should* you stop an investigation? At what point do you take the off-ramp to the more convenient goal of *probable* instead of continuing the investigative pursuit and perhaps later being able to state the problem, the cause, with *certainty*? Like being able to say, *this..is..the..cause*. Must economics and cost-benefit considerations enter into the decision-making process?

He guessed that in all fairness and reason there had to be a limit somewhere, though, as some pursuits were fruitless. Like a doomed aircraft and its unfortunate souls lying sunken beneath a thousand fathoms of seawater. The evidence was unreachable and you had little choice but to settle for the probables as the cause. That much was clear.

But strictly within the context of the NTSB's marching orders to seek probable causes, and using deductive reasoning after much sifting of evidence, Ryan's case had been right on the money: pilot error compounded by the presence of drugs. A reasonable person in possession of the facts couldn't have concluded otherwise. And he, Mitchell Hardison, sure as hell hadn't.

And he'd been wrong. *Perception is reality, Mitchell.* Well, damn.

So what was missing? How much further down the investigative highway should he have gone (assuming they'd let him) before diving for the off-ramp to the destination of *probable* cause? On the other hand, maybe pursuing it further wasn't the issue in Ryan's case. Maybe he had missed something along the way after all?

Then what was it he *should* have seen, been aware of, intuitively calculated, deduced, induced, but didn't? Or...what had he ignored?

Methinks the lady doth protest too much. Shakespeare.

Yes, he'd thought Ryan's protestations a desperate and contrived attempt to salvage her own skin. He had seen such actions of the guilty many times and had programmed himself to ignore all but documented fact. And so, Mitchell Hardison, you grabbed for the obvious when all else lead you nowhere. And maybe you were just a little pressured to do it as well. Pressured by yourself, not them, to show them just how valuable you are.

"An early out, Mitch. Saves a lot of face..."

Yeah, maybe he was a little pressured by them too. Just a little.

But then consider the other side of the coin, Mitchell, my man. Outside influences aside. You crusade tirelessly on the issue of human failure in the cockpit, do you not? Indeed. And what of yourself? Your failures? Was it not because of your self-programmed myopia involving Ryan that you had allowed yourself to become thoroughly hoodwinked by the cunning of an aged and wheelchair-ridden psychotic? A psychotic and de-mented mind, perhaps, but nevertheless capable of perceiving the weaknesses of others, yourself included, and predicting and manipulating their behavior to achieve the end so desired. Um-hmm. You bought Sylvia Edelbrock's *probable cause,* Mitchell. Stepped in it, didn't you?

Perception is reality...

Except that the vigorously protesting lady-pilot whom you scoffed relentlessly had made it otherwise. Anne Ryan had changed the ending.

He rocked on his heels as he stood puffing vigorously on his cigar, nodding as he stared at the passing traffic. Yeah, she sure as hell had. And Anne Ryan had changed forever the way he would approach aircraft accident investigations.

Probable cause be damned.

Mitchell Hardison spat and crushed out his cigar as he began walking down the steps. "Thanks for the lesson, Ryan. I owe you one."

And no, he'd be damned if he'd take an early-out.

SEVENTEEN

Anne lay back against the bed pillows, exhausted, her body flaming with the heat from her terrible burns. Three weeks, Levinson had said. Three weeks and she could likely leave the hospital unless infection set in. He had used the word *assume* a good deal: assuming no infection, assuming the corneas of her eyes healed satisfactorily, assuming grafts were not later determined necessary, assuming...

God, how badly she wanted out of here, to get on with her life, whatever that may be...

Whatever that may be...

Would she fly again? First must come the privilege. So here was that word again: *assuming* the criminal charges would be set aside, as Lorenzo had indicated, and *assuming* that the NTSB would reverse its position of pilot error, as Hardison had said, and *assuming* the FAA would reinstate her license in light of all of the above, then in all likelihood she *could*.

But assumptions aside, there remained the vision of the little girl, Toni, sitting on her frightened father's lap in the passenger cabin of the doomed aircraft she had commanded not that many months ago, a vision that would be forever seared into her brain, thus driving a wedge between the could and would of her flying. Still it was impossible for her not to remember the little girl, and she remembered her often, without remembering also the grisly photographs of lumpy body bags lying in snow beside the steaming carcass that had once been an airliner. Her airliner. Like it or not, extenuating circumstances aside, all forty-seven of them had been her responsibility and they were now very much dead. Always would be.

That she had tried her best and failed to save them in those terrifying moments mattered not. The passage of time does *not* heal all wounds. No matter what was said, how it was said, what perspective was gained, what logic and reason was used by those well-meaning persons who would seek to set her straight, it would never be *okay*. She could never look upon it any differently than she was at this moment. They died at her hands, however innocent she may have been.

No, she would never fly again.

Anne passed from these thoughts into a fitful and shallow sleep.

He sat hunched on a stool in the basement beneath a single bulb hanging from the ceiling, toying with the creatures in the small crate, poking at them with a stick and watching with satisfaction as their segmented tails whipped and struck in response. There were a dozen of them, and their crustacean bodies made little clicking noises as they scuttled about, climbing over one another, seeking prey.

In another box were the mice. Two of them. He reached in and gently removed one, then stroked its back with his forefinger as he held it close to his face. It twitched its tiny nose at him curiously, and then began washing its face with its paws. Then he lowered it into the crate with the twelve creatures and withdrew his hand quickly as they descended upon it. Their tails bucked and snapped furiously as the mouse skittered about in a frenzy of fear, and then the needle pointed venom bulb on one of the tails struck home. Then another, and another... For seconds the mouse lay in agonizing convulsions. And then it was over.

Centruroides Exilicauda, they were called. They were the largest and most venomous scorpions in all of North America, several inches in length and indigenous largely to Mexico. Collectively, a dozen of them could kill a human. The neurotoxins in the venom concentration from so many would cause anaphylactic shock then respiratory failure, he knew. He had seen it happen long ago. In his country. In Mexico.

Anne stirred in her restless sleep, responding to some stimulus that had rescued her from the nightmares. Gradually she became aware of something touching her neck, and suddenly her eyes blinked open to the semi-darkness of her hospital room.

"Hi," he said gently.

"Oh, Jesus, it's you. For a moment I thought—"

"Not Jesus, just David. David Levinson."

"I felt something, something touching my neck."

"Just taking your pulse. Nothing to get excited about." He looked down at her bandaged hands and wrists.

Anne took a deep breath and let it out in a rush. She had had the dream again, a dream of slapping a screaming and flailing Overmeyer who was shouting, *"Watch out! Watch out! Watch out!"*. A dream of suddenly tumbling end over end, and of the cataclysmic crash that followed. And then there were the body bags...

"You had the dream again, didn't you."

She squeezed her eyes shut too hard, compressing the inflamed corneas; then came the stinging tears and she turned her head away. "Yes."

"Do you want to talk about it?" he asked, resting his hand on her forearm.

337

She turned toward him, glanced at his hand on her forearm, felt a gentle and meaningful squeeze. Long suppressed emotions suddenly washed over her, spawned not only of relationships with men that lacked sensitivity, gentleness, but of a deep-rooted need for simple human contact. Contact with someone whom she trusted, someone who cared and had no other agenda. She had reached desperately for Sylvia's faux nurturing and had been burned badly, figuratively as well as literally. But this man had saved her life, more than once, and he was a good man. Selfless and sensitive. Safe. She rested a bandaged hand on his "No."

David Levinson nodded. "I guess I probably wouldn't either. But I just wanted you to know that I'd listen if you wanted me to. I haven't got any ax to grind, Anne."

"I know."

He gently took her bound hand from his and placed it at her side as he rose to leave.

"Wait...please." She reached and touched his elbow. "Don't go just yet."

"Are you okay? Do you need anything?"

"Yes, I...I need you to stay with me for a while. Just...be with me."

It was a risk, bordering on questionable conduct, but he took it nonetheless. He touched her forehead, feeling for fever, found none and then caressed her cheek with the backs of his fingers. His fingertips lingered beneath her chin and he gently turned her face toward him. "I'll stay with you as long as you wish, Anne."

In minutes her eyes had closed, their lids occasionally fluttering as she settled once again into troubled sleep. There were muted noises coming from the corridor and he looked at his watch, saw that it was nearly eleven p.m. The nurses' shift was changing. A thin shaft of light from the corridor was all that illuminated the darkened room, but it was enough that he could see her face and watch her breathing. Not so long ago he had sat at her side just as he was tonight, watching her chest rise and all, watching for signs that she might stir and at last awaken from the coma.

He thought of the months that followed, of the physical progress she had made under his tutelage in spite of the odds, of her brief encounter with addiction to pain medication, of the psychological damage inflicted upon her by the authorities, that old woman, and most of all by herself.

He thought of her life and how it must have been before the world had come crashing down upon her. How, her friend Gordy had said, she had existed in a narrow world of her choosing. How, David Levinson thought, it had so closely paralleled his own. Her focus on flying, his on medicine, nearly at the exclusion of all else. Just as Regina Dotzer had known that his personal life was a cipher, so had Gordy known Anne's as well. He supposed that his relationship with Regina was much like Gordy's with Anne: close yet platonic.

He had read of her affair and later entanglement with that man, Edelbrock, and wondered what it was that drew women to men of his sort. As a doctor he understood body chemistry, but not that variety. On the other hand he wondered also what, if anything, drew women to men of his own sort. Whatever sort that might be.

Because somewhere along the way he, the mild-mannered, average looking and otherwise benign David Levinson, MD, had fallen in love with Anne Ryan.

He found what he was looking for by the fireplace in the study. An eight-inch fireplace match would do, and he selected one. He took the back stairs and once again descended into the dankness of the basement where one by one he offered the matchstick to the scorpions. How simple it was; they grabbed hold with their pincers. He lifted them out of the wooden crate and shook them off into the shoebox. Then he carefully taped the lid shut while they scuttled about in frenzy inside the box.

339

He looked at his pocket watch and saw that it was after eleven. It was time. He ascended the stairs to the kitchen and made his way through the cavernous mansion, looking around for the last time. He left through the service entrance where his pickup was waiting, then climbed in and set the shoebox on the seat beside him. For a few minutes he sat in the darkness, listening to the night sounds until his vision adjusted. Pale light from a half moon bathed the expansive grounds, and he sighed and shook his head as he looked about. The fruits of his labors were everywhere, but now he must leave, never to return. There would be one stop before he made the long drive to the border. To the land of his birth. To Mexico.

He must first stop at Queens Memorial Hospital. He must avenge the señora's death.

David Levinson suddenly jerked awake and raised his head slowly, the muscles in his neck painfully protesting the awkward position to which they'd been subjected. He'd dozed off while sitting at her bedside, but still she slept, her bandaged hand resting upon his. His bladder was calling and he looked at his watch. Five after midnight. Too much coffee earlier. In another hour he'd be reminded again, such was his ritual with caffeine.

He gently placed her hand at her side and rose slowly to his feet and stretched, careful not to wake her. He wandered out into the quiet corridor, blinking, the lights too bright, and made his way silently past the nurses' station toward the men's room nearby.

"Dr. Levinson?"

Too late. It mattered not whether you were on duty or off, whether you were dressed in white hospital tunic and slacks or in tee shirt and jeans, it was always the same. Doctors were never off duty. He turned, "Yes? Oh! Regina, what are you doing here so late? I thought you left at eleven."

340

She smiled, "What do you think nurses do—keep regular hours? Someone calls in sick and they ask you to fill in, what do you say? Sorry, I'm tired, see you tomorrow?"

"I'm sorry, I didn't—"

"I'm just kidding, David. You know me; I'm just as bad about it as you are. If I'm needed, I do it. Simple as that." Regina inclined her head toward Anne's room, "How's she doing?"

David stifled a yawn and rubbed the stubble on his cheeks. "Okay, I guess. Physically, at least. But I'm worried about how she's punishing herself, how she keeps having those terrible dreams, and—"

"Maybe you should ask Halstead to look in on her, maybe have a talk."

"She doesn't want to talk about it, and I'm certain that she'd resist a shrink. Maybe some things are better left alone, maybe in time what's troubling her will go out with the tide."

Regina held his gaze. "You know better than that."

David shrugged and turned toward the men's room. "Nature calls."

"David?"

"What?"

"Come here," she said, crooking her finger at him. He leaned on the countertop and she motioned him closer, studying his face as though examining some curious object, "You're in love with her, aren't you?" she whispered.

The speed at which traffic passed his aging pickup was frightening, yet he was determined to finish what he had vowed to do. It was a matter of honor. He was unaccustomed to traffic, even at this hour, he had driven so little for so long. Señor Pennington had usually done the driving, had taken him to town when needed, but now he too was gone. And soon the authorities would loot and close the mansion. He would have to leave anyway.

He missed his native Mexico; it would be good to return. Return to the remote high mountains south of the great Chisos where the air was still fresh and pure, where traffic was two burros passing on a steep and narrow trail. There he would be welcome, the people would welcome him as one of them, without condition, without question, and the years that had passed would shrink to mere days as though he had never left. This was where his people went when they wished never to be seen again.

La ciudad de los muertos. The city of the dead.

David relieved himself then walked past the nurses' station winked at Regina, and stepped quietly into Anne's room. Still she slept, but she was restless, mumbling, an occasional whimper escaping her seared lips. He felt a lump in his throat, his eyes misting as he watched her personal torture repeating itself.

He felt so damned helpless, so thoroughly incapable of exorcising the demons ravaging her mind and feeding upon her corrosive guilt. There was a nearly overpowering urge to reach for some instrument, some medication, some machine or other device used to heal the body, but there was nothing. Nothing for the mind. Physiological technology had made quantum leaps in only a few decades, astonishing revelations in just the past few years and many more were within reach. Yet treatment of the mind and its ills remained in Gothic times, stalled largely in a quagmire of conflicting theory, depending upon whether you were a Freudian or a Jungian. The power of physical medicine compared to psychological was like comparing the neutron bomb to a firecracker.

He stood by her side in the sliver of light from the corridor and watched the now rapid cadence of her breathing, the jerking muscle movements, knowing the terror she must be enduring as the nightmares once again consumed her. To wake her in the midst of this would frighten her even more, even though for only seconds; the severity would be too great. She would have to work through it.

He reached for a tissue and wiped the beads of perspiration from her brow, then bent and gently kissed her there. As he straightened he saw that she had suddenly calmed, the hurricane of emotion stilled as though she were in the eye of it. It was a good time to leave. For a while, anyway. He had decided to make a nightlong vigil of it.

"Bring me a cup, would you?" Regina asked, as he stepped into the elevator.

"Black?"

"The blacker the better. Some of that French Roast stuff, if it isn't yesterday's."

He looked at his watch as the doors began closing. "That could mean it was brewed ten minutes ago."

"Day before, then. You test it. If you survive, bring me some."

The main floor cafeteria was a twenty-four hour affair, nearly deserted now. Two interns and a nurse were quietly chatting over by the windows. He knew none of them, but nodded anyway as he passed. In a far corner sat one of thousands of New York's derelicts, alternately nursing a cup and a brown-bagged bottle, his heaping shopping basket bearing the Kroger logo moored close by. He nodded at him too, and then headed for the steaming pots along the counter. The coffee tested okay, and well it should for a buck twenty-five.

He sat down several tables away from the derelict, even farther from the other medical types, not wishing to be drawn into conversation, least of all with the interns and the nurse, and the derelict was least likely to engage him. He wanted most just to be with his thoughts, however confused they were.

He knew her well, yet he knew her not at all. As her physician of many months he knew well every physical aspect of her being. He knew intimately how she responded to pain, to the process of healing, to emotional conflict, to daunting challenges in the face of overwhelming odds, to failures, and even to humor--his, if you could call it that. He had been by her side nurturing her through it all, at least through all that was within the realm of his responsibilities and capabilities as a physician.

But he knew virtually nothing of the person that was Anne Ryan. He knew nothing of her in an interpersonal sense. She seemed kind enough to others, but was she really? Instead of chastising someone's obvious faults, would she instead seek and dwell on the positive aspects of individuals? Was she selfish or selfless? Was she of the habit of doing something nice for someone—without being caught at it? Or was she of the sort that kept a ledger of quid pro quos? If stung would she offer the offender a second chance? And what habits did she possess that might, over time, annoy someone to the point of distraction? Would she cheat at Monopoly?

He knew her not at all. So just what was it that so attracted him to her?

He had stuffed it far away in a dark corner of his mind, ignoring it, but still it seeped out when he dwelled on thoughts of her. Perhaps logic and reason, his professional thought processes that ruled both sides of his life, nudged it free to remind him. And when it did he would shun the notion and turn away from it.

Ah, but there was no denying it, really, and he knew it. David Levinson was simply a lonely man.

As he sat sipping his coffee in the nearly deserted cafeteria, occasionally nodding and waving back at the derelict who guffawed heartily each time, he at last came to terms with himself. That he loved her he was certain, even though it may be fueled by loneliness. He was as certain of this as one could be, given that as far as he knew he'd never experienced the emotion. Oh, there had been a woman now and then, infrequently, but seldom intimately. The truth was, no one had aroused his interest sufficiently to cause him to…well, to go to the trouble of engaging in emotional involvement. And worse, he had observed too often in others the resulting agony of disentanglement. He was far too absorbed otherwise, and early on, at least, the distractions of ntering into and exiting from relationships would have been atal to his career. He knew that much of himself.

Anne Ryan, he was certain, would understand these things if ver they were to compare notes.

He wondered if by some stretch of the imagination she had ver...ever thought of him as someone other than her doctor. Whether she also had become...afflicted. He chuckled briefly, oud enough that the interns and the nurse looked at him curi-ously.

What was so funny? The word *twitterpated* had popped into his mind. Yes, twitterpated. That was what it was. That's what Flower had said to Bambi a hundred years ago at an age when Levinson had gotten his first toy doctor's kit. And that was his present state of mind. He was thoroughly...smitten. Suddenly he burst out laughing, and across the room the derelict shared in the joke, barking a loud guffaw through gums that held no teeth.

He parked his pickup in the sprawling lot next to the aged monolith that was Queens Memorial Hospital, turned off the ig-nition and sat for several moments listening to the ticking of the engine as it cooled. It would not be difficult, he knew. Manuel had provided him with the proper clothing and identification and had shown him a hand-drawn sketch of the general layout of the corridors, the elevators, and the entrances where, at this hour, he could readily enter and exit. The name sewn on the breast of his green janitor's shirt was *Pancho*, matching the name on the plastic ID tag, but not the picture. The man in the picture was younger, considerably more robust, yet he was dark and also of Latino descent. It was close enough, Manuel had said. You have merely lost weight. Not to worry.

In cadence with the ticking of the engine were the rustling, scratching sounds coming from within the shoebox on the seat beside him. They were annoyed.

He pulled out his grandmother's pocket watch, held it to the glow of the parking lot lights, and then snapped it shut. It was

345

time to go. The building was all but asleep. It was time for him to mop the floors on the seventh floor.

She surfaced from a deeper, more peaceful sleep and hovered on the border of wakefulness until a noise and voices in the corridor parted the curtain to consciousness. She lay there for moments disoriented, blinking her grainy eyes until the damaged corneas stung and she winced. She could hear one of the nurses conversing with someone, bantering, then questioning.

"So where's Artie tonight? Out sick like the others?"

There came a squishing, slopping sound, then a clatter and the rolling of wheels on hard surface. She turned her head toward the doorway just as a swarthy man in dark green work clothes went past, his back to her door, humming quietly to himself while sloshing a mop, then pushing his cart forward. "Si señorita, ma'am. Artie, he not well. Back soon. Maybe tomorrow."

"And you're—"

"Pancho."

"Okay, Pancho, but before you finish go down the hall to 7017. The patient in bed two threw up on the floor a couple of minutes ago."

"Right away, señorita."

Anne closed her eyes, wishing that David were still there. Not that she wanted to talk; it was just that…just that she wanted him close by. To once again feel the warmth of his hand resting upon her arm.

"I'll stay with you as long as you wish, Anne…"

His words had been a solace she hadn't known since childhood. Since she was seven. They were the exact words her father had used when he had put her to bed, told her stories, and comforted her as both a father and a mother because her mother had left, never to return. Only instead of calling her Anne, he had called her *monkey* because of the way she had clung to him.

"I'll stay with you as long as you wish, monkey…"

Still the memory of his words evoked a lump in her throat, tightness in her chest. They were the last words he had spoken to her. His aircraft had exploded over the Gulf of Mexico the following day.

She wondered how long ago David had left, whether he had stayed for a while, had watched her in sleep. Would he be back tonight? She closed her eyes and lay there thinking of him, entertaining thoughts of a man, physical thoughts, something she hadn't done in a while. She could feel her body stirring, emotions awakening that had been suppressed for longer than she cared to remember. With Warner it had been no more than a hearty slapping of meat upon meat, emotions on a level no higher than that of the humping of animals. But what would it be like with someone…someone who cared? With a gentle, loving person, not an animal like Edelbrock had been. Someone like David.

She sensed someone nearby and opened her eyes.

"Are you okay? Need anything?" Regina asked quietly.

"Maybe a little water."

Minutes later she felt herself drifting off once again…

He saw that the nurses' station was about sixty feet from her door, and on the same side of the corridor. And the sole nurse was deep in her paperwork. That meant someone could quietly enter and leave her room without being seen from the station.

He pushed the cleaning cart past the station, smiled at the nurse who looked up briefly, and said, "Buenos noches, señorita. I clean the drinking fountains and then I am finished. Okay?"

"Sure, Pancho. Thanks," she said, returning to her paperwork.

He stopped just before the door to her room. There was a drinking fountain there and he squirted Lysol foam on it and began polishing. He looked back toward the nurses' station, saw that the alcove in which the nurse sat prevented a view of the corridor.

He would do it now.

Carefully he reached into the cart and retrieved the shoebox from among the cleaning supplies, then looked about the corridor once again and saw that it was deserted. Then a thought suddenly struck him: he had forgotten to turn off the elevators as Manuel had described. Manuel had said to go down to the second floor, take each of the two elevators to the sixth floor, pull out the red *stop* buttons, and then take the stairs to the seventh floor. This he was to have done after he had gotten the cleaning cart up to the seventh floor.

But it was too late now; the nurse would become suspicious.

His breathing became rapid as he held the box carefully in his hands, felt the scratchy scuttling within, and stepped into the nearly dark room. For moments he stood there, listening, while his eyes became accustomed. Then he saw that her eyes were closed, her breathing slow and steady, and that only a sheet covered her body. He listened for the sound of someone approaching, but there was nothing. All was quiet.

Slowly he knelt at the foot of her bed and set the box on the floor. Then slowly, carefully, he tugged the sheet free from the corner of the mattress and lifted it, exposing her bare feet. He saw that her feet were over to one side, away from him, not in the center. That was good. There was room for the creatures to wander before finding what they sought, and her feet would tent the sheet, allowing them more freedom of movement, freedom to explore and locate warm crevices... But he must be careful not to get them too agitated; they must not strike too soon. He would need time to get away.

Blood drummed in his ears as he held the sheet up with one hand and removed the tape from the box top with the other. Carefully he lifted the box to the level of the mattress, tipped it and shook gently. Three, four, five...eight...eleven. There. All twelve were scuttling about, disoriented, and he slowly lowered the sheet and tucked it.

He stood quickly, crossed himself and left. It was done.

David downed the dregs of his coffee, debated about another cup but decided against it. He rose from his chair and stretched, smiling at the interns and nurse still on break, and waved good-bye to the derelict. He sauntered over to the counter, selected a clean go-cup and filled it for Regina.

He stood waiting at the elevators when an unfamiliar voice behind called his name.

"David? David Levinson? Is that you?"

He turned and saw the older man in green scrubs and static-proof slippers smiling uncertainly at him. "Ben? Ben uh…"

"Moranski. You got it. God, David, how the hell are ya?" he said, taking David's hand and pumping it vigorously. "Been years." He thumbed David's white tunic, "Didn't know you worked here too. Thought you'd be in private practice by now."

He smiled at the surgeon who'd been his mentor in medical school, had gotten him his appointment for his residency. "Haven't been there, haven't done that, Ben, but it's good to see you too."

Moranski slapped his shoulder, "That's the spirit. Right here on the front lines is where it's at. Always has been, always will be. We practice medicine here, make 'em whole again. Those guys with their shingles out, they gotta run a business. Hell, they're not doctors anymore, they're brokers, clearing-houses for the sick and injured. A person goes in to see the doctor, and who do they get to see? The fucking nurse practitio-ner. What the fuck do they know? And when they do get to see the doctor, somewhere in a three-minute slot among eighty other patients, he sticks a stethoscope between their tits, says *hmmm,* then charges their insurance and refers them to a specialist. See? Just a fucking medical clearinghouse." He tapped Levinson's chest with a thick finger, "They don't practice medicine. We taught 'em how, but they get the sniff of a dollar and that's the end of it."

The elevator dinged and David turned and saw the door open. "Ben, uh, it's great to see you again, but I've got to go got a patient to see, and she's—"

Moranski raised his eyebrows. "The coffee for her? Room service?" He jabbed David in the ribs and bawled with laughter.

David stepped quickly into the elevator, punched seven and grinned at Moranski as the doors began closing. "We'll have to get together soon, Ben. Catch up on old times. I'll call you."

The night shift had its compensations, Regina thought. For one it was quiet. The janitor had come and gone, the floors were now clean, the patient status board clear, at last she could get some work done. And there was a good deal of it. The afternoon shift must have been chaos, for the present they had left for her, a formidable stack of paperwork, was daunting.

She had just begun entering chart data into the computer when there came a sonar ping on the patient status board. She swiveled around, saw that it was bed two in 7017 again. The elderly woman still wasn't tolerating the medication, probably, and had likely vomited again. She rose from her chair and walked out into the corridor, hoping the janitor, Pablo, or whatever his name had been, was still around to clean it up. She looked in the direction of Anne's room where he had been cleaning the fountain, but the hallway was now deserted, the cleaning cart gone. There was nothing in the opposite direction either.

Well now, that was odd. The elevator banks were directly across from the nurses station, yet she hadn't seen Pablo—no, it was Pancho, leave with the cleaning cart.

Frowning, Regina strode quickly toward Anne Ryan's room for a look, but the insistent pinging of the status board drew her attention and she turned around and hurried to room 7017.

The steel shaft of the knitting needle stabbed again and again into her breast, forearm and thigh, and the old woman's de-

monic shrieking assaulted her ears until she swung the heavy .45 automatic with all of her might into the side of Sylvia's head, mashing cartilage and bone. Great gouts of warm blood suddenly sprayed Anne's face as she swung the automatic again, this time catching Sylvia full in the face, and at last the terrifying shrieking stopped.

Anne suddenly awoke, whimpering with fright, her face bathed in sweat and her heart pounding. For moments she lay there disoriented, blinking and gasping for breath. Then she felt a tickle on the inside of her thigh and she reached with a bandaged hand and rubbed it.

"YEEOWWWW!" she screamed. The sudden terrible pain in her thigh felt like someone had jabbed her with a white-hot poker. *"Ah, god, god, OWWWW,"* she wailed, writhing and twisting onto her side. Suddenly the pain struck again, this time on her buttocks and more agonizing than before. The pain seared into her brain, her shrieking and bellowing now tearing at her vocal cords as she flailed and beat on the mattress with bandaged hands.

The elevator doors opened and David saw that the nurse's station was unattended. He looked left and right, but the corridor was deserted. He set Regina's coffee on the counter, then glanced at the status board and saw the light illuminated for 7017 but it wasn't flashing. That meant she was there, had answered a call. He drummed his fingers on the countertop, waiting.

"YEEOWWWW!" came the sharp, high-pitched and inhuman scream from the down the corridor, and David spun around, knocking the coffee over, searching for the source. It had sounded like a cat, a big cat, and a cat in terrible agony being tortured or abused by some—

"Ah, god, god, OWWWW!"

David slipped and stumbled in the spilled coffee, then sprinted toward Anne's room.

"Jesus, god, god, oh god, OWWWWW, ah-ah-ah ow wOWWWW!"

He ran for her doorway and smashed his shoulder painfully on the jamb as he turned in, then collided with a janitor's cleaning cart and fell, cracking his knee on the tiled floor. He quickly gathered himself and snapped the light on, saw Anne, her face horribly contorted by excruciating pain, flailing her arms frantically on the bed, shrieking demonically. He rushed to her side and took her by the shoulders, forcing her back on the bed. "What? *What*, Anne? What's *happening*? Are you having the nightmare—?"

"YEOWWWWW! AH-AH-GOD! ARRRHHHHHHHH—BITING, BITING, LEGS—"

David froze, still holding her shoulders, her body thrashing wildly. Suddenly he grabbed the sheet and tore it away. "*My GOD!*" he yelled, his mouth agape as he saw the ugly brown creatures swarming about her legs and thighs. Instantly he knew what they were. They were more than three inches long, the largest he had ever seen, and their segmented tails containing the venom bulb and needle-sharp stinger snapped and stuck at one another as they scuttled about. For a second he stared eyeswide, disbelieving, then he reacted without thinking, instinctively grabbing two of them poised near her genitals.

Regina rushed into the room and stopped short. "David! What—what is it? What are--?"

"YAHHHRRRGGGG!" he bellowed in terrible pain, casting away the two creatures, both of which had struck him. Yet still he grabbed for more, growling and gargling like an enraged bear, and they struck him repeatedly as he swept them away with his hands and arms and stamped on them.

Regina screamed and ran to Anne's side, grabbed her about the shoulders and dragged her from the bed, then picked her up bodily and laid her upon the other bed. Then she rushed to the nurses' station, yelled the security, emergency and stat codes over the paging system, and ran back to help David.

352

Anne laid moaning and writhing on the bed, but worse was the condition in which she found David. He lay on the floor convulsing, his breathing ragged, and vomit oozing from the corner of his mouth. She knelt to help him and quickly recoiled. Three of the vile creatures were crawling across his chest, their pincers raised, squaring off with one another as though ready to engage in battle. Suddenly they were at it, thrashing and striking, their tails snapping downward as they struck at one another and missed, the needle-like stingers piercing the thin fabric of David's shirt.

But David Levinson was beyond feeling the pain.

Regina quickly looked about the room, saw a whiskbroom amid the spilled contents of the overturned cleaning cart, grabbed it and swept the scorpions off his chest. They skittered across the floor and she went after them, leaping and stamping until she was certain they were dead.

Suddenly the small room was alive with people, uniformed guards, ER staff, and what seemed to be every attending physician and surgeon within earshot of the paging system. One pushed his way through and quickly knelt at David's side. He was in green scrubs pocked with blood, an older man, obviously straight out of emergency surgery. He reached for the carotid artery in David's neck and held two fingers there, then hung his head and shook it slowly. "David. Ah, David. Damn."

They wheeled her on a gurney into emergency, fast; there wasn't a moment to lose, her heart rate was rapid, there was fever, vomiting, and then came the convulsions. For an hour they labored over her in teams, a veritable tug of war with the effects of the venom as she lapsed in and out of a coma. They counted at least five impact points where she had been stung. One of the doctors, a Chilean intimately familiar with the creatures, had known of cases where people had been stung as many as four times by the *Centruroides Exilicauda* and survived, but never five. The survival rate depended largely upon the patient's general health, age, and whether there were multiple stings by the same scorpion, or whether each was from a different one. The concentration of venom was, of course, significantly greater in the latter case, he said. And when annoyed—pissed off, as he put it in his native language, they tended to inject more of their deadly toxins.

They concluded that due to the degree of swelling surrounding the impact points on her genitals, thighs and buttocks and by the severe reaction she was suffering, that Anne Ryan had been stung by five different scorpions. Her prognosis was poor.

At last they had done all they could and transferred her to intensive care. Anaphylactic shock had set in. There was now little to do but wait. They didn't know her religious choice, if any, and Captain Gordon Rosenberg, whom Regina remembered as being Anne's best friend, was away on a trip. So Regina decided to play it safe and a priest had been called to administer the last rites.

The three men and one woman stood shoulder to shoulder beneath the dripping awning at graveside, heads bowed, as the minister spoke eloquently yet simply of the person that was Anne Ryan. Mitchell Hardison and Titus Wofford had given him what he needed to know, and Regina Dotzer too, but Gordy Rosenberg had given him far more. He alone knew best of the stouthearted courage that had sustained her through life, of her selfless character and how she had unknowingly shaped or otherwise fulfilled the lives of others.

Anne loved humor, Gordy knew well, and when asked to share a few words of her with those gathered, words that would typify Anne, he said simply, "Just so you'll all know her as I did, Anne never even cheated at Monopoly."

"Amen," said Titus.

he trail was dry and dusty, narrow as well as steep, but the
ure-footed burro plodded lazily along in the rugged and remote
mountains of Coahuila, Mexico. The rider nudged the burro to
one side, removed his wide-brimmed sombrero and held it to his
chest as two others passed on the way down. "Buenos dias,
Señor, Señora," he said. "Voy a casa, ahora." I go home, now.

Home to the City of the Dead.

"Vaya con dios, Señor," said the woman.

John Haviland Williams

EPILOGUE

Mitchell Hardison stepped forward and shook the minister's hand, thanked him, then turned and spoke a few words with Gordy and Titus and left.

Rain drummed on the awning sheltering the few mourners, and Hardison took the offered umbrella and made his way through the puddles to his aging Ford. He slammed the door, turned the key in the ignition and switched the wipers to high. He sat for a few moments, watching Gordy and Titus standing together, Titus's huge hand on Gordy's shoulder, consoling him.

Too bad, he thought. Too bad he couldn't tell them. Only he and a handful of others at the Department of Justice knew that the casket was empty. That the woman formerly known as Anne Ryan, still in critical condition but now recovering in an unidentified federal facility, had been taken beneath the protective wing of the Federal Witness Protection Program.

He slipped the Ford into gear and drove slowly out of the cemetery.

Lillian Attebury sat alone on the sofa in her son Donald's living room in Detroit, contentedly babysitting the grandchildren reading the newspaper and watching them gleefully constructing ships and castles and other fascinating things with building blocks.

Donald's youngest crawled up beside her and snuggled in close. She wrapped an arm about the adorable two year-old and shook her head wistfully. In two months she would turn ninety eighty-eight years her granddaughter's senior. Lord, she had seen and experienced much in all those years. Only a year ago she had been found wandering about in the snow and frigid night air at La Guardia, dazed and shaken, in shock but uninjured from a devastating airline crash that had killed many yet spared her. She remembered well her wailing, *"Why me? Why spare me, God?"*

Until now the answer had eluded her.

Snuggled beside her was the answer to her wailing, she now knew. These children needed their grandmother, wanted her, and loved her. And there was much she could teach them.

She sighed and continued reading *The Detroit Free Press* while the two year-old snuggled next to her pretended to read as well. She read with interest a story that touched close to home, to that terrifying night of a year ago. It was the story of Maria Gugliotti, mother of Dominic Gugliotti who, with his wife and four daughters, had perished in the La Guardia tragedy. Maria was a pensioner, also a widow, now lacking any family whatever. Yet as the story described, she had recently come into a great deal of money from an anonymous source. Someone had simply mailed her a certificate for 5,000 shares of stock in TransCon Airlines. And it was genuine, worth a small fortune.

Who in the world would do such a thing? Lillian wondered. A lottery winner showing off, no doubt. Someone who did nothing to earn it and who could well afford to part with it.

The End

John Haviland Williams

ABOUT THE AUTHOR

Probable Cause is John Haviland Williams' second novel. His first, *Angels Fly High*, was written in 1992. A private pilot for 35 years, both novels evidence his deep and continuing interest in aviation safety.

A certified public accountant by profession and the former Auditor General of the State of California, he has also written and published six accounting textbooks and training manuals, three of which were published by the U.S. Office of Personnel Management.

Mr. Williams and his wife live in the foothills of Northern California, where he now writes full time and pursues his other passions of backpacking and snowshoeing in the Sierra Nevada Mountains.

Made in the USA
San Bernardino, CA
13 August 2019